The Trainer's Dictionary:

HRD Terms, Acronyms, Initials, and Abbreviations

Angus Reynolds

22 Amherst Rd. Amherst, Massachusetts 01002

413-253-3488 1-800-822-2801

The Trainer's Dictionary

First Edition

First Printing, April 1993

Library of Congress Cataloging in Publication Data

Reynolds, Angus S. 1936-

The Trainer's Dictionary

1.

ISBN 0-87425-219-9

Manufactured in the United States of America

Contents

Preface v

How to Use This Dictionary vii

How This Book Was Written xi

A Word of Caution xv

Terms — A through Z 1

Essential HRD Vocabulary 271

Acronyms and Abbreviations 275

An Invitation 289

Preface

Have you ever noticed that commonly used terms appear differently in authoritative books in the HRD field? For example, is it posttest, post-test, or post test? Clearly, it must be possible for all of us to write these terms in the same way. A number of excellent glossaries were developed to help address this need for one part of the field or another. Still, people have often commented that they wished there were a dictionary of HRD terms. Our field is 50 years old and needs one.

I set out to develop a dictionary useful to those involved with any aspect of the HRD equation: a practical instead of academically oriented or theoretical book. In particular, I decided there would be no definitions that would look as if they had been written by a lawyer, or worse, as if they had been evolved by an academic to cover every base and withstand debate and the attacks of others who already know the terms.

I am indebted to the many individuals whose earlier efforts to provide clarity on these terms made my task easier. Also, I am grateful for the help of many university and public librarians, and Amanda Stroud, in particular, for their help.

Since no one can know every area of HRD well, I requested the help of experts to review the terms for accuracy and completeness. They have been generous in supplying their wisdom. Nevertheless, the responsibility for error is mine alone.

My challenge was to provide definitions for terms you encounter to help you be more effective and professional in whatever part of the field you work. If I have succeeded, you will find practical definitions that you can apply in the real-world situations you face.

Angus Reynolds
New York, New York
January, 1993

How to Use This Dictionary

This dictionary contains several features to enhance its ease of use and value to people who work in the field and to the many others who need terms but who do not work in, or are new to, the field. They will help you find the terms you need. Possible use strategies include all terms which may be found directly, the 100 most essential HRD terms, a basic HRD vocabulary, and acronyms and abbreviations.

All Terms

First, needed terms can be located directly in alphabetical order. Most terms are listed in their fully spelled-out forms. The spelled-out form of an acronym or abbreviated term may be identified in the acronym and abbreviation listing to assist you in locating the correct dictionary entry.

Many HRD terms belong to a specialized vocabulary used by people who work in a particular part of this very large and diverse field. The same terms may not be used at all by people who work in other parts of the field. This dictionary includes terms needed by practitioners who use these specialized vocabularies:

biographical
career development
cross-cultural/international
cost-benefit
evaluation
facilities
general
instructional delivery
instructional meetings
instructional resource
instructional systems design
legislation
landmark events
media

management development
military
organizational development
presentation
publication/data base
quality
roles and competencies
service
sales & marketing
theory/research
technology-based instruction
training management
technical & skills training

In order to eliminate duplication, synonymous terms are only defined in one place in the dictionary. Terms with a similar or same meaning are marked *See* to refer to the defined synonymous term.

You can also locate words by indirect reference. Suggestions of terms that are related to an entry are marked *See also*. Terms that are distinctly different or contrasting and antonyms are suggested by *Compare with*. The sample entry below shows some of these features.

The 100 Most Essential HRD Terms

To help people new to the field get up to speed quickly, an initial vocabulary of 100 terms are marked *essential 100 term*. The 100 terms were judged essential by the dictionary's panel of experts for a beginning professional HRD vocabulary.

Most similar words were eliminated from the 100 Essential Terms list, since a user looking at one term would be lead to the other by its proximity or *See also* reference. For example, "facilitation" was eliminated because the term "facilitator" will serve the same purpose for the user.

Some individuals are included among the terms in this dictionary. Individuals, although recognized as important by their very inclusion, were eliminated from the 100 Essential Terms list to make way for operative terms.

These terms form a survival level vocabulary. The essential 100 terms are also listed beginning on page 271 to assist vocabulary building efforts.

Basic HRD Vocabulary

It is difficult to determine the exact terms a particular practitioner will need. Terms used most frequently in a particular organization may not appear in the essential 100 grouping. Therefore, all of the terms that two or more members of the expert review panel considered part of a basic HRD vocabulary are marked *basic term*. The wide range of expertise represented resulted in a rich vocabulary. This presents the potential for vocabulary building by studying unfamiliar terms.

Acronyms and Abbreviations

Acronyms and abbreviations, along with the words that form them, are listed in a separate section beginning on page 275. This may speed finding the term, although not the definition, when all you want to look up is an acronym or abbreviation. Dictionary entries are listed by their fully spelled-out terms, not according to their abbreviated ones.

Use the Acronyms and Abbreviations section to

- look up only the fully spelled-out term of an acronym or abbreviation, not the definition;
- determine where to find a definition in the dictionary if the spelled-out term of an acronym or abbreviation is unknown to you.

A Sample

The following sample term shows a typical entry—one for "machine lettering."

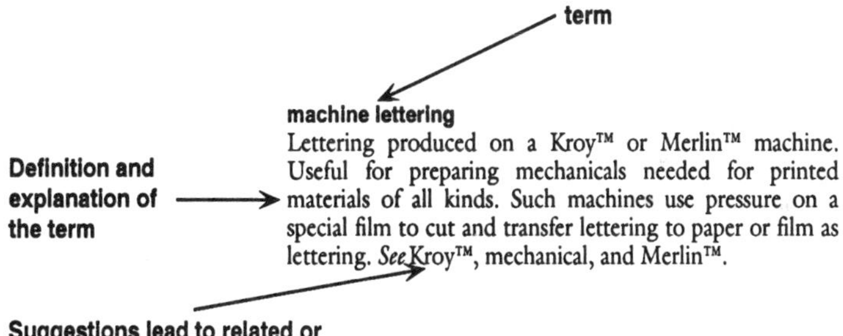

You could have found the term in a variety of ways.

- You could have found the term directly.
- You could also have found it after reading the entries for Kroy™, mechanical, or Merlin™, all of which would indicate *See also* machine lettering.
- If it were an *essential 100 HRD term,* you might have come to the entry from that separate listing.
- If an acronym were commonly associated with the term, you could have come to the entry by way of the Acronyms and Abbreviations section.

Most of these work in reverse. From a particular entry,

you might choose to look in the Essential 100 Terms listing, the entries for related terms, or the entries for terms that are different or opposite.

How This Book Was Written

This book grew from the determination to correct the fact that the HRD field, unlike many others, suffers from lack of a dictionary. Its roots, however, are in the *Glossary of Computer-based Learning Terms,* developed in 1980 to meet a similar need in that area. The glossary sold briskly for the cost of reproduction and postage, based on kind mention made by the editor of *Training* magazine. That glossary has required, and has received, constant update ever since. It was later incorporated in *Computer-Based Training Today,* published by ASTD in 1987. It is altogether appropriate to recognize that several other noteworthy glossaries were developed for other areas of interest and that several books have excellent glossaries.

The next level of growth was required in 1991 when I wrote the third edition of *Selecting and Developing Media for Instruction,* published by Van Nostrand Reinhold in 1992. Because of the same need for definitions, I created a glossary to cover the entire media field. During that experience, I decided to construct a dictionary to serve the entire HRD field.

The dictionary was created during nearly two years of pointedly reading a wide range of books and periodicals, and, more interestingly, of recording the verbal use of terms by people in the field. Quite often the words used orally somehow don't seem to find their way into print.

It was obvious from the outset that any worthy dictionary must include input from a diverse group of HRD experts. With that in mind, a panel was invited to review the manuscript and identify terms that needed correction as well as to suggest other terms that were missing. In addition, with the needs of the dictionary's user in mind, the expert panel also identified the essential 100 terms and those that form the basic vocabulary. The contribution that the following professionals made to this book as members of the expert panel is gratefully acknowledged.

Karl G. Albrecht
Margaret Bedrosian
Chip R. Bell
Mary Broad
Donald Crippen
John Eldridge
C. E. "Gene" Hahne
Ned Herrmann
Greg Kearsley
Donald L. Kirkpatrick
Malcolm Knowles
Zandy Liebowitz
Oliver London
Leonard Nadler
Michael Marquardt
Mary McCain
Patricia McLagan
David C. Paquin
Thomas A. Parks
Richard Phillips
George M. Piskurich
Tom Reeves
William Rothwell
Sivasailam Thiagarajan
Joyce W. Tuck
Ron Zemke

In addition, I wanted the dictionary to be both more complete and useful to HRD practitioners in all English-speaking countries. To achieve this, professionals from Australia, Canada, and the United Kingdom were invited to serve as correspondents. Each had served previously as the President of his professional HRD society. The correspondents identified terms that should be identified as specific to United States usage. Then they suggested terms that are encountered by practitioners in their countries. The able assistance of the following correspondents is deeply appreciated:

John Fricker, United Kingdom
Les Lear, Canada
Les Pickett, Australia

All of this effort notwithstanding, it was impossible to produce definitions on which everyone agreed. Numbered multiple definitions were prepared to reflect these differences.

The large number of terms that are used was as much a surprise to me as it is to most people who see them for the first time. One consideration was whether to cut some of them out. This is at odds with wanting to provide a complete resource. In the end, the fact that people are not bothered by the inclusion of dictionary terms they currently do not need prevailed. Most people value a dictionary because they know that the day may come when they will be glad to have the other terms it contains.

Some ordinary non-HRD English words, such as "larynx," appear among the terms. These are presented because they are encountered by HRD people who need to know what they mean. Not every HRD practitioner whom I have met knows that term, but it is heard in presentation skills training.

One area that cried out for standardization is hyphenation. For example, as asked in the Preface, is it posttest, post-test, or post test? All three versions may be found in reputable and authoritative publications. I have tried to respcct common usage if any is identified.

Most commonly encountered statistical and research terms are included. Not everyone will need them, but they will be there when the time comes. I worked in the field for over 20 years before working in an HRD office that had a research textbook in which a definition could be found—and then it was a difficult definition to follow at that.

I wrote a computer-based learning (today called a technology-based learning) glossary because many specialized words are used in that area. If there are many in this dictionary, it is not because I have a bias toward them. The expert panel and I made every effort to gather *all* of the terms used in every area of HRD. Rapid advances in technology-based instruction continue to swell the number of terms that occur in instructional settings. There simply *are* a lot of technology-based learning terms.

Individuals are also the subject of some entries. Many pages could be written about each individual named, so the entry provides only highlights of the person's accomplishments. Most of them have written many books. Generally, only one book is included in an entry for an individual. Every effort was made to identify and recognize people who developed the techniques defined. No one was intentionally omitted.

Some people questioned the inclusion of terms related to the quality process in this dictionary. Others felt that even more quality process terms should be included. Quality process terms are included here because they are now commonly used by many HRD practitioners in the ordinary course of their work. The choice and number of terms is intended to serve that need.

Hundreds of thousands of people in the military participate in the complete range of HRD activities every day. Military terms are included in this dictionary, not because I or members of the expert panel favor war, but to include this large, active, and often ignored sector.

Some terms are included even though they describe things that are no longer often seen or that did not catch on. However, because people continue to talk and write about them, it seemed a disservice to the reader to omit providing definitions for them.

Laws and government programs are listed in the body of the definitions. Dictionary users must recognize that they are subject to change at any time. Their entry is in the body of the definitions because they retain an historical context.

Periodicals and professional associations are also included in the dictionary. Both of them change as well. In this case, they are listed in the body of the definitions, rather than separately, to ease the user's task in finding them.

The appropriate symbol is displayed when a technique is known to be trademarked or copyrighted. Any omission is unintentional.

The occasional inclusion of "U.S." in a definition may appear gratuitous to users in the United States. It was placed there as a flag to users from other countries, signalling that the term is specific to U.S. usage.

A Word of Caution

Terms appear in this dictionary because they are written and spoken in our field. Some of them describe techniques or concepts you might consider using. Every effort has been made to avoid judgments of the usefulness or value of the contents of terms defined.

Remember, inclusion is recognition of use of a term, not endorsement of a method. In the interest of completeness, terms are included that describe fads and techniques that I do not endorse. Also, they are not necessarily endorsed by any of the experts who reviewed the dictionary prior to publication. You should take care when selecting tools and techniques for personal or organizational use.

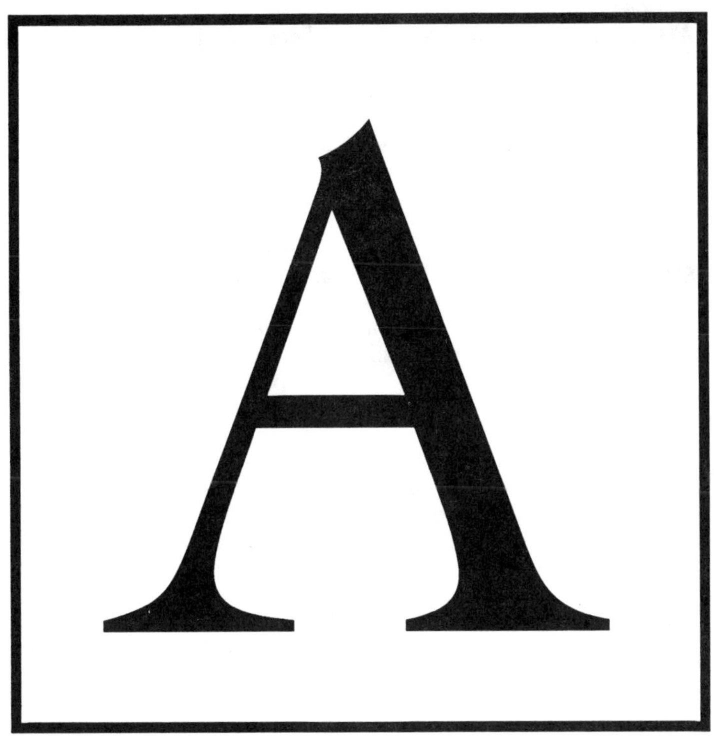

ABA design
See reversal design.

Abilene paradox
A concept, developed by Jerry Harvey, to describe the management of agreement. The Abilene paradox is based on family outing plans with which no one wanted to disagree.

abscissa
The horizontal axis of a graph.

absolute standards
Qualitative or quantitative performance standards. Absolute standards usually provide a written description of behavior, value, or output expectations of the employee. *See also* performance standard *and* criterion-referenced evaluation.

abstract game
An instructional game with little or no formal subject matter content. *See also* process-centered game.

Academy of Human Resource Development
A scholarly association serving the interests of the HRD academic community. Members pursue the study of HRD issues. Fellows of the academy, who must have adademic service, are selected from the membership.

Academy of Management Executive
A periodical of interest to HRD practitioners involved in management. *Academy of Management Executive* is published by the Academy of Management.

Academy of Management Review
A periodical of interest to HRD practitioners involved in management. *Academy of Management Review* is published by the Academy of Management.

accelerated learning
1. Attempts to improve instruction through use of characterisics of effective instruction and teaching the learner more effective learning stategies.
2. A system of learning designed to improve rate of learning and overall retention by incorporating creative and andragogical learning techniques. *See also* suggestopedia.

accelerative learning
See accelerated learning.

acceptance
A stage in the concept life cycle model. Acceptance is usually performed by the end user. *See also* concept life cycle.

access
1. The authority or ability to communicate with a distant computer.
2. The process by which information contained either in one part of a computer is available to another part of the computer or to the user.
3. In OD, the ability to communicate as a more powerful person, or to explore categories of information.

access floor
A floor that allows access to cables in an open space below the floor surface. This eases interequipment connections. *Also called* raised floor.

accessories, game
Added equipment that aids in the conduct of a game. For example, dice.

accountability *basic term*
An area of responsibility for specific performance, outcomes, and results to an individual, group, or organization.

accreditation
A formal process for sanction of instructional programs by an organization recognized to conduct the process. *Compare with* certification *and* licensure. *See also* Ontario Society for Training & Development (OSTD).

accreditation of prior achievement (APA)
See accreditation of prior learning (APL).

accreditation of prior experience (APE)
See accreditation of prior earning (APL).

accreditation of prior learning (APL)
Through a systematic and valid assessment process, an indivdual's skills and knowledge can be formally recognized and credited regardless of how, when, where, or why they were obtained. Slightly different terms are used frequently in different countries. APL is preferred in the U.K., prior learning assessment is preferred in the U.S., and recognition of prior learning is preferred in Australia. *See also* prior

learning assessment (PLA) *and* recognition of learning (RPL).

acetate
See transparency.

achievement motivation
A theory mainly concerned with motivation developed by David McClelland, John Atkinson, and others. Achievement motivation attempts to measure how four factors influence achievement-oriented activity. The factors are (1) expected probability of success, (2) incentive value of success, (3) perceived difficulty of the task, and (4) intrinsic interest that the task holds for the subject. *See also* McClelland, David.

achievement test
Measurement of learner's abilities. Achievement tests are usually used to measure existing, as opposed to newly acquired, abilities. *Compare with* aptitude test.

acquisition test
See criterion (referenced) test.

acronym
A word made from the initial letters of a phrase, but pronounced as a word. Acronyms are common in technology-based learning. For example, WYSIWYG, pronounced wizzy-wig, stands for "What you see is what you get."

Across the Board
A periodical of interest to HRD practitioners involved in management issues. *Across the Board* is published by the Conference Board.

action
1. *See* response.
2. The sixth step in action research.

action centered leadership (ACL)
A model developed by John Adair involving a dynamic interaction which takes into account the needs of the task, the team, and the individuals concerned.

action learning
A method for personal and organizational development developed by Reginald Revan. Action learning involves small groups that take on tasks in the organization to act on and change. The results are reported for review and learning.

action maze
A programmed-type case study that is conducted manually. Learners choose from alternatives at decision points. A case description provides the information needed to reach the first decision point. It also provides options from which to select. After a decision, the group is provided the next "frame." It explains the consequences of their decision and contains more information. The case continues in this manner. Variations are to allow groups to reorganize according to individuals' choices of action or to allow groups to make up their own possible actions at each decision point. *See also* case study *and* incident process. *Compare with* situation simulation.

action-reflection learning
Instruction in the form of an actual business problem for teams of learners to solve together. *Compare with* simulation.

action research *basic term*
An OD term originated by Kurt Lewin to describe research similar to applied research. Rather than being intrusive action, action research is interventionist and pro-

Continued on next page

duces ideas for change. These changes are introduced, and continued research determines the effects of the change. The process continues in this manner. *See also* Lewin, Kurt *and* organization development (OD).

action science
An OD intervention theory and method developed by Chris Argyris. Action science is concerned with improving how organizations diagnose problems, decide how to respond, and then implement solutions. *See also* Argyris, Chris *and* organization development (OD).

action title
On visuals, a meaningful title that concisely conveys the central message. *Also called* interpretive title.

active listening *basic term*
Differentiating between the cognitive and emotional content of the message, and communicating these to the speaker. An active listener makes inferences regarding feelings expressed by the speaker while listening, and reflects these back for verification.

active participation *basic term*
Instructional activities in which learners are involved in the learning experience. For example, CAI. *Compare with* passive participation.

activity-centered learners
Learners who participate in learning activities because of interest in the activity rather than in its objectives or outcomes.

activity network diagram
A quality process management and planning tool used when the task is a familiar one with sub-tasks of known duration. The activity network diagram is useful when tasks on a project can be done sequentially and/or simultaneously.

activity-oriented learner
A learner who pursues instruction primarily for social contact and human relationships. *Compare with* goal- *and* learning-oriented learner.

adaptation *basic term*
Changing existing instructional materials to suit organization, instructor, or learner needs.

adaptive learning
An individual's or organization's learning from experience and reflection.

ad hoc group
See task-oriented group.

adjunct game
An instructional game that reinforces initial learning from another source. For example, a quiz game can be used to review and reinforce the learning from a reading assignment.

Adler, Alfred
A psychologist who was a contemporary of Freud. Adler's concept of the creative self stressed the positive, active role individuals play in shaping their own goals and personality. His work is reflected in some of the theories and principles used in HRD today, especially those related to self-concept.

Administrative Management Society
A professional society of interest to some HR professionals.

administrative service charge
A fee charged by some HRD departments for providing routine and standard services within the organization. The charge represents an equitable charge for providing the service. For example, 10% may be charged for processing tuition refund applications. *Also called* charge back, internal price, and transfer price. *See also* profit center *and* cost center.

administrator
The HRD role of providing coordination and support services for the delivery of HRD programs and services. *See also* HRD Roles and Competencies Study.

adult *basic term*
An individual who performs adult roles. For example, spouse, parent, or full-time worker.

adult basic education *basic term*
Instructional programs for undereducated or functionally illiterate adults. *Also called* remedial education. For example, multiplication or citizenship. *See also* adult education *and* general educational development (GED).

adult education *basic term*
1. Learning activities engaged in by adults in either a formal or informal educational setting for the purpose of bringing about change or growth. *See also* adult learning theory, andragogy, continuing education, experiential learning, and human resource development (HRD).
2. The field of study that examines the disciplines of adult learning and the delivery of instructional programming for adults.
3. Loosely, any educational program provided for adults.

Adult Education Quarterly
A periodical of interest to HRD practitioners involved in adult education. *Adult Education Quarterly* is published by the American Association for Adult & Continuing Education.

adult ego state
In transactional analysis, one of three states: parent, child, and adult. The adult is the position of mature, objective action. The combinations of these states in human interactions are the basis of transactional analysis. *See also* transactional analysis (TA).

Adult Learning
A periodical of interest to HRD practitioners involved in adult education. *Adult Learning* is published by the American Association for Adult & Continuing Education.

adult learning *basic term*
1. A process in which the instructional needs of adults, as perceived by themselves or others, are met through organized learning activities. *See also* adult learning theory *and* andragogy.
2. An inclusive term for any instruction for adults. *See also* adult learning theory *and* andragogy.
3. Loosely, a synonym for andragogy. *See also* andragogy.

adult learning, phases of
Three phases that describe the process of engaging in learning, originated by Alan Tough. The phases are (1) deciding to begin, (2) choosing a plan, and (3) engaging in learning.

adult learning theory
1. Loosely, adult learning principles and practices, especially those advanced by Malcolm Knowles under the term andra-

Continued on next page

gogy. *See also* adult education; andragogy; experiential learning; Knowles, Malcolm; and social learning theory.
2. A body of learning theory focused on adults.

adult learning understanding
The HRD competency of knowing how adults acquire and use knowledge, skills, and attitudes; understanding individual differences in learning. *See also* HRD Roles and Competencies Study.

advance organizer *basic term*
Information about the potentially meaningful material to be covered by instruction presented before that instruction. A research-based practice, developed by David Ausabel, to prepare the learner to receive and remember the substance of the instruction. Two types of organizers are identified: expository (new material) and comparative (similarities and differences).

adventure game
See adventure training.

adventure training
An outdoor activity that involves physical participation, usually by team members. Adventure training activities usually have high and low challenge activities and problem-solving tasks. A particular type of adventure training is called ropes training because of its use of rope-based challenges. *Also called* adventure game.

affective *essential 100 term*
Outcomes based on the development of attitudes or feelings rather than knowledge. Deals with the attitudes and motivation of the learner. Affective responses reflect the feelings of the learner toward the instructional environment.

affective conflict
Emotional clashes between members of any group. *See also* affective.

affective domain *basic term*
The area of human learning associated with attitudes, feelings, interests, opinions, world views, and values. *Compare with* cognitive domain *and* psychomotor domain.

affective learning
Learning in the affective domain. *See also* Bloom's taxonomy and cognitive science. *Compare with* cognitive learning *and* psychomotor learning.

affective objective *basic term*
A learning objective specifying the acquisition of particular attitudes, values, or feelings. Affective objectives deal with the affective domain. *Also called* attitudinal objective. *See also* learning objective.

affective responses
Responses that reflect the feelings of the learner toward the instructional environment.

affiliation-offensive language
Words that will insult, offend, or at least upset members of an audience simply because of their identity. For example: antiminority, antireligious, politically touchy, or sexist statements.

affinity diagram
A quality process management and planning tool used to make sense of disparate verbal information. The affinity diagram is useful to find major themes in a large number of ideas, opinions, or issues.

after action review (AAR)
A method of providing feedback to units by involving participants in

the training diagnostic process in order to increase and reinforce learning. The AAR leader guides participants in identifying deficiencies and seeking solutions.

after think steps
Things the learner must weigh after completing the steps of a process. *Compare with* before think steps *and* during think steps.

Age Discrimination in Employment Act
U.S. legislation that prohibits discrimination against persons over 40 years old in any employment decision. *See also* older worker.

Agency for International Development (AID)
An agency of the U.S. State Department that is a frequent funding sponsor of international HRD projects.

agenda *basic term*
The list of topics to be covered in a presentation or meeting. *See also* moving agenda chart.

agenda-setting buzz group
An andragogic method of gathering goals-data from participants. The buzz group team members may determine the objectives and areas of discussion or all of the course content. Alternatively, such buzz groups can meet after the program is underway to recommend courses of action for the remaining time. *See also* buzz group.

agree-disagree statements
A list of true-false statements provided to a group for agree or disagree response to the sentences as stated. Small groups then alter the statements so that the whole group can accept the revised statement. *See also* consensus.

Alberta Society of Human Resource & Organization Development (ASHROD)
A professional society for HRD practitioners in the Province of Alberta. *See also* HR Canada.

algorithm *basic term*
See Figure on next page.

alphanumeric
Both letters and numerals. *Compare with* graphic.

alpha test
The internal test of software under development before external testing or distribution. This term is also applied to development of technology-based courseware. *Compare with* beta test.

alter ego
A learner who serves as a consultant during role play.

alternate form reliability
One method of determining the reliability of a test based on two essentially equivalent forms of the test. On readministration, subjects receive the alternate form of the test. *See also* split-half reliability *and* test-retest reliability.

alternative hypothesis
The logical opposite of a null hypothesis. *Also called* research hypothesis. *Compare with* null hypothesis.

American Association for Counseling and Development
A professional society of interest to some HR professionals.

American Journal of Distance Education
A periodical of interest to HRD practitioners involved in distance learning. *American Journal of Dis-*

Continued on next page

algorithm *basic term*

1. Organization of any task into the exact sequence of steps needed to accomplish it. Algorithms replace continuous prose as a means for communicating complex rules and regulations and can be used as the basis of a job aid. *See also* job aid.
2. In a job aid, a format used when decision-making rules are too complex for flowcharts that show the relationship between representation in a decision table. Job aid algorithms have the appearance of simple input data, rules, and outcomes. *See also* job aid. *Compare with* cookbook, decision table, and heuristics.

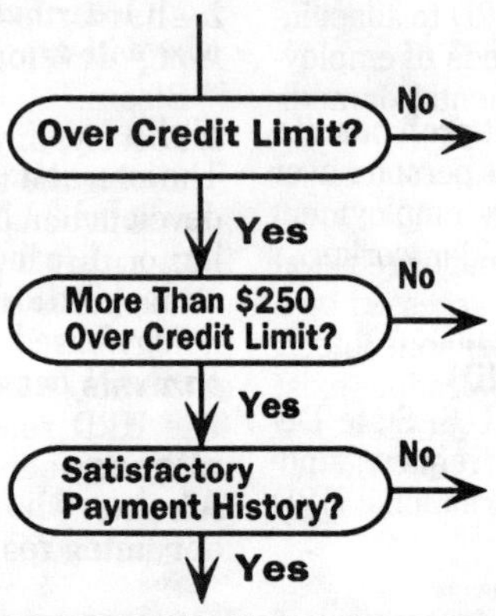

tance Education is published by the Pennsylvania State University.

American Management Association (AMA)
A professional society of interest to some HR professionals.

American Marketing Association
A professional society of interest to some HR professionals.

American Production and Control Society
A professional society of interest to some HR professionals.

American Psychological Association (APA)
A professional society of interest to some HR professionals. The publication guide of the APA is the most commonly used standard for serious HRD writing.

American Quality and Productivity Management Association
A professional society of interest to some HR professionals.

American Society for Adult and Continuing Education
A professional society of interest to some HRD professionals.

American Society for Quality Control
A professional society of interest to some HRD professionals.

American Society for Training and Development (ASTD)
The largest professional society for HRD practitioners in the United States.

American Society for Training Directors
A professional society formed in 1944, subsequently renamed as the American Society for Training and Development (ASTD).

Americans with Disabilities Act (ADA)
Legislation effective in 1992 that requires, among other employment provisions, HRD to adapt instruction to the needs of employees with physical, mental, or medical impairments.

America Online
A commercial information retrieval service that can be accessed by a computer over a telephone line. A large number of sublocations exist based on user interest. *See also* Compuserve, DIALOG, ORBIT, and Prodigy.

amortize
In budgeting, accounting for the costs of a capital investment over the projected lifetime of the training program for which it is purchased and used.

analog *basic term*
In technology-based instruction, a technology type that is based on continuous measurement. Analog technology is now being replaced by digital. For example, analog videodisc versus compact disc. *Compare with* digital.

analogy
A representation that is similar in form or function to the desired concept but is somehow different. Analogy is an effective method of teaching concepts. One classic example is comparing fractions to slices of a pizza.

analysis
1. The first of five phases in the ISD process. In analysis, the following are identified: ideal performance, actual performance, gaps between ideal and actual, areas that can be addressed by instruction and other actions, and potential solutions. *See also* design, development, implementation, and evaluation.
2. The fourth of six levels of learning developed by Benjamin Bloom.
3. Loosely, any process of determining the scope and nature of instructional materials needed to satisfy a given performance need. *Also called* diagnosis.

analysis/assessment roles
The HRD role cluster including evaluator, needs analyst, and researcher. *See also* HRD Roles and Competencies Study.

analysis of variance (ANOVA)
In statistics, a method of determining the significance of the difference between the means of two groups. Can be used to compare two or more groups. *Compare with* T-test.

analytic learner
A person who learns by breaking up things or ideas into parts and examining them to see how they fit together. *See also* learning style.

andragogics
The ideological and methodological systems that order the process of andragogy. *See also* andragogy *and* andragology.

andragogy *essential 100 term*
(Pronounced an'-dra-go-gee. The "gee" sounds like gee wiz.)
1. The art and science of helping adults learn. A European term

Continued on next page

introduced into the English-speaking adult learning vocabulary by Malcolm Knowles. Andragogy is based on the Greek *andr-* (man, as opposed to boy) and *agogus* (leader). A contrast is usually made with pedagogy—teaching children. Andragogy makes specific assumptions about how adults perceive and react to learning situations. Andragogy emphasizes self-directedness, utilization of the learner's experience as a resource for learning, and involves sharing in the diagnosis of needs, formulation of objectives, building and doing of learning plans, and evaluation of the process. *See also* adult education; adult learning; adult learning theory; and Knowles, Malcolm. *Compare with* pedagogy.
2. Life- or work-centered learning.
3. Instructional principles based on the way adult learners differ from children.

andragology
The scientific study of andragogy and andragogics. *See also* andragogics *and* andragogy.

animation *basic term*
Objects drawn, selectively erased, and repositioned to produce apparent movement on a video or computer display. For example, liquid flow though a system or movement of the needle of a gauge.

answer judging
The process of comparing a learner's response to the predetermined correct answer. Answer judging refinements are an important characteristic for comparison of authoring systems.

anticipatory change
Adjustment that occurs when an organization attempts to identify external changes that are expected to occur in the surrounding business environment. Anticipatory change allows the organization to take advantage of the change.

anticipatory learning
An individual's or organization's learning in order to meet needs that are projected for the future. The anticipatory learning sequence is vision-reflection-action.

Antiope
A French videotex system. *See* videotex. *Compare with* Prestel *and* Telidon.

application
1. An instructional technique based on the use of knowledge and skills in real-life situations, provided in instructional settings.
2. The third of six levels of learning developed by Benjamin Bloom. *See also* Bloom's Taxonomy.
3. *See* computer application.

application (program)
See computer application.

application-oriented objective
A statement, in behavioral terms, of what learners should be able to do when they apply their learning to specific tasks.

applied behavioral science
1. The key principles and research findings from such academic disciplines as psychology, sociology, anthropology, and archeology.
2. Called by some the theoretical basis for HRD.

applied billing entry
Time spent on specific projects, activities, or clients. Time for which a client can be billed. *Also called* billable time.

applied creative teaching and learning
Whole brain technology applied to the design and delivery of instruction.

applied rate
The number of hours billed to projects divided by the total hours paid in a given time period. The applied rate has been called the most important indicator of productivity.

applied research
See research.

apprenticeship *essential 100 term*
HRD activities provided to develop a skilled tradesperson. An apprentice participates in a formal program with basis in law and written agreements. The apprentice serves under a master or journeyman on a one-on-one basis for one to six years in a formal program. Most programs run for three to five years. Apprenticeship is commonly established by a single employer or group of employers working alone or with a union. *Also called* apprenticeship training. *Compare with* Youth Apprenticeship.

appropriate technology
1. A concept based on the use of new technology that is operable and maintainable by the user.
2. Sometimes used, incorrectly, to refer to low technology.

aptitude *basic term*
A capacity to engage in behavior. There are different scientific opinions regarding to what degree aptitudes are a function of heredity or are expandable through learning experiences.

aptitude test
A test or battery of tests designed to infer a person's capacity for a particular type of behavior in a single field or in several related fields. *Compare with* achievement test.

arbitrary sample
A sample in which members of the population were selected without an obvious basis. Such selection is *not* random and cannot be used for research. *See also* random sample.

areas of responsibility
Job duties. *Also called* key results areas in some organizations.

argumentatio
A rhetorical term for the rational arguments presented to support the conclusion of a speech. A key feature of a good presentation.

Argyris, Chris
A professor at Harvard University, as well as a leading researcher and theorist on behavioral science applications to organizational life. He has made important contributions to OD, including his double loop learning concept.

arithmetic mean
See mean.

Army Program for Individual Training (AR-PRINT)
The program which defines the U.S. Army's requirements and capabilities for all individual training.

Army School of Training Support (ASTS)
A military establishment tasked with supporting the British Army training system through R&D, course design, consultancy, training aids evaluation, training technology, and validation.

Army Trainer
A periodical of interest to HRD practitioners involved in military training. *Army Trainer* is published by the U.S. Government Printing Office.

Army Training and Evaluation Program (ARTEP)
The U.S. Army's collective training program. ARTEP establishes unit training objectives critical to unit survival and performance in combat. ARTEP combines the training and the evaluation process into one integrated function. The ARTEP is a training program and not a test. The sole purpose of external evaluation under this program is to diagnose unit requirements for future training.

art director
In video production, the person in charge of the look of the program. The art director may be responsible for the storyboard, set decoration, props, wardrobe, and location scouting.

articulated media
Media that reinforce each other.

artifacts, game
Materials and equipment used in an instructional game. For example, a deck of cards.

artificial intelligence (AI)
A field of computer science that deals with designing computer software which can reason and solve problems. AI includes expert systems: computer programs that offer advice and form the basis of performance support systems. *See* expert system, job aid, and performance support system.

artificial reality
See virtual reality.

artwork
The graphics prepared for print, film, or video. Artwork includes captions, charts, drawings, graphs, maps, photos, sketches, and titles.

Asia Pacific Journal of Human Resources
A periodical of general interest to HRD practitioners. Asia Pacific Journal of Human Resources is published by the Australian Human Resource Institute.

Asian Region Training and Development Organization (ARTDO)
(Most often called by its acronym ARTDO, pronounced ar′-toe. "D" is nearly silent.) An umbrella organization consisting of representatives from the regional Associations. *See also* International Federation of Training and Development Organizations (IFTDO).

aspect ratio
A film or television image viewing area's ratio of width to height. The aspect ratio is expressed in terms of relative width and height values. For example, the aspect ratio of a television screen is 3 x 4.

assembly effect
A group's collective ability to achieve a productivity level greater than the sum of the individuals working alone.

assessment *basic term*
1. Testing.

2. Any evaluation of the degree of success of learners.
3. A critical examination and estimate of the present value or status of a person or activity and need for change.

assessment center
Usually a process rather than a physical place, an assessment center evaluates the knowledge, skill, and attitudes of people to support their development and career and job placement. *See also* assessment center method.

assessment center method
basic term
A widely used formal method of data collection for evaluating the performance of individuals, involving feedback provided by a group of specially trained observers called assessors. The individuals being assessed participate in simulation exercises that enable them to demonstrate a particular skill, knowledge, or ability. The assessment center method was initiated to select foremen from among candidates and is often used to select candidates for senior level management positions. Research has validated the assessment center concept and it enjoys the confidence of a wide variety of organizations.

assessment of prior experiential learning (APEL)
See accreditation of prior learning (APL).

assessor
A member of the assessment staff of an assessment center. *See also* assessment center method.

assistant director
In video production, the person who prepares the actors and deals with other matters assigned by the director.

associate producer
In video production, the person who performs whatever task, special service, or function is required by the producer.

association
The connection made between an input (stimulus) and an action (response). For example, a person responds with the letter "A" when hearing the code "dih-dah." *See also* operant conditioning *and* stimulus.

Association de Dirigentes de Capacitacion de Argentina
A professional society for HRD practitioners in Argentina.

Association for Development of Computer-Based Instructional Systems
A professional society of interest to some HRD professionals.

Association for Educational Communications and Technology
A professional society of interest to some HRD professionals.

Association for Humanistic Psychology
A professional society of interest to some HRD professionals.

Association for Quality and Participation
A professional society of interest to some HRD professionals.

Association of Human Resource Systems Professionals
A professional society of interest to some HR professionals.

Association of Internal Consultants
A professional society of interest to some HRD professionals.

Association of Management Consulting Firms
A professional society of interest to some HRD professionals.

Association of Training and Employment Professionals
A professional society of interest to some HRD professionals.

Association of Visual Communicators
A professional society of interest to some HRD professionals.

assumptive question
A question used to assist learners to see the correct response. An assumptive question provides a hint to its answer. For example: "A gatevalve will work best in that situation, won't it?"

Atlantic Regional Society for Human Resource Development
A professional society for HRD practitioners in the maritime provinces of New Brunswick, Newfoundland, and Nova Scotia. *See also* HR Canada.

attention arousal set
An explanation for the enhancing effects of rehearsal on performance. Rehearsal helps performers set pretension levels and maintain attention to task-relevant cues.

attenuate
1. To reduce the level of an electrical audio signal, usually with a volume loudness control.
2. To reduce sound levels acoustically through the use of absorption material.

attitude change
1. A modification of development of opinions or feelings toward persons, ideas, causes, and events.
2. The goal of affective instruction.

attitudinal objective
See affective objective.

attributes
Qualitative data that can be recorded for analysis.

attribute weights
A value assigned to the characteristics of an instructional approach for purpose of comparison in cost-benefit analysis.

attrition
1. In research, *see* mortality.
2. In business, the turnover or loss of customers.

audience analysis
1. For oral presentations, assessment of how to shape the presentation for that audience. *Compare with* target population analysis.
2. Loosely, the process of determining the needs of specific participants for a planned program. *See also* target population analysis.

audience qualification
On the spot determination of the characteristics, background, or readiness of participants unknown to a presenter. Brief audience qualification is often done to ensure the planned program will be appropriate for the actual attendees.

audience reaction team
Members of the audience who react to a presenter to seek clarification of the material presented.

audio
The medium that involves words or sounds delivered to the learner's ear by a method other than voice. *Compare with* print.

audioconferencing
Communication between more than two people or groups, in different locations, by voice via a telecommunications network. Audioconferencing is often used for meetings. *See also* audio teleconferencing. *Compare with* video teleconference.

audiographics
Simultaneous transmission of audio and graphics across a telecommunications network.

audiographic teleconferencing
A distance learning method using a telephone and still frame video communication using a facsimile device or electronic blackboard between two or more locations. *Compare with* audio teleconferencing, computer conferencing, and videoconferencing.

audio motion visual
The medium that involves motion images in combination with audio. For example, videotape with sound. *Compare with* motion visual.

audio-print
The medium that involves printed materials in combination with audio. *Compare with* print.

audio-projected still video
The medium that involves projected still video images in combination with audio. *Compare with* print.

audiotape
Recording of sounds, a presentation, or a discussion, using magnetic tape. Audiotape is a medium that can support learning effectively, although it is used less often than it merits. *See also* cassette.

audio teleconferencing
1. Two-way (or more) audio-only communication for the purpose of learning.
2. A distance learning method using a speakerphone that allows groups in separate locations to hold a discussion. *Compare with* audiographic teleconferencing, computer conferencing, and videoconferencing.

audio-tutorial
An audiotape recording that directs the learner to activities according to a planned instructional sequence. An inexpensive but effective method.

audiovisual (AV) (A/V) *basic term*
Devices involving either sight, sound, or both for instruction.

Audio Visual Management Association
A professional society of interest to some HRD professionals.

audio-workbook
A courseware package that includes both audiotape and print media. Audio-workbooks are self-instructional.

audit, organizational
An evaluation of an organization's activities and status in various or all areas. For example, operations, production, or communications. *See also* audit, training.

audit, training
A technique used to evaluate activities to identify opportunities to improve the organization's overall HRD program.

aural learning preference
An individual learning style based on preference for listening. *See also* haptic, interactive, kinesthetic, olfactory, print, and visual learning styles.

Ausabel, David
A learning theorist best known for the development of the advance organizer concept. *See also* advance organizer.

Australian Human Resource Institute (AHRI)
A professional society of interest to HRD practitioners. *See also* Australian Institute of Training & Development (AITD).

Australian Institute of Management (AIM)
A professional society of interest to some HR professionals.

Australian Institute of Training & Development (AITD)
A professional society for HRD practitioners. *See also* Australian Human Resource Institute (AHRI).

Australian Training Review
A periodical of general interest to HRD practitioners. *Australian Training Review* is published by the National Centre for Vocational Education Research.

author
1. A person who creates a technology-based learning course material. *Compare with* programmer.
2. A person who creates instructional material.

authoring
To prepare a technology-based learning program, often using an authoring language or authoring system. *See also* author language *and* authoring system.

authoring aid
See authoring system.

authoring station
The computer and associated peripherals at which an author creates technology-based lessons. In some cases, there is no difference between an authoring station *and* a learning station.

authoring system
Special type of program that eases the programming of CAI courseware by enabling a content expert to interact with the computer in everyday language. Unlike an authoring language, it does not need programming knowledge or skill. *Also called* authoring aid *and* authoring utility. *Compare with* author language.

authoring utility
See authoring system.

author language
A computer language used specifically for creating CAI (including multimedia) courseware. For example, the learning-specific Tencore™ as opposed to a general purpose computer language such as FORTRAN. Author languages provide greater capabilities than authoring systems at the price of the greater effort required to learn them. *Also called* authoring language. *Compare with* authoring system.

autogenic training
Self-generated regulation of tension levels used in stress management. Autogenic training does not use specific biofeedback on recorded internal events. Instructions are presented to encourage relaxation.

automated apprenticeship training (AAT)
A training technique in which the learner receives tutorial guidance through pictures with accompanying sound when provided opportunity to practice.

auxiliary device
A device connected to a technology-based learning system and controlled by it. For example, an oscilloscope, audiotape, videotape, or videodisc. A videodisc controlled by a computer for learning purposes is termed interactive video. In computer terminology these are called peripheral devices. *Compare with* interactive video.

A/V skill
The HRD competency of selecting and using audio/visual hardware and software. *See also* HRD Roles and Competencies Study.

average
See mean.

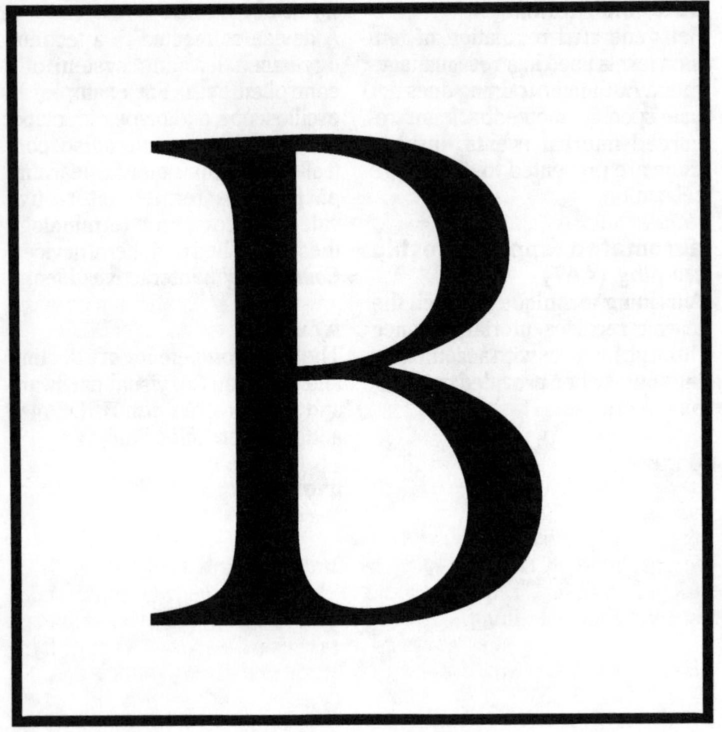

background
That portion of a visual that provides relief for text and objects in the foreground.

back-up (material)
Material important to support a learning activity, but not an essential part of its design characteristics.

balance
The design principle that orders the arrangement of elements of a visual.

balance, play
Adjustments made to a game to ensure that no player gets an undue advantage. Also, adjusting a game to ensure players at different levels can play on an equal basis.

balanced instructional style
An instructional approach based on equal emphasis on both content and experience. Other styles include facilitative, directive, Socratic, and disseminational.

barrier
1. A communication blockage.
2. A difficulty in achieving a goal.

barrier to transfer
Any factor that inhibits the success of transfer of learning to the job. For example: lack of reinforcement on the job. *See also* transfer of training.

baseline (performance) data
Data collected before an intervention. Baseline data are useful for identifying instructional needs and comparing postinstructional improvements to preexisting conditions.

basic education
See adult basic education.

basic research
See research.

basic skills *basic term*
Job-related basic skills are literacy skills (reading, writing, and speaking English) and computational skills. Basic skills programs often aim at raising learners from their preexisting level of ability to 6th- or 7th-grade level. *Compare with* remedial training, retraining, and second-chance training.

Basic Skills Enhancement Program (BESEP)
A program offered through a business-education partnership by the United Auto Workers and Ford Motor Company Employee Development and Training Center working with local U.S. school districts.

batch processing
A method in which all the data are fed to a computer at one time and processed at the same time. Rarely seen in today's interactive computing, batch processing may still be used to process large quantities of inputs, for example in business games.

battle focus
The process of deriving peacetime training requirements from wartime missions.

battle task
A task which must be accomplished by a subordinate organization if the next higher headquarters is to accomplish a mission-essential task. Battle tasks are selected by the senior commander from the subordinate organization's METL. *See also* mission essential task list (METL).

baud
The unit of measure of data-transmission speed used for comparison of hardware capabilities for technology-based learning. Baud originated in the era of telegraphy and is now used interchangeably with "bits per second."

baukasten principle
See modular principle.

before think steps
Things the learner must weigh before completing the steps of a process. *Compare with* after think steps *and* during think steps.

behavior *basic term*
1. One of the three required parts of a learning objective that describe what the learner will be able to do after instruction. *Also called* performance. *Compare with* condition *and* criterion. *See* performance.
2. The third level of Donald Kirkpatrick's summative evaluation model, focusing on the learner's new or changed job performance produced by instruction. Collected by questionnaire, usually 30, 60, or 90 days after the completion of instruction. It asks the manager how well the training has enabled the employee to do what's needed to get the job done. Some HRD departments send a similar form to the trainee. *See also* Evaluation Model, Four Level; learning; reaction; and results.

Continued on next page

3. The general psychological term for performance.
4. Any activity, overt or covert, capable of being measured.

behavioral anchor
A common behavior for a particular job. A behavioral anchor is identified, ranked, and weighted by experts familiar with the job.

behavioral career path
A type of career path based on behaviors. *See also* career pathing, historical career path, and organizational career path.

behavioral change *basic term*
Modification of people's actions in their own environment.

behavioral contract
An agreement between two parties to implement behavioral change. One party specifies the performance changes they wish to make and the steps to achieve them. The other party commits to provide agreed supportive resources.

behavioralism
Synonymous with behaviorism. *See* behaviorism.

behavioral modeling
See behavior modeling.

behavioral modification
See behavior modification.

behavioral objective *basic term*
A learning objective specifying the acquisition of a particular new behavior that the participant should be able to execute after instruction. Deals with the cognitive domain. *See also* learning objective *and* Mager, Robert.

behavioral skills output (BSO)
A specific curriculum design method.

behavioral transfer intention
A learner's commitment to apply newly learned specific key concepts or skills. *See also* transfer of training.

behavior frequency count
A method of gathering analysis data. Behavior frequency count is based on counting the number of repetitions of a particular behavior during a specific period of time.

behaviorism *essential 100 term*
A major school of psychology focused on observable, measurable, behavioral change. Behaviorism is usually associated with B. F. Skinner, but also is based on the work of Edwin Guthrie, Clark Hull, Ivan Pavlov, Edward L. Thorndike, John B. Watson, and others. Skinner is particularly associated with the behaviorist theory known as *operant conditioning.* Skinnerians developed programmed instruction, behavioral learning objectives, and behavior modification techniques. The power of reinforcement theory is based on reward of successive approximations, which are small steps toward the ultimate learning objective. Synonymous with behavioralism. *See also* behavior modification; cognitive learning; operant conditioning; punishers; reinforcement; reinforcer; and Skinner, B. F.

behavior modeling *basic term*
An instructional technique used to change the behavior of learners by showing them a sample of the correct behavior. Behavior modeling is based on carefully prepared presentations showing the *model* or an ideal enactment of the

desired behavior. Learners then try to emulate what they have seen. The total skill is usually presented before learners try out any behavior themselves. The model may be presented by video or instructors in a skit; however, the latter method may vary each time repeated. Sometimes called interactive modeling.

behavior modification *essential 100 term*
The process by which a person's particular *behavior* or behavior pattern is intentionally changed to some specified new behavior or behavior pattern, usually through use of external factors with reward, punishment, or recognition. *See also* behaviorism; operant conditioning; Pavlovian conditioning; and Skinner, B. F.

behind obstructions
In audio recordings, the barrier between the speaker and the audience.

bell (shaped) curve
See normal curve.

belonging and love needs
One of the levels of needs in Maslow's hierarchy of needs. *See also* hierarchy of needs.

benchmarking *basic term*
1. Evaluating one's own practices and then comparing them to another company's. Benchmarking is frequently used in the quality process.
2. Identifying notably successful practices used by other individuals or organizations who are toughest competitors or recognized as leaders. The benchmarked practices are implemented to upgrade one's own results. *Also called* competitive benchmarking. *See also* best practices.
3. Comparing performance of technology-based systems on the same test. Tests may be common or locally developed.

benchmark position
See job model.

benefits model
A cost-benefit analysis model. The benefits model links the benefits of a program with its goals. Unique relationships are identified for each instructional system. *Compare with* resource requirements model, life cycle model, and productivity model.

Berne, Eric
Developer of transactional analysis (TA). TA is a method of analyzing interpersonal communications. Berne published TA concepts in *Games People Play*. *See also* transactional analysis (TA).

best and final offer
A purchaser asking a qualified bidder to amend the price asked. A part of the negotiation process.

best practices
A process involving interviews of other companies to learn the reasons for their success. *See also* benchmarking.

Betacam
A hand-held combination camera and recorder using a professional quality Beta videocassette recorder. *Compare with* camcorder.

beta test
The formal test of under-development courseware and draft documentation by selected users before external testing or distribution. Users test the functionality

Continued on next page

and determine whether operational or utilization errors still exist. Beta testing is one of the last steps before release of the product. Also used to describe the testing of surveys and questionnaires. Beta test is also written ß test. *Compare with* alpha test.

beta test site
External organization that conducts a beta test.

bid
A proposal for project work. A part of the negotiation process. *See also* request for proposals (RFP).

bidders list
A list of qualified vendors maintained by a contracting office. Individuals and companies who want to be added to the list usually must follow a specified procedure, such as completing a simple form.

big media
The overall mode of instruction for a course, such as instructor-led training or CAI. Auxiliary items to support instructor-led instruction. *See also* media. *Compare with* little media.

billable time
See applied billing entry.

billing cost per applied person day
The amount needed to cover salary, fringe benefits, and overhead costs for one person for one day.

bimodal distribution
See Figure.

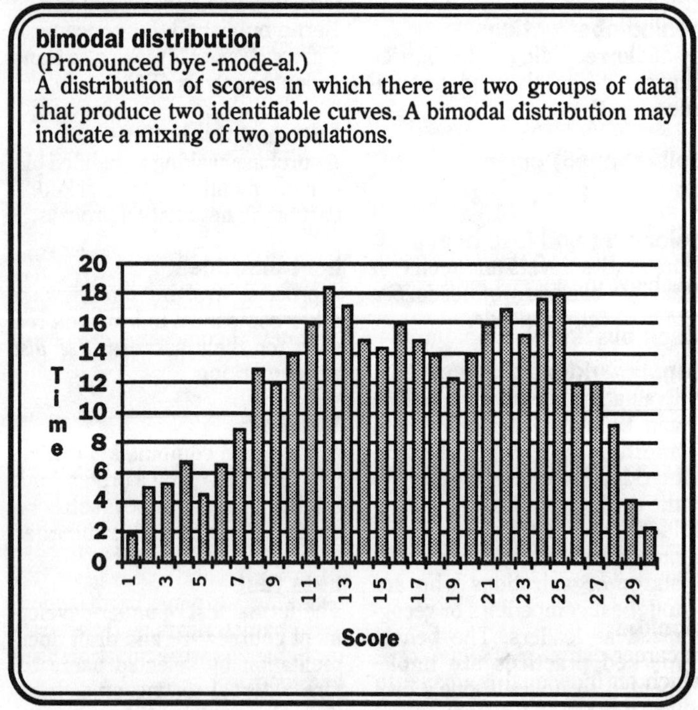
bimodal distribution
(Pronounced bye'-mode-al.)
A distribution of scores in which there are two groups of data that produce two identifiable curves. A bimodal distribution may indicate a mixing of two populations.

biofeedback
A class of techniques that use equipment to provide information to subjects about a variety of internal events, including heart rate, electromyography, autonomic events, respiration, brain frequencies, finger temperature, and peripheral vasoconstriction. The goal of biofeedback is to allow the learner to regulate the desired bodily changes without instrumentation. *See also* conditioned emotional response.

blackout curtains
Draperies used to block out nearly 100 percent of the window light from outside the room. They are used to maximize the darkness within the room for media presentations. *Also called* blackout drapes.

blackout drapes
See blackout curtains.

Blake, Robert R.
Codeveloper, with Jane Mouton, of the *Managerial Grid®* and grid theory concept. *See also* Managerial Grid® *and* Mouton, Jane.

blending
The process of combining sounds to achieve the desired audio effect.

block busting
A creativity training term to describe various ways of identifying and sidestepping blocks to understanding a problem or conceiving possible solutions. Block busting is used against perceptual, emotional, intellectual, expressional, or environmental blocks. *See also* creativity training.

blocked
In career planning, a situation in which an individual is unable to advance because the next logical career position is occupied by someone who is unlikely to move.

block of instruction
A group of related instructional units or modules covering a major subject area.

block scheduling
The traditional practice of scheduling groups of learners for the same instruction at the same time as each other. *Compare with* modular scheduling.

block "X" concept
An instructional design that identifies and groups lesson materials that do not require sequencing into a separate block identified as Block "X." Students may complete these materials concurrently with the regularly scheduled lessons of other blocks.

Bloom, Benjamin
An educational researcher best known for his *Taxonomy of Educational Objectives*. *See also* Bloom's taxonomy.

Bloom's taxonomy *essential 100 term*
A taxonomy of learning objectives developed by Benjamin Bloom. He addressed affective and cognitive learning outcomes in hierarchical fashion. His taxonomy was adopted by many developers and is applied to the development of a large body of instruction today. The taxonomy cites six cognitive behaviors: knowledge, comprehension, application, analysis, synthesis, and evaluation. There are five affective behaviors cited: receiving, responding, valuing, organization, and characterization. Psychomotor behaviors were not addressed by Bloom.

blueline
A document ready for the final check for typographical errors before printing. Brownline is a synonym for blueline.

board game
A game played on the surface of a specially designed board. For example, Monopoly™. Board games have been developed for a wide variety of instructional purposes.

boards
Synonym for platform. *See* platform.

body
1. The middle and largest part of a presentation. The body always includes the main points and content of the presentation. *Compare with* introduction *and* conclusion.
2. The main part of a lesson.
3. The core part of a document.

body language
See nonverbal communication.

boilerplate
Preprepared text that can be inserted in more than one future document. Boilerplate is often inserted in proposals for contracts.

boom operator
In video production, the person responsible for a boom microphone.

brain dominance *basic term*
1. The tenet, proposed by Ned Herrmann, that since each human being applies the two hemispheres of their brain asymmetrically, HRD activities that account for the potential differences that affect the learning are assumed to have better success. *See also* brain lateralization *and* whole brain learning.
2. The tendency for people to prefer either intuitive/emotive or analytical/rational ways of thinking.

brain dominance profile
The product of the Herrmann Brain Dominance Instrument, a questionnaire to assess brain dominance devised by Ned Herrmann. The profile provides a metaphor for the subject's brain quadrant preferences. *See also* whole brain learning.

brain dominance technology
The study of the relationship of brain dominance to learning. *See also* brain dominance, brain lateralization, and whole brain learning.

brain lateralization
The differentiation of brain functions in the right and left cerebral hemispheres and the right and left halves of the limbic system. Ned Herrmann has characterized the cerebral left hemisphere as logical, analytic, and mathematical, in contrast to the cerebral right as the conceptual, holistic, and synthesizing. The left limbic has been characterized as organized, linear, and sequential, in contrast to the right limbic which is interpersonal, emotional, and feeling. The encouragement of information processing by both sides of the brain is also a prime concern in creativity training. *See also* brain dominance, creativity training, and whole brain learning.

brainstorming *essential 100 term*
A group process for encouraging uninhibited generation of ideas

commonly used in real problem-solving situations. A technique developed by Alex Osborn. Brainstorming can help a group identify a large number of ideas in a short time. Includes both structured and unstructured brainstorming. Brain-storming is often used interchangeably with creative thinking and think tank. *See also* creativity training *and* nominal group technique.

brainstorming process
The brainstorming process includes three phases: generation, analysis, and action planning. Activities include generation, recording, amending, consolidating, establish evaluation criteria, evaluation, planning for action.

brainstorming rules
The basic rules applied to brainstorming sessions emphasize idea generation and recording of all ideas. The recorded ideas are usually posted. Criticism and evaluation of ideas must be postponed until all suggestions have been recorded. *See also* brainstorming *and* brainstorming process.

branching
In technology-based learning, the process of directing the learner to one of two or more paths through instructional material on the basis of replies to questions. Branching can also be responsive to learner-directed ideas such as deciding to see a glossary. *Compare with* linear.

breakdown, communication
See communication breakdown.

breakeven center
A form of financial arrangement for the HRD function. Fees and prices are established to enable the department to reach a breakeven point at year end. Higher prices may be established for popular or frequently offered programs to offset losses on other needed programs or services. *Compare with* budget item center, cost center, and profit center.

breakeven model
A cost-benefit analysis model that identifies the point at which the costs of a training approach equal the benefits. *Compare with* resource requirements, model life cycle model, and productivity model.

breakeven point *basic term*
The point in time at which the cost of a new and old approach are equal. At any time after the breakeven point the more costly method will be less costly. Identification of the breakeven point is important in cost-benefit analysis.

breakout session *basic term*
Conference sessions related to a general session. Breakout sessions may be concurrent sessions but all will address the same topic or a variation of it. *Compare with* concurrent session, general session, and track session.

briefing
1. A synonym for presentation. The briefing term and technique are often used in military training.
2. An introductory session describing the background and rules of play of an instructional game or other activity.

brightness
The amount of light emitted from a surface such as a screen; usually measured in foot-candles, foot-lamberts, or lux.

British Institute of Management (BIM)
A professional society of interest to some HR professionals.

British Psychological Society (BPS)
A professional society of interest to some HR professionals.

broadband
Communications channels such as broadcast television, cable television, microwave, and satellite that are capable of carrying a wide range of frequencies.

brownline
See blueline.

BRS
A commercial information retrieval service that can be accessed by a computer over a telephone line. A large number of data bases may be searched. *See also* ORBIT *and* DIALOG.

Bruner, Jerome
A psychologist best known for study of cognition in concept attainment. *See also* concept attainment *and* cognitive development theory.

BS 5750
A standard of the British Standards Institute which is awarded to organizations, irrespective of their size, on the basis of achieving quality as applied to the HRD function. *See also* ISO 9000.

budget item center
Provision of a budget for the operation of the HRD function. This approach makes HRD an overhead cost. *Compare with* breakeven center, cost center, and profit center.

build
The generation of explanatory and support material and visuals.

builder
One of five career value structures identified by Edgar Schein. The others are technocrat, climber, searcher, and stabilizer.

bullets
On visuals, dots or other graphics before key points that highlight each item.

Bureau of Apprenticeship and Training
A unit of the U.S. Department of Labor that sets the framework and basic standards for conduct of apprenticeship training in the U.S. *See also* apprenticeship *and* National Apprenticeship Act.

business competencies
Competencies are described in the HRD Roles and Competencies Study as having a strong management, economics, or administration base. They include business understanding, cost-benefit analysis skill, delegation skill, industry understanding, organization-behavior understanding, organization-development-theories-and-techniques understanding, organization understanding, project-management skill, and records-management skill. *See also* HRD Roles and Competencies Study.

business game *basic term*
An instructional game based on one or more of the financial or management disciplines. Typical game objectives are to maximize profit, sales, market share, or return on investment. Learners manipulate the variables of the busi-

ness and observe the effect of those changes. *Also called* business simulation. *See also* games.

business partner
A newly popular term to describe a formal symbiotic relationship between two companies. The best known example is the formal program that associates much smaller companies with IBM as business partners.

business plan
A formal document that specifies the mission, vision, objectives, financial considerations, and action items which an organization has formulated to accomplish its business goals in a defined time period, usually one or more years. A business plan is often the basis for internal approval or external financing. *See also* strategic plan.

business simulation
See business game.

business understanding
The HRD competency of knowing how the functions of a business work and relate to each other; knowing the economic impact of business decisions. *See also* HRD Roles and Competencies Study.

butcher paper
See newsprint.

butterflies
See stage fright.

button
A potentially active spot on the screen that branches the user to another location in the program when chosen. Buttons may look like real-world buttons, take the shape of a familiar object, or be unseen by the learner.

buzz group *basic term*
A small group technique named for the buzzing sound of multiple intensive discussions. Subgroups of six or fewer participants who are part of a larger group usually all meet in the same room for a limited period of time. Each group agrees on chairperson and recorder roles. The group discusses the topic assigned, called the team task. At the end of the specified work period they report back to the whole group. Buzz groups are useful to develop agendas, react to a presentation, develop questions or points, stimulate thinking, or recommend courses of action.

buzz session
A short period in which participants discuss a given topic.

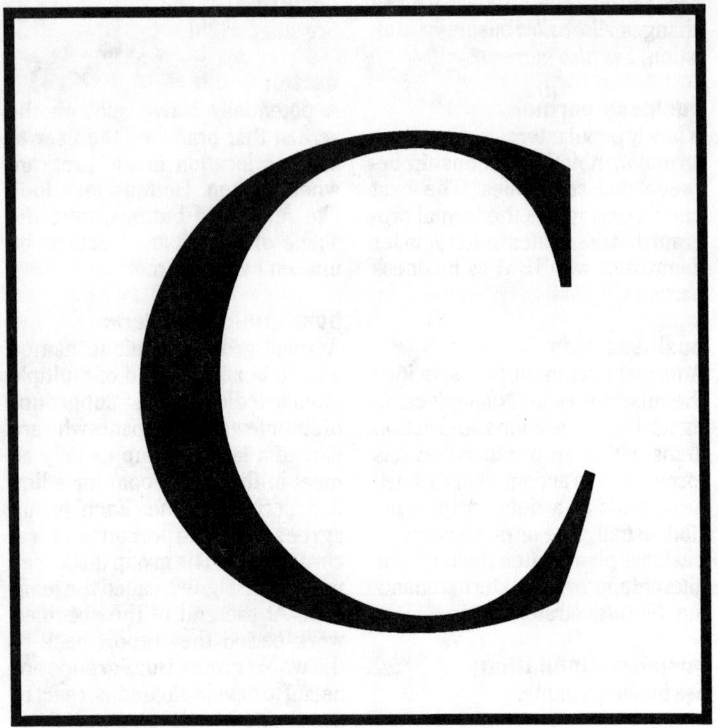

cable television
Delivery of taped or live TV programming over a controlled system to a specified audience by means of coaxial cable. Similar to closed-circuit TV (CCTV). *See also* closed-circuit TV (CCTV).

California Management Review
A periodical of interest to HRD practitioners involved in management. *California Management Review* is published by the University of California at Berkeley.

camcorder
A lightweight, hand-held video camera and recorder in a single unit.

cameraperson
In small video productions, the person in charge of setting up the lights and running the camera. In larger productions, up to three people may share this work.

camera ready
Copy ready to be photographed for printing.

Canadian Jobs Strategy (CJS)
An assortment of Federal programs, administered through Employment and Immigration Canada, emphasizing long-term training and development assistance to both individuals and employers. In Canada, most HRD-

related programs are administered at the provincial level.

canned instruction
See off-the-shelf programs.

canned programs
See off-the-shelf programs.

card back
In instructional games, the back or design side of a question card.

card face
In instructional games, the front or question side of a question card.

card game
An instructional game based on playing cards or other types of cards.

cards
1. The cards used in instructional games.
2. The pages (screens) within a Hypermedia stack.

card sort survey
A manual method of gathering analysis data. A card sort survey is based on subjects sorting prepared index cards containing statements into several piles. For example, the piles might be labeled "really want," "don't care," and "really don't want" training or information on a given subject. A data base may be used to achieve the same results.

career
1. The pattern and sequence of jobs and responsibilities which characterize one person's work over time.
2. Development in a particular vocation or profession to which personal commitment is given.
3. For career development purposes, includes aspirations, attitudes, and values.
4. Loosely, a life-long series of work-related activities.

career counseling
Helping individuals plan their careers.

career development *essential 100 term*
1. A planned, structured process of interaction between a representative of the organization and the individual. Career development enables employees to grow within an organization and results in their optimal utilization. *See also* organizational career development.
2. The results of implementing a career plan.
3. The name applied to the field related to careers.

career-development-theories-and-techniques understanding
The HRD competency of knowing the techniques and methods used in career development, and understanding their appropriate uses. *See also* HRD Roles and Competencies Study.

career goal
The career end-result an individual hopes to achieve. *Compare with* career objective.

career ladder
See career path.

career management
Systematically preparing, implementing, and monitoring of an individual's career plan. Career management may be driven by the individual, or the organization, or both.

career objective
A specific career step an individual hopes to achievewithin a predeter-

Continued on next page

mined time. *Compare with* career goal.

career path *basic term*
A structured sequence of work assignments and experiences. A career path provides employees the opportunity to participate in many aspects of a career area for the purpose of preparation for career growth. Includes detailed descriptions of interrelationships between jobs in an organization, expressed in terms of the training, education, experience, and behaviors required for movement between jobs. Used by career planners to advise an employee. *See also* historical path, organizational path, and behavioral career path.

career pathing
See career path.

career planning *basic term*
Planned programs for the development of employees of an organization. Includes identifying and exploring career opportunities, setting goals, establishing direction, and choosing the means by which to attain the goals. The output of this process is the career plan.

Career Planning and Adult Development Journal
A periodical of interest to HRD practitioners involved in career development. *Career Planning and Adult Development Journal* is published by the Career Planning and Adult Development Network.

career plateau
A career level from which it is difficult to progress.

career progression ladder
See job progression ladder.

career resource center
A function or location provided by the organization to offer formal career planning guides or processes to help employees determine their career interests, values, and competencies; educational references; job-finding skills; management and supervisory training; and occupational guides.

career strategy
In career planning, criteria for considering alternatives, evaluating options, making choices, and measuring success.

Carl Perkins Vocational Education Act
Legislation for a U.S. program to fund and expand vocational education.

carousel
The most popular type of 35mm slide tray. Carousel refers to the circular shape and rotation of the tray.

carrel
A carrel consists of a desk-like work area and chair, or sometimes a more elaborate setup. The distinguishing characteristic of a carrel is a partition separating the learning activity of one learner from the adjacent carrel. Carrels may also have shelves, storage, and functional areas for computer or audiovisual equipment. *See also* learning station. *Compare with* workstation.

case analysis
A specific, comprehensive, analytical process that produces a case report. Historically accurate cases are considered to be best. Case analysis is often completed by a group because of the extensive

effort required. The product is called a case report. *See also* case study.

case discussion
The process of following a specified sequence of activities using a case study. *See also* case study.

case incident
A brief description of a specific situation. The case incident is used as the bases for discussion and problem solving. A case incident is smaller than a case study. *Compare with* case study.

case method *essential 100 term*
An instructional technique that presents real or fictional situations or problems for learners to analyze, to discuss, and to recommend actions to be taken. It is based on the concept of discovery learning. The information given in the study realistically simulates the experience where only limited information is available. Learners are presented case information. Usually each learner determines a solution. Then groups of students discuss the problem to arrive at a group solution. Then, the entire group discusses the case. Finally, the class is advised of the historical solution to the problem. Emphasis is on decision making. A case study can be used to start a general session, or as part of a small group session. The well-known case study method originated at Harvard University. Harvard case studies have a worldwide reputation. *See also* case study.

case report
An objective body of information that forms a case in a case study. It is the product of the case analysis process. Well-written reports provide multiple inside views and applicable interpersonal relationships. *See also* case study.

case study *basic term*
A written account of an event or situation to which learners react. *See also* action maze, case method, case report, and incident process.

case study method
See case method.

cassette
A self-contained audiotape, videotape, or film case.

cast
In video production, anyone working in front of the camera.

casting director
In video production, the person who gathers actors from whom a producer will select. The casting director may choose the smaller parts or recommend actors for major roles.

cathode ray tube (CRT)
CRT refers to the screen technology commonly used in oscilloscopes, television sets, and computer terminals. *Compare with* VDT, LCD, plasma panel, and video monitor.

caucus
A meeting, often of a subgroup. Caucusing is a method sometimes used for before-instruction meetings with learners.

causal coefficient
In cost-benefit analysis, a value assigned to causal links between attributes of an instructional approach and its outcome.

cause and effect diagram
See Figure on next page.

cause and effect diagram
Information representation in the general shape of a fish skeleton. The diagram thoroughly lists subcategories and illustrates the relationship of ideas to one another. The cause and effect diagram can be used to record the ideas produced by brainstorming. *Also called* fishbone diagram *and* Ishikawa diagram. *See also* seven quality process tools.

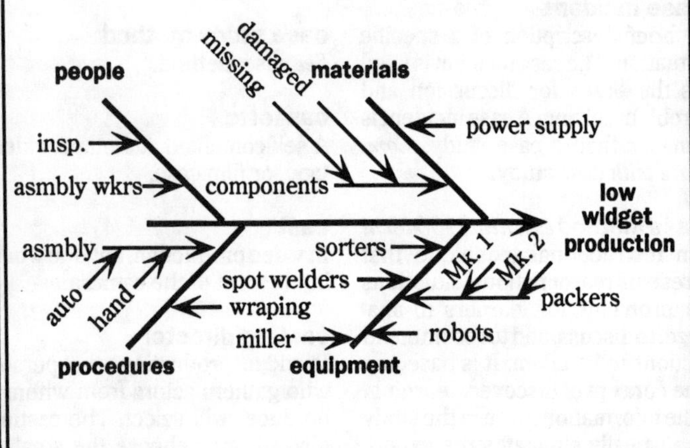

CBT Directions
A periodical of interest to HRD practitioners involved in technology-based learning. *CBT Directions* is published by Weingarten Publications, Inc.

CD redbook audio
A sound file format that will play on any audio CD or CD-ROM player.

CD-ROM drive
The drive needed to retrieve data from a CD-ROM format disc. *See also* compact disc read only memory (CD-ROM).

CD-ROM player
See CD-ROM drive.

CD-ROM XA
A compact disc format designed for interactive multimedia. A hybrid of CD-ROM and CD-I. *Compare with* compact disc-interactive (CD-I), compact disc read only memory (CD-ROM), and digital video interactive (DVI).

CD rot
See laser rot.

CEEFAX
A system of information distribution via broadcast television operated by the British Broadcasting corporation. *See also* Teletext *and* videotex.

centered (justification)
Type centered in the document or screen. *Compare with* flush right or left *and* ragged justification.

Center for the Application of Psychological Type
An organization established to conduct research and provide services to users of the Myers-Briggs Type Indicator. *See* Myers-Briggs Type Indicator (MBTI).

centering
Placing a copy of graphic material in the middle of the layout.

centrality
A position in a communication network requiring the fewest linkages to transmit a message to every other member.

central tendency
In statistics, the overall term that includes the average, mean, and median of a group of scores.

cerebral left quadrant
The quadrant of the brain associated with logical, analytical, quantitative, fact-based functions. *See also* brain dominance and whole brain learning. *Compare with* cerebral right quadrant.

cerebral mode thinking processes
One of four whole brain learning descriptors. Cerebral mode thinking processes includes cerebral left and right quadrants. *See also* whole brain learning. *Compare with* limbic mode thinking processes.

cerebral right quadrant
The quadrant of the brain associated with holistic, intuitive, synthesizing, integrating functions. *See also* brain dominance *and* whole brain learning. *Compare with* cerebral right quadrant.

certification
See professional certification.

chaining
Linking a series of discriminable responses together in a particular order. The completion of each response provides the stimulus for the next response. Chaining may involve verbal or motor responses. *See also* association, discrimination, and operant conditioning.

chalkboard *basic term*
Surface which can be written on with chalk. Chalkboards were known as blackboards when they were made from slate. Research indicates that green is the preferable color. Since airborne chalk is harmful to computer drives, technology-based classrooms use dry erase boards called whiteboards. *Compare with* whiteboard.

change
1. The second phase in Kurt Lewin's three-stage process, in which the existing equilibrium is disrupted by bringing about a favorable imbalance between driving forces and restraining forces. *See also* transfer of training.
2. The global forces that produce dynamic effects in organizations. Change is the force that generates the need for much HRD.

change agent *essential 100 term*
1. In OD, any person or group responsible for initiating or implementing organizational change. A term originated by Kurt Lewin. *See also* Lewin, Kurt *and* organization development (OD).
2. A person, who understands organizational and personal change dynamics and seeks to affect a different condition in an organization.

Continued on next page

3 A consultant who works with the client system to apply valid knowledge to the client's problems.

change management
A process whereby organizations and individuals proactively plan for and adapt to change.

Change Model
A model developed by Kurt Lewin. The change model represents the modification of any existing social system through a three-stage process from unfreezing to change to refreezing.

channel
1. The conduit through which information to be communicated is conveyed.
2. A specific frequency for reception or transmission.

channel capacity
The number of items of information that an individual can effectively process at one time.

character
1. Any alphanumeric representation in any language. *See* alphanumeric, graphic.
2. Specifications of a role in role playing.

charette
An intensive planning session. In a charette community, members critique a major plan or model, contribute suggestions, and ask difficult questions. This leads to a discussion of the problems, with all working to resolve conflicting desires and to actively plan together.

charge-back *basic term*
In HRD accounting, the process of charging costs to the department receiving an HRD service. The receiving department may agree to pick up the bill for travel, meals, and lodging for all participants in advance of a program. It may also agree to be charged for facilitator fees, participant materials, and other program-specific costs.

chart *basic term*
1. Any two-dimensional visual.
2. A misnomer for a graph.
3. A flipchart or poster chart.

cheat sheet
A slightly negative slang name for a job aid. Some employees place a negative connotation on job aids because of traditional reliance on instruction and memory.

check disc
A reduced quality test videodisc produced from the tape master to verify contents and placement before production.

checklist
A quality control document used to record preliminary data based on sample observations. Check sheets record data on the frequency of an event or problem. In the U.S., events are usually recorded by four vertical lines with a fifth horizontal line drawn through the first four to represent a group of five. *Also called* check sheet *and* tally sheet. *See also* seven quality process tools.

child ego state
In transactional analysis, one of three states: parent, child, and adult. The child is the spontaneous, experimenting, exploring or dependent side of the human personality. The combinations of these states in human interactions are the basis of transactional analysis. *See also* transactional analysis (TA).

Chilean Association for Training and Development
A professional society for HRD practitioners in Chile.

Chinese Society for Training and Development
A professional society for HRD practitioners in Taiwan.

chi-square
(Pronounced kye—rhymes with dye—square.)
One of the most frequently encountered non-parametric tests. Chi-square is used to study data that falls in two or more categories to determine whether they differ significantly from expected proportions or each other.

chroma
The color portion of a video signal. *Also called* chrominance. *See also* luminance.

chrominance
See chroma.

chronemics
An area of nonverbal communications based on time concept.

chunking
The process of dividing or combining training material into small, easier-to-deal-with portions. Research establishes ideal portions as between 5 and 9 pieces of information.

Chyron
(Pronounced kye′-ron.)
The process of preparing textual graphics for inclusion in a video-based presentation. For example, "Insert a chyron here." Chyron is a brand name of text generator.

circle chat
See cracker barrel session.

circle introduction
A game used for mutual group introductions. Each person adds their own name to the growing list of those who preceded them until the group is completed.

clarifying questions
1. A question that requires a specific answer. Clarifying questions are used to probe for increased detail and to promote full understanding of a response. *Compare with* open question *and* direct question.
2. A question intended to reduce the ambiguity of a position or statement.

class A presentation
A presentation given top-quality visual treatment.

classical conditioning
See Pavlovian conditioning.

classification
A system of security levels placed on verbal and visual information by military and private sector organizations.

classroom response system
Equipment that provides feedback to the instructor or whole group based on selections on devices available to each learner. Classroom response systems can make lecture-based sessions interactive. The instructor, and sometimes the students, can instantly see the percentage of responses to any question. This permits the instructor to vary the pace or content based on exact need.

classroom style
See Figure on next page.

clearinghouse *basic term*
1. Any organization established to

Continued on next page

classroom style
An arrangement of tables and chairs in a meeting room. Usually set up in straight rows. *Compare with* theater *and* conference styles.

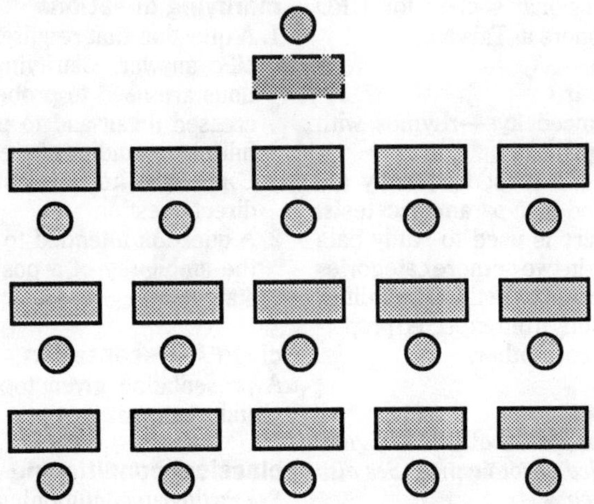

gather information on a topic for use by a wider group of individuals or organizations.
2. A centralized center for purchasing instructional programs.

client *essential 100 term*
1. In consulting, the person responsible for the outcome of a project for which a consultant has been employed. The client may be a different person from the initial contact or sponsor who secured a particular consultant. *Compare with* stakeholder.
2. A person or organization that is the sponsor or recipient of an intervention.
3. The person who can terminate the consultation without recourse to anyone else.

client-centered relationship
In consulting, a relationship between consultant and client based on the needs of the client. *See also* client, client system, and helping relationship.

clientele
See client.

client system *basic term*
1. In consulting, the organizational unit most directly affected by a consultant. The client system *may* be led by the client. *See also* client.
2. In organization development, the target for change.

climate *basic term*
1. Favorable or unfavorable conditions for learning.

2. The condition of morale within an organization.
3. Loosely, the atmosphere in an organization.
4. The emotional or affective environment within which behavior or learning will occur.

climate management
See climate setting.

climate setting *basic term*
Activities that establish a climate conducive to learning. Climate setting is closely aligned with adult learning. The two components of climate are organizational climate and instructional climate. *Also called* climate management.

climate setting activity *basic term*
Any activity to develop group readiness for instruction. *See also* climate setting.

climber
One of five career value structures identified by Edgar Schein. *Compare with* technocrat, builder, searcher, and stabilizer.

clinic *basic term*
1. A group learning activity focused on improving a specific skill of participants who have at least some experience. Clinics are similar to workshops except that the attendees provide the cases. They differ from seminars, which are more general. *See also* workshop. *Compare with* seminar.
2. A group learning and problem-solving activity focused on relevant common interests to diagnose, analyze, and seek solutions to specific individual and programatic problems.

clip art
1. Traditionally, convenient, preprinted, camera-ready art, such as graphics, logos, borders, and banner heads. Clip art is cut from paper sheets and pasted directly on pages to be processed for publication.
2. Computer files that provide the same functionality as the traditional paper clip art. Electronic clip art is "cut and pasted" into the target document. *See also* clip media.

clip media
Already-developed animation, sound, and motion video computer files that provide the same functionality as clip art. Clip media speeds creation of multimedia programs. *See also* clip art.

clock hour
See instructional hour.

closed-circuit television
See closed-circuit TV (CCTV).

closed-circuit TV (CCTV)
CCTV is a limited network cable system serving classrooms with either taped or live video with, or without, audio.

closed communication
1. Constraints placed on sending and receiving of messages by individuals or groups. Open communication is important in the instructional setting. *Compare with* open communication.
2. A condition in which people interact defensively and do not share information.

closed response question (item)
In written questioning, a question in which the respondent is asked to select one of several answers

Continued on next page

provided. *Also called* selected response. *Compare with* open response question.

closure

1. In consulting, the end of the consultation. *Also called* disengagement, separation, and termination.
2. One of six gestalt principles about perception. *See* gestalt perception principles.

cluster approach

An instructional approach independent of logical chronology or procedure. Learners directly identify information needed to achieve the instructional goal.

coaching *basic term*

A process through which an individual supports the learning or performance improvement of another via interactive questioning and other means of active support. The coaching instructor observes the learner, provides hints, help, and feedback in a positive way as needed. Coaching is sometimes incorporated in on-the-job training.

coaching skill

The HRD competency of helping individuals recognize and understand personal needs, values, problems, alternatives, and goals. *See also* HRD Roles and Competencies Study.

coalition

A temporary alliance among two or more members of a group. A coalition is typically oriented to overcoming a difference of opinion on how to achieve the group goal.

codec

A coder-decoder used in videoconferencing to convert and reconvert analog signals such as video or voice into digital form for digital transmission.

coding

1. Programming in computer language. *Compare with* authoring.
2. Preparing information for storage or input.

coercive change *basic term*

In organization development, a change process characterized by nonmutual goal-setting and imbalanced power with one-sided deliberateness. *Compare with* indoctrination, planned change, technocratic change, interactional change, normative-re-educative change, persuasive change, socialization change, emulative change, and natural change.

cognitive *essential 100 term*

Outcomes based on the enhancement of knowledge and understanding of, or related to, mental processes, particularly information processing. *Compare with* affective *and* psychomotor.

cognitive apprenticeship

An instructional approach based on emulation of craft apprenticeship. In a cognitive apprenticeship learners are provided the opportunities for extended practice on authentic tasks while working under a master performer-instructor.

cognitive development theory

In developmental psychology, a theory concerned with growth in the processes of perceiving, thinking, and knowing. Swiss psychologist Jean Piaget described cognitive processes developed through four stages from early childhood to adult.

cognitive dissonance *basic term*
1. Disorientation due to the incompatibility and conflict of two contradictory messages received by one or more senses. A term used in marketing and advertising that applies to the learning site as well.
2. Incompatibility of a written or spoken message with the visuals that were developed to deliver the same message.
3. Loosely, disorientation and distress due to a discrepancy between words and behavior.

cognitive domain *basic term*
The area of human learning associated with intellectual skills, such as assimilation of information or knowledge.

cognitive feasibility theory
A theory of learning for advanced knowledge. Cognitive feasibility theory recommends a multiple perspective approach to content via multiple analogies.

cognitive learning *basic term*
In Benjamin Bloom's taxonomy, changes in knowledge, comprehension, application, analysis, synthesis, and evaluation. *See also* Bloom's taxonomy *and* cognitive science. *Compare with* affective learning *and* psychomotor learning.

cognitive map
1. An instructional technique of creating a map of concepts related to examples. The cognitive map diagram shows which concepts are relevant to each.
2. The internalized association between a goal, a behavior(s), and an awareness of the environment in which the goal is located.

cognitive modeling *basic term*
An instructional technique similar to behavior modeling. Cognitive modeling converts mental processes to observable graphic media. For example, checklists, flowcharts, job aids, and worksheets. *See also* behavior modeling *and* social learning theory.

cognitive network (cognet)
Usually called by its acronym, an instructional approach based on all participants completing assigned readings and answering the same questions before meeting. In a cognet, only specific subgroups read identical material. Subgroups may be assigned reading with contrasting viewpoints. Before the whole group meets, the subgroups meet to prepare group answers to share with entire group.

cognitive objectives *basic term*
A learning objective specifying the acquisition of particular knowledge or information dealing with the cognitive domain. *See also* learning objective.

cognitive psychology
The branch of psychology that emphasizes the way the brain collects, organizes, and retrieves information in order to understand human behavior.

cognitive science
An interdisciplinary scientific field focused on discovering the mechanisms of the mind and the way in which mental processes combine to yield human behavior, beliefs, and understanding. *See also* affective learning, behaviorism, cognitive learning, and psychomotor learning.

cognitive style *basic term*
A categorization of a person's pre-

Continued on next page

ferred method of learning, based on the concept that individuals think and learn differently.

cognitivism
A learning theory concerned with the internal person and with insight or discovery.

cohesion
The sum of intermember attraction, instrumental value of the group, and risk taking. Members of a cohesive group feel a sense of belonging, interpersonal influence, and teamwork.

cohesiveness
The degree to which group members are committed to the group.

cohort system
A set of procedures designed to increase group cohesion by strengthening friendship ties and a sense of belonging.

cold storage training
Instruction that does not apply immediately and, therefore, is easily forgotten. *Compare with* refresher training.

collaborative learning
An instructional approach in which learners share responsibility for learning with instructors or facilitators. In collaborative learning, they work together to determine how the learning session should progress.

collective training
Unit training to prepare cohesive teams and units to accomplish their combined arms missions on the integrated battlefield.

colloquy *basic term*
A discussion, usually in front of an audience, between teams representing different points of view. Often in a colloquy, one group consists of resource persons or experts and the other represents the audience. Resembles a panel in that all members take an active part. In some cases, the audience may participate depending on the rules established for that colloquy. A colloquy provides better audience participation than a panel. *See also* debate, forum, panel, and speech.

color
In instructional design, an element that can be employed to emphasize relationship, focus attention, or provoke a psychological response.

color graphics adaptor (CGA)
CGA is the low end color video system available for IBM and compatible computers. CGA has less resolution than EGA (enhanced graphics adaptor) or VGA (video graphics adaptor).

Combat Training Center Program
A U.S. Army program established to provide realistic joint service and combined arms training in accordance with Army doctrine. It is designed to provide training units opportunities to increase collective proficiency on the most realistic battlefield available during peacetime.

combined training
Training involving elements of two or more forces of two or more allied nations.

command
In technology-based learning, specific words or code used to tell the computer what to do. In compari-

son, a menu choice is a simpler way to achieve the same result.

command training guidance (CTG)
In U.S. military training, the long-range planning document published by division and brigade (or equivalents) in the active and reserve components to prescribe future training and related activities.

Commerce Business Daily (CBD)
A periodical providing legal notice of all U.S. federal contracting information. The CBD is a primary source of information on RFPs for U.S. government HRD projects. *See also* request for proposals (RFP).

commercial information retrieval service
A data base that can be accessed by a computer over a telephone line. Commercial information retrieval service may be included as a service in an organization's learning center. Usually, large number of data bases may be searched. *See also* BRS, DIALOG, and ORBIT.

common cause
In quality improvement or TQM training, a source of variation that is part of the random variation inherent in the process itself. The common cause origin can usually be traced to an element of the system correctable only by management.

common-skills-first principle
An instructional approach based on teaching foundation knowledge and skills early in a course of instruction. The common-skills-first principle is used frequently in technical instruction.

communicatee
The intended receiver of the concepts and ideas that are communicated. *See also* communication. *Compare with* communicator.

communication
The process of creating understanding between the originator of a concept and the receiver. *See also* communicatee *and* communicator.

communication breakdown
A cessation of communication.

communication networks
Communication patterns within a small group. For example, circle, wheel, chain, and star.

communication skills *basic term*
The skills associated with the transfer of information in either oral, written, or pictorial form. Communication skills include both reception (e.g. listening and empathy) or expression (e.g. concluding and describing). Oral and written communication skills are often valued and measured separately.

communicator
One who generates and communicates concepts and ideas. *See also* communication. *Compare with* communicatee.

community simulation *basic term*
A large group role play in which staff members play the roles as key community figures. A learner is selected to go into the community to perform a particular task. The learner proceeds to and interacts with each figure who is considered relevant to performing the task. This continues until the task has been accomplished or until

Continued on next page

the trainee is asked to leave the community.

compact disc (CD) *basic term*
Any of several 12-cm compact disc formats. Because of the inherent advantages of all of the smaller digital disc systems, they will eventually replace the larger 12-inch analog videodisc. *See also* CD redbook audio, CD rot, compact disc-interactive (CD-I), compact disc read only memory (CD-ROM), and digital video interactive (DVI).

compact disc-interactive (CD-I)
Usually called by its initials, a compact disc format designed for interactive multimedia. A 12-cm CD-I disc holds a comprehensive mix of up to one hour of video, 7,000 still images, audio, computer text and graphics, and interaction capabilities. One competitive format for interactive multimedia. *Compare with* CD-ROM, CD-ROM XA, and DVI.

compact disc read only memory (CD-ROM) *basic term*
Usually called by its initials, a compact disc format designed to store large amounts of text or picture data. A CD-ROM provides enough storage for five encyclopedias on a 4.75-inch (12-cm) disc. CD-ROMs are read by a laser. The format is not compatible with either CD-I or DVI. *Compare with* CD-I, CD-ROM XA, and DVI.

company games
Games used by organizations for in-service development of their employees.

compatible
Elements or individuals that work smoothly and correctly together.

compensatory programs
HRD programs designed to help minority groups enter the workforce or to advance.

competency *essential 100 term*
An area of personal capability that enables one to perform. For example, a knowledge, skill, attitude, value, or other personal characteristic. Competency is necessary for the acceptable performance of a task or achievement of an outcome.

competency analysis
The assessment and definition of the competencies needed for success in a given job. *See also* competency assessment, competency model, and needs analysis.

competency assessment *basic term*
The process through which the competencies of an individual are identified and evaluated against the needs of a specific job or profile. *See also* competency analysis, competency model, and needs analysis.

competency-based curriculum
An instructional sequence based on objectives-centered instruction. *See also* competency model.

competency-identification skill
The HRD competency of identifying the knowledge and skill requirements of jobs, tasks, and roles. *See also* HRD Roles and Competencies Study.

competency model *basic term*
A way of describing the requisite abilities, personal qualities, and skills needed to perform a specific job for an organization, an organi-

Competency models can be constructed through expert judgment, group participation, research, and task or output analysis. *See also* competency-based curriculum *and* needs analysis.

competency study
The process of identifying and describing the knowledge, skills, and behavior necessary for the acceptable performance. *See also* HRD Roles and Competencies Study.

competition
1. In instructional games, a contest between two or more participants, against a standard or simply against the forces of chance.
2. Interference of prior learning with new learning. Cues provided suggest an incorrect connection with the new learning. *Compare with* facilitation.

component display theory
A theory, developed by M. David Merrill, composed of instructional design principles related to specific tasks. The theory is implemented in the lesson design system (LDS). *See also* lesson design system (LDS).

composite design
A design involving a combination of at least two basic design structures.

composite video
The output of certain computers and videocassette players.

composite whole brain learning group
A group that is balanced in thinking and learning styles across the spectrum of mental possibilities.

comprehension *basic term*
1. A synonym for understanding.
2. The second of Bloom's six levels of learning. *See also* Bloom's taxonomy.

comprehensiveness
In HRD, the degree to which an instructional package contains support material.

compressed speech
A method of reducing the listening time for prerecorded audiotape. The tape can be played at up to two and one-half the original speed without unacceptable distortion. *Also called* time compressed speech.

compressed video
Video images that have been processed to facilitate storage and transmission.

compression (of digital information)
Reduction of the amount of information stored to represent an image.

Compuserve
A commercial information retrieval service that can be accessed by a computer over a telephone line. A large number of sublocations exist based on user interest. *See also* DIALOG, ORBIT, and Prodigy.

computer application *basic term*
1. Commonly used practical programs. For example, word processing, spreadsheets, data bases, graphics, and communications.
2. Any technique for applying computer technology to the solution of a variety of human endeavors (manual tasks).

computer assisted instruction (CAI)
Usually called by its initials, CAI is the use of a computer to deliver instruction. The modes of CAI are drill and practice, modeling, tutorial, and simulation. This is the preferred term. It is synonymous with CAT and CAL. CAI, along with CMI and CSLR, are the components of CBL. Unfortunately, some HRD people say "CAI" when they mean CBL. *See also* computer-based learning (CBL). *Compare with* computer managed instruction (CMI) *and* computer supported learning resources (CSLR).

computer assisted learning (CAL)
A synonym for computer assisted instruction. *See* computer assisted instruction (CAI).

computer assisted training (CAT)
A synonym for computer assisted instruction. *See* computer assisted instruction (CAI).

computer-based education (CBE) *basic term*
Since computer-based learning (CBL) was originally developed in a university setting, the term education was naturally applied to it. Therefore, CBE is the oldest of the several synonymous terms in use. *See also* computer-based learning (CBL).

computer-based instruction (CBI) *basic term*
The meaning is identical to computer-based learning, but is preferred by some users in industry. *See* computer-based learning (CBL).

computer-based learning (CBL) basic term
See Figure on next page.

computer-based reference (CBR)
Storage and retrieval of reference materials using a computer. For example, job performance manuals for quick information access.

computer-based training (CBT) *basic term*
1. The meaning is identical to computer-based learning, but is preferred by some users with a training focus. *See* computer-based learning (CBL).
2. Loosely used by some practitioners as a synonym for computer assisted instruction. *See* computer assisted instruction (CAI).

computer competence
The HRD competency of understanding and being able to use computers. *See also* HRD Roles and Competencies Study.

computer conferencing *basic term*
A distance learning method using computers. Computer conferencing participants leave messages for each other (asynchronously) and do not usually access the conference simultaneously (synchronously). *Compare with* audio teleconferencing, audiographic teleconferencing, and videoconferencing.

computer directed training system (CDTS)
An instructional system that involves dependent subsystems (functional software and courseware) and related documentation. Functional software enables use of hardware by the course designer to code course material and by the

computer-based learning (CBL) *basic term*
Also called technology-based learning in recent years. CBL is the umbrella term that includes all forms of use of computers in support of learning. The components of CBL are CAI, CMI, and CSLR. CBL was defined by Donald Bitzer as, "anytime a person and a computer come together and one of them learns something." The meaning of CBL is identical to CBE, CBI, and CBT, but preferred by HRD people who focus on the learner, rather than on the instructor. *See also* computer assisted instruction (CAI), computer-based education (CBE), computer managed instruction (CMI), and computer supported learning resources (CSLR).

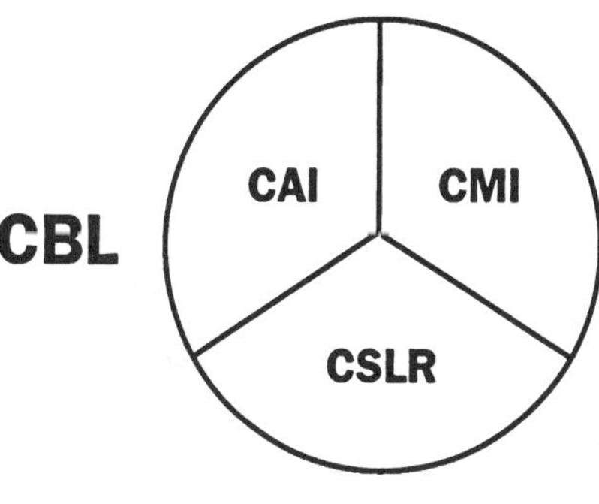

learner to interact with courseware. A CDTS does not necessarily include CMI. *See also* computer assisted instruction (CAI), computer-based learning (CBL), and computer managed instruction (CMI).

computer game
In HRD, an instructional game that involves the use of a computer.

computer language
Software with instructions used in programming. *See also* author language *and* authoring utility. *Compare with* application program.

computer literacy
See computer competence.

computer managed instruction (CMI) *basic term*
See Figure on next page.

computer managed learning
A synonym for computer managed instruction. *See* computer managed instruction (CMI).

computer managed training (CMT)
A synonym for computer managed instruction. *See* computer managed instruction (CMI).

computer model
See modeling.

computer-readable
Storage of information in a form that permits direct computer access. Computer input is also possible by scanning printed or typed text on paper, but such text is not considered computer-readable.

computer managed instruction (CMI) *basic term*
The aspect of CBL that includes testing, prescription generation, and record keeping modes. CMI, along with CAI and CSLR, are the components of CBL. *Compare with* computer assisted instruction (CAI) *and* computer supported learning resources (CSLR).

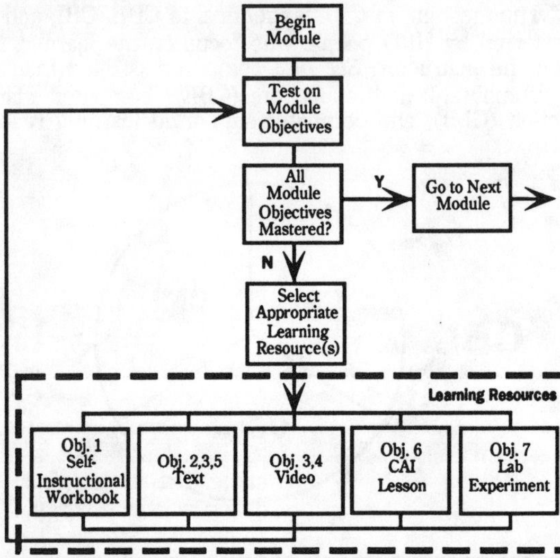

Begin Module
Test on Module Objectives
All Module Objectives Mastered?
Y
Go to Next Module
N
Select Appropriate Learning Resource(s)
Learning Resources
Obj. 1 Self-Instructional Workbook
Obj. 2,3,5 Text
Obj. 3,4 Video
Obj. 6 CAI Lesson
Obj. 7 Lab Experiment

computer supported learning resources (CSLR)
Usually called by its initials, CSLR is any form of computer support for learning other than those that teach (CAI) or test, prescribe, or keep records (CMI). The modes of CSLR are communications, data base, hypermedia, and performance support systems. CSLR, CAI and CMI are the components of CBL. *Compare with* computer assisted instruction (CAI) *and* computer managed instruction (CMI).

computer teleconferencing
See teleconferencing.

computer terminal
See terminal.

concept attainment
How people come to grasp concepts and make differentiations between categories. The three principles of cognition described by Jerome Bruner are motivation, structure, and sequence.

concept learning
The formation of an abstraction of an aspect of a group of objects or events common to all of them. Concept learning enables a person to classify experiences.

concept life cycle
A model developed by Jerry Gilley to illustrate stages of acceptance and use of HRD concepts. Consists of exposure, acceptance, maturity, and decline.

concept map
A specific document format used in structured writing. The concept

map is one format useful to introduce new topics or terms.

conceptual learner
A person who learns by conceiving thoughts and ideas; to generalize abstract ideas from specific instances. *See also* learning style.

conclusion
The final part of a presentation. Sometimes called the summary. The conclusion often includes a review of the main points of the presentation. *Compare with* introduction *and* body.

concurrent session *basic term*
Conference sessions held at the same time as each other. Concurrent sessions offer the participant a choice of topic. *Compare with* breakout, general, and track sessions.

concurrent training
Scheduled training designed to train groups of learners simultaneously on different tasks. These tasks may or may not be related. For example, a military leader may subdivide the unit at a rifle range into firing orders. Soldiers who are not firing may train on preliminary marksmanship instruction, target detection, soldier decontamination procedures, or map reading.

condition *basic term*
One of the three required parts of a learning objective. Condition describes the circumstances under which the performance or outcome of learning will be tested. It states what items or circumstances will apply, be provided, or be withheld. It may include manuals or tools the trainee will have to work with.

conditioned emotional response (CER)
In the context of biofeedback, refers to learned responses (feelings) to stressful situations. *See also* biofeedback.

conditioned response *basic term*
A behavior established by use of a reward. The conditioned response remains even after the reward is removed. For example, Pavlov's classic experiments where dogs became conditioned to salivate when a bell rang. *See also* behaviorism; behavior modification; reinforcement; and Skinner, B. F.

conditions of learning
A prescriptive taxonomy developed by Robert Gagne and others, published in a book by the same name. The conditions of learning describe how instruction should be designed to meet the learning outcomes.

conference *basic term*
1. A large meeting of individuals from different organizations for the purpose of gaining information on a specific topic of common interest. Large, multifaceted conferences are often held annually. *See also* convention.
2. A meeting of individuals from different organizations or departments to discuss and resolve mutual problems. Conferences may also be used to exchange information.

conference program book
A document resulting from a plan for a conference, used by the conference staff. The conference program book includes conference design, contact telephone numbers, exhibit information, procedures, room diagrams, and site floor plan.

conference style *basic term*
A room arrangement with tables and chairs. Usually set up so that participants can see one another. Arrangements include a single table or tables arranged in U-shape, square-shape, hexagon-shape, herringbone, and V-shape. *Compare with* theater *and* classroom styles.

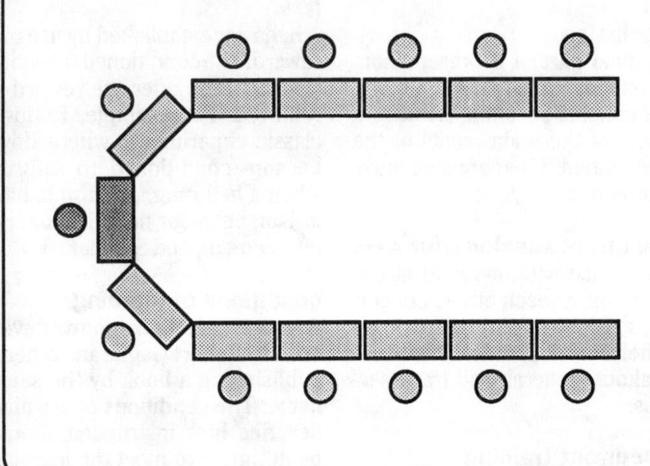

conference style *basic term*
See Figure.

configuration
In technology-based instruction, the optimum type and number of hardware components and other devices.

confirmation
Notification to the learner of the correctness of his or her response. *See also* feedback *and* knowledge of results.

conformity
Uniform behaviors exhibited by members of a group. Conformity is due to members' choosing the behavioral alternative least subject to negative social influences from among conflicting alternatives.

confound
In research, when something unexpected and extraneous to the experiment happens to one of two groups—but not the other. The confounding event could affect the outcome.

connect the dots
One of the most common of all exercises used with groups. Connect the dots is based on a blank page with nine dots. The instructions include a prohibition against lifting the pencil from the paper, so the puzzle cannot be solved without exceeding the implied boundary of the dots—the correct way. Use of this exercise illustrates that people's creativity is often confined by their self-imposed limitations. Thinking outside the dots is a com-

mon metaphor for breaking out of mindsets.

consecutive interpretation
Translation of a speaker's message into another language after it is spoken. In HRD situations this limits any presentation to half the material or makes it last twice as long. *Also called* consecutive translation. *Compare with* simultaneous translation.

consensus *basic term*
1. A collective opinion or general agreement.
2. A decision process for resolving conflicts. When all group members feel able to accept the group decision on the basis of logic and feasibility, consensus is reached and the judgment becomes a group decision.
3. The degree of personal commitment members feel toward a group decision.

constraints
Limiting or restraining conditions or factors, such as policy considerations, time limitations, environmental factors, and budgetary and other resource limitations.

constructed response question
See open response question.

construct validity
The extent to which a user can be sure a test represents its intended purpose. For example, how well a test matches the objective(s) it is supposed to measure. Constructs are developed to explain the relationship. Construct validity is often used in affective-oriented and other hard-to-measure programs. *See also* validity. *Compare with* content validity *and* criterion-related validity.

consultant *essential 100 term*
A person who provides needed information, help, and perspective. Consultants may be employees of an organization (internal) or under contract with the organization (external) because of competence, status, reputation, or experience. Strictly, this term should not be used to describe a person from outside the organization who only provides instruction. *Also called* resource person. *See also* change agent, client, client system, and organization development (OD).

consultant network
In organization development, a group formed as a resource within an organization. It serves as an OD skills bank that can be drawn upon to solve problems.

contact hour *basic term*
One hour in which both the instructor and learner are present together for the purpose of learning. Contact hours are used to define the length of instruction. *Compare with* instructional hour.

contamination
In research, when the control group receives some portion of the experimental methods or materials intended for the experimental group.

content *basic term*
The subject matter of instruction.

content-centered game
An instructional game in which the subject matter plays an important role.

content derivation
Specification of instructional content to facilitate accomplishment of each objective. Content derivation ensures that learners will study

Continued on next page

only what they need to know, as opposed to irrelevant content and things they know already.

content expert
See subject matter expert (SME).

Content-Performance Matrix
A taxonomy described by M. David Merrill that provides technical experts a basis for designing instructional materials.

content validity
The representativeness of questions on a test. *Compare with* construct validity, criterion-related validity, and validity.

contiguity
One of six gestalt principles about perception. *See* gestalt perception principles.

contiguous learning culture
The milieu or environment in which people are encouraged and enabled to learn in an ongoing, continuous basis.

Contingency Model
A model of group leadership developed by Fiedler. The contingency model incorporates general predictions of leader effectiveness in selected situations based on selected scores of group leaders.

continuing education *essential 100 term*

1. Instructional programs for adult learners that include formal degree programs and various nontraditional experiences. Programs are conducted in business, colleges and universities, government, industry, and nonprofit organizations. *See also* adult education.
2. Mandated HRD activities that individuals must engage in to retain certification, licensure, or standing. This term does not apply to the formal education or other programs required to enter the field. *Also called* mandatory continuing education. *Compare with* adult education.

continuing education unit (CEU) *basic term*
A CEU is a unit of measurement based on 10 contact hours of instruction. Following an approval process, instruction conducted outside formal institutions of learning can award CEUs that may be accepted toward credit at institutions of higher education.

contract (learning)
See learning contract.

contracting
The second step in action research.

contractor
See vendor.

contrast ratio
The ratio of brightness of an image's brightest and darkest areas.

control chart *basic term*
See Figure on next page.

control group (C-group)
Subjects in an experiment who do not receive the experimental treatment. *Compare with* experimental group.

controller
In an instructional game, the person who directs activities.

control limit
In quality control, a line (or lines) on a control chart used in statistical control as a basis for judging the significance of the variation

control chart *basic term*
In quality control, a chart that identifies the amount of variability in a process used as an aid in achieving and maintaining statistical control. A control chart plots data to distinguish between normal and abnormal variation. Similar to a run chart with upper and lower control limit lines established at a fixed interval from the average. *See also* control limit *and* seven quality process tools.

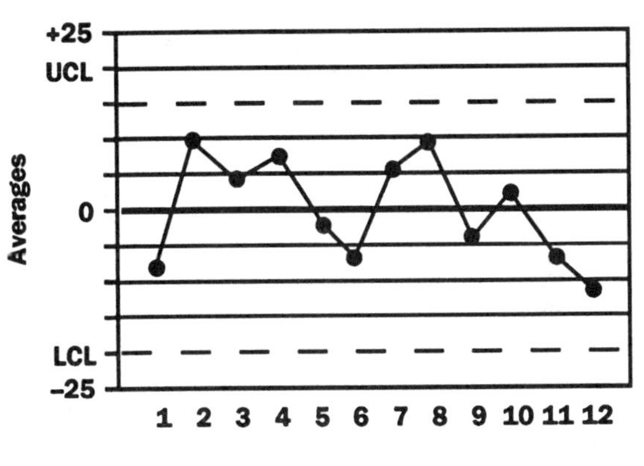

from subgroup to subgroup. The cause of plotted variation beyond a control limit is investigated. *See also* control chart.

convention *basic term*
A large meeting of individuals. A convention is distinguished from a conference by attendees who represent units of a parent organization. Conventions often pursue problems of common interest to the delegates attending. Large, multifaceted conventions are held annually. *Compare with* conference.

convergent thinking *basic term*
A logical, rational, systematic stage of problem solving that narrows the focus of consideration and seeks consensus on conclusions. *Compare with* divergent thinking.

cookbook
1. A guide for conducting sequential activities in any area of instruction.
2. One job aid format. For example, numbered steps with illustrations to help the user, and clarify points that are difficult to describe. *See also* job aid. *Compare with* algorithm *and* decision table.

cooperative education *basic term*
Skills training focused on vocational subjects. Cooperative education is usually conducted jointly between an educational institution and an organization. Participants receive academic education, related vocational instruction, and on-the-job training.

copyfitting
Adjustment of text to fit a page.

copy stand
A stand used to photograph flat objects.

cordless microphone *basic term*
A microphone that transmits a signal to the amplifier. Cordless microphones permit freedom of movement and gestures. Do not confuse with non-cordless lavaliere microphones. *Compare with* lavaliere microphone.

corpus collosum
The bundle of 200 to 250 million axion fibers connecting the left and right hemispheres.

correlation coefficient
A measure of the strength of the linear correlation between two variables. Designated by the "Pearson r" which ranges from +1.0 to -1.0. Correlation does NOT imply causation.

correspondence study *basic term*
Self-instructional study using materials provided by a distant instructor and institution. Communication between the instructor and learner is usually in writing forwarded by mail. In some countries, correspondence study is called distance learning. *See also* self-directed learning.

cost avoidance
A form of cost justification based upon eliminating or reducing existing or future costs. For example, travel and equipment cost. *Compare with* cost reduction.

cost-benefit analysis *basic term*
A method of evaluating the implications of alternative HRD plans. Cost-benefit analysis determines whether a project will save an amount equal to or greater than its cost and lost opportunities. A technique for assessing the relationship between results of outcomes of HRD programs and the cost required to produce them. *See also* return on investment (ROI).

cost-benefit analysis skill
The HRD competency of assessing alternatives in terms of their financial, psychological, and strategic advantages and disadvantages. *See also* HRD Roles and Competencies Study.

cost center
One financial arrangement for funding the HRD function. The cost center approach is based on the HRD department receiving a budget for all its operations. The HRD department then provides the HRD services to the organization. *Compare with* breakeven center *and* profit center.

cost-effectiveness
A comparative evaluation derived from the analyses of alternatives (actions, methods, approaches, equipment, support systems, team combinations, etc.) to achieve an objective. Analyses focus on the interrelated influences of cost and effectiveness in accomplishing the specific mission or objective.

cost pattern
The relationship of costs and the impact of alternate instructional approaches. *See also* resource requirements model.

cost proposal
One of two parts, technical and cost proposals, sometimes required in RFPs. The cost proposal

sets forth the price for each component described in the technical proposal. *Compare with* technical proposal. *See also* request for proposals (RFP).

cost reduction
Decrease of current expenditures. *Compare with* cost avoidance.

Council on the Continuing Education Unit (CCEU)
An organization focused on the relationship between business and higher education in the U.S. The CCEU is the source of Standards of Good Practice in Continuing Education. *See also* Continuing Education Unit (CEU).

counseling
A step in the supervisory process where a particular job performance issue is discussed in detail with the employee, with the goal of resolving the problem.

counseling, game
Advice and support for participants during or after an instructional game.

counseling skill *basic term*
The HRD competency of helping individuals recognize and understand personal needs, values, problems, alternatives, and goals. *See also* HRD Roles and Competencies Study.

count the Fs
One of the most common of all exercises used with groups, based on a short sentence of common words. Use of this exercise illustrates that people are often not careful enough and fail to see what is actually present.

course calendar
A document that outlines the progress of a course on a day-to-day basis.

course chart
A qualitative course control document that includes the course identity, length, and other required data, that lists major items of instructional equipment, and that summarizes the subject matter covered.

course control documents package
Collected documents that pertain to a single course used to control the quality of instruction. For example, the package might contain plan of instruction, syllabus, course chart or essential data form, lesson learning objectives, and instructional plan or lesson outline.

course description *basic term*
A document that includes the course goal(s), objectives, and a course calendar. The course description usually defines how, when, where, why, and by and for whom, a course will be conducted. *Compare with* course management guide *and* program of instruction.

course goal
A broad statement that outlines in general terms what the student is to learn, as opposed to stating learning goals in specific measurable or behavioral terms. *Compare with* learning objective.

course management guide
A document designed for the instructor, containing all necessary information for the implementation, maintenance, and evaluation of a specific course. *Compare with* course description *and* program of instruction.

course map
A document that outlines a course and shows the various relationships between the lessons and modules. A course map usually takes the form of a diagram or flowchart.

course objective *basic term*
The knowledge, skills, and attitudes the learner is expected to have acquired at the end of the course. Sometimes referred to collectively as terminal objectives. *Compare with* learning objective.

course prerequisites
A description of what students must be able to do before entering the instruction in question. For example, a prerequisite for the advanced electronics course is intermediate electronics.

course training standard
A course control document. A course training standard prescribes the qualitative requirements of a formal course in terms of tasks, knowledge, and proficiency levels (extent of training). *Compare with* specialty training standard.

courseware *essential 100 term*
All instructional material necessary for a learner to complete his or her course, in whatever media required, including manuals, visual aids, and hardware or software. This term is not restricted to technology-based learning.

cousins' group
A group composed of participants from the same organization. Participants usually come from different work groups and do not include supervisors with subordinates. Cousins' group is a term borrowed from OD. *Compare with* strangers' group *and* family group.

covert
Hidden. For example, covert learning objectives.

covert response
A learner response that is not displayed outwardly. A covert response is one that the learner presumably makes but which is neither recorded nor otherwise available to an observer. The covert response does not necessarily have a negative or critical connotation. For example, a learner "thinks" a response.

covert role playing
In role play, the situation where special instructions are given to one or more parties, but not to all. Usually material must be read and assimilated before the role play can begin. *Compare with* open role playing.

cracker barrel session *basic term*
Conference sessions providing participants the opportunity to discuss topics of interest in an informal atmosphere. In some cases, a resource person may be available at a cracker barrel session. Topics may be predesignated or open. *Also called* a swap shop. *Compare with* peer session.

craft training
Instructional programs conducted for skilled tradespeople, such as machinist or welder. Craft training is often part of an apprenticeship program with organized labor involvement.

creative organizational learning
Learning in an organization that

promotes risk-taking, creativity, and innovativeness.

creativity training *basic term*
HRD activities addressing creative thinking or problem solving. Creativity training usually includes methods and techniques for encouraging the creative process and integrating them with rational approaches to problem solving, decision making, and other tasks. *See also* brain lateralization, brainstorming, and synectics.

credentialling
See professional certification.

crew
In video production, anyone working behind the camera.

criteria
See criterion.

criterion *basic term*
One of the three required parts of a learning objective that states the minimum competency or performance level that the student must attain by the end of instruction. A properly stated criterion allows the designer and learner to measure success. Criterion is often based on time limit, accuracy, or quality. For example, the learner must be able to assemble the gear box within ten minutes or the learner must identify seven of ten blueprint errors to pass the test. The plural of criterion is criteria. *Also called* standard *and* proficiency. *Compare with* behavior *and* condition.

criterion-based test
See criterion test (CT).

criterion-referenced evaluation *basic term*
An evaluation method in which each question or performance is written from, and can be related back to, an objective in the learning process. The concordance of performance, instruction, and test is called the instructional triad.

criterion-referenced instruction (CRI)
See performance-based instruction.

criterion-referenced test (CRT)
See criterion test (CT).

criterion-related validity
The relationship of a test to an outcome that is the primary variable of interest.

criterion test (CT) *basic term*
A test that measures individual proficiency of absolute criteria as defined by specific learning objectives. CTs do not seek to determine how well a learner performed in comparison with other learners as do norm-referenced tests. If given immediately after learning sequences, it is a test of acquisition. If given considerably later, it is a retention test. If it requires performance not specifically learned during instruction, it is a transfer test. *Also called* criterion-based test, criterion-referenced test, performance checks, or skill checks. *Compare with* norm-referenced test.

Critical Events Model (CEM)
A systematic method for the development of instruction developed by Leonard Nadler. *See also* instructional systems development (ISD).

critical incident *essential 100 term*
1. An event, occurance, or action

Continued on next page

that is critically important to an outcome. Critical incidents are those which make the difference between success and failure in performing a job. In designing learning, critical incidents are often selected as the basis of learning activities.
2. In customer research and in quality analysis, it is usually an event that critically influences the customer's perception of quality.

critical incident method *basic term*
The identification and analysis of participant's actual experiences to better understand real problems or the role the critical incident plays in the career. The critical incident method is also known as the peak-experience approach. The participants are asked to describe the details of an incident that changed their lives. This method is used extensively in upper management or executive development programs.

critical mass
The individuals, or percentage of individuals, in an organization that must be trained or change their behavior before other individuals will willingly do the same.

critical reflectivity
An introspective process in which participants formulate a personal perspective of themselves and their world.

critical task
See task.

critique *basic term*
1. An analysis of a past experience or performance to enable improvement in the future.
2. A conference design procedure used by the coordinator, secretariat, sponsor, and new design committee to analyze a past event. Participant evaluations may provide data for the critique.

cropping
Marking the edges of a photograph to establish the area to be printed.

cross-cultural *basic term*
Interactions that incorporate information and values of a second culture on an equal basis with the original culture.

cross-cultural instruction *basic term*
Activities to increase individual's awareness of and sensitivity to differences in cultures.

cross-cultural instructor
An instructor in a situation in which the learners are from a different culture.

cross-cutting loyalty
Shared loyalties held by members of competing groups.

cross-fade
In audio, a dissolve from one sound to another.

crossover point
See breakeven point.

cross training
See retraining.

cueing *basic term*
Provision of stimuli to learners suggesting that the instruction to be received will be relevant and useful for evoking recall and usage of instruction received. Cueing is accomplished through as-

sertions, expectations, and questions.

cultural barriers *basic term*
Difficulties, often unsuspected, based on the differences in the two (or more) cultural backgrounds of the parties. Identification and reduction of cultural barriers is usually the focus of cross-cultural training.

cultural bias
See ethnocentrism.

Cultural Diversity at Work
A newsletter of interest to HRD practitioners interested in cultural diversity. *Cultural Diversity at Work* is published by the Gildeane Group.

cultural intervention *basic term*
In organization development, an intervention focused on organizational culture through examination of established practices, precedents, and traditions.

culture
1. The unspoken pattern of values that people develop and practice unconsciously as they grow up. Culture varies significantly, even within one country.
2. In OD and HRD, unspoken patterns that guide the behavior of the people in an organization. It specifically includes attitudes and practices that are difficult to change. For example, "That's the way we do things around here." *See also* organizational culture.

culture audit
An in-depth review of a group's or organization's culture.

culture shock *basic term*
The adverse reaction experienced by persons who travel to an unfamiliar place or work in an unfamiliar setting. Culture shock is common among employees working in a foreign country. One manifestation of culture shock is homesickness.

curricula
The plural of curriculum. *See* curriculum.

curriculum *essential 100 term*
1. The largest instructional component. A curriculum is made up of two or more courses.
2. A collection of formal and informal learning events that work together to support learning over time.
3. The subject areas within a specified course of study.
4. A specific plan for instruction or learning.

curriculum design *basic term*
1. The planning of instruction. *See also* instructional systems development (ISD).
2. A blueprint for the development of a curriculum.

curriculum development *basic term*
The construction of an instructional entity from conception through implementation. *See also* instructional systems development (ISD).

curriculum guide *basic term*
A document listing all learning-enhancing programs and services of an organization, institution, or HRD department. *Also called* curriculum catalog.

custom courseware *basic term*
Courseware that is developed specifically for one organization. *Also called* custom-designed learning.

customer first team
Line level service improvement groups.

customer first workshop
Events conducted to develop specific criteria for service quality at the front line. Customer first workshops are conducted by senior managers for their staff members. *Also called* customer service workshop.

customer focus
Attention to customers as a business matter of first priority.

customer service objectives
Objectives to achieve optimal customer service on a continuous basis.

customer service plan
A formal description of how each customer service objective will be achieved.

customer service workshop
See customer first workshop.

cut
A change from one visual to another instantaneously.

cyberspace
An artificial environment designed to permit (mental) freedom of movement and exploration. *See also* virtual reality.

cycle of service
A concept, developed by Ron Zemke, of analyzing all of a customer's moments of truth outlined in sequence from need identification to need fulfillment.

cyclic game
In instructional games, a term used to describe those games that pass through a number of stages which are similar or identical to previous stages.

CYCLOPS
An audiovisual teaching system developed by the British Open University. CYCLOPS included audiocassettes, television monitor, and computer component.

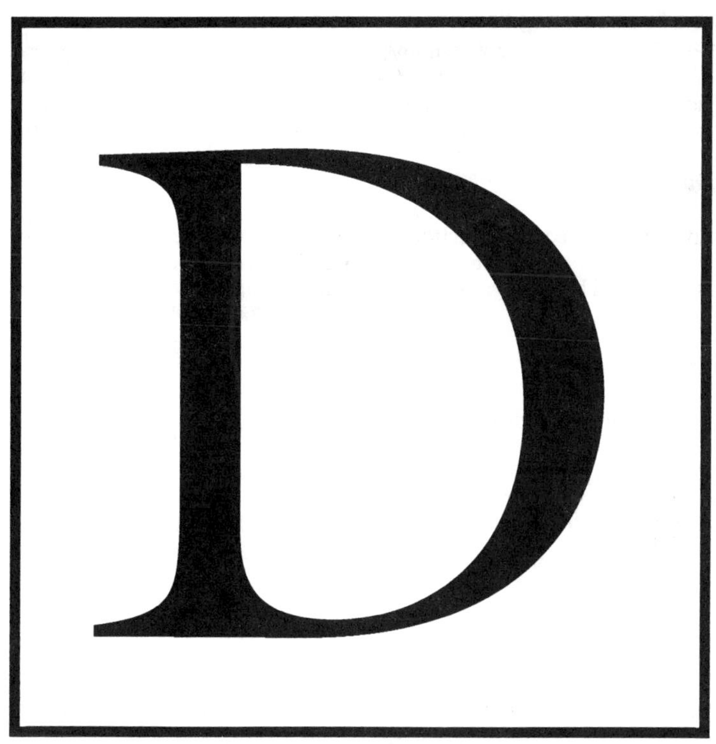

DACUM (developing a curriculum) *basic term*
Almost always called by its acronym, DACUM is analysis conducted by bringing all concerned parties together. Typical analysis questions are addressed and resolved on-the-spot. The process moves more quickly than a conventional analysis. Care must be exercised to avoid superficial results. *Also called* DACUM analysis.

DACUM chart
A chart used in the DACUM process. The DACUM chart is often wall-size.

data, continuous
See continuous data.

data, discrete
See discrete data.

data base *basic term*
Collection of information, organized for retrieval. For example, the individual HRD records.

data-based intervention
A specific technique in action research. First, data are collected. Then the data are presented to the group. As a result, a process of self-analysis is begun. *See also* action research, organization development (OD), and survey feedback.

data reduction skill
The HRD competency of scanning, synthesizing, and drawing conclusions from data. *See also* HRD Roles and Competencies Study.

Data Training
A periodical of interest to HRD practitioners involved in instruction for systems personnel. *Data Training* is published by Weingarten Publications.

data training
The term used to describe any learning activities directed at the development of the computer users of the organization.

datum
Singular of data.

debate *basic term*
A highly structured and formal presentation by several individuals or teams. Each offers a different point of view about an identified issue. Debate differs from a colloquy in that each presenter speaks in turn with no direct response or discussion. During a debate, the audience does not interact. A debate is not a form of communication or exchange of ideas. It is a win-lose form of intellectual combat. Audience members may change their mind as a result of listening, but the participants usually do not. *See also* audience reaction team *and* forum.

debriefing *basic term*
Review and discussion of the processes and outcomes of any instructional activity. Debriefing is used after role plays and simulation games. Debriefing facilitates participants reflecting on their prior experiences, gaming insights, and sharing for mutual learning.

debugging
In technology-based learning, error identification and correction in any courseware. Originally meant identifying and removing errors from computer programs.

decile
In statistics, points marking a distribution into ten parts. For example, the third decile is located at the 30th percentile. *See also* percentile.

decision
In a group, a choice from among available alternatives that is validated through member consensus.

decision logic chart
See decision table.

decision making *basic term*
The process of choosing among alternatives. In a group process exercise, no best or correct answer can be validated by any means other than consensus.

decision-making skills
Skills associated with making rational judgments on the basis of available information.

decision table
One job aid format. Decision tables list rules for actions to assist in the decision-making process. A decision logic chart represents the inputs likely to occur for a given situation and recommends a course of action or, if appropriate, alternative actions. The rules may not look like computer code, but they usually follow the same sort of "if—and if—then" sequence. *Also called* decision logic chart. *See also* job aid. *Compare with* algorithm *and* cookbook.

decision tree
A diagram that is the basis of a technique for making choices based on the relationships and implications of one decision to others. Decision trees are often incorporated in job aids. Named because of its branching structure.

decline
A stage in the concept life cycle model. *See also* concept life cycle.

deductive approach
Moving from observations of the whole to generalize the specific parts. The deductive approach is preferred by some individuals. *Compare with* inductive approach.

delegation skill
1. The HRD competency of assigning task responsibility and authority to others. *See also* HRD Roles and Competencies Study.
2. One of the basic topics that is included in practically any supervisory skills training program.

delivery *basic term*
1. A phase in the ISD process, usually called implementation. *See also* implementation.
2. The oral quality of a presentation. The style with which a speech or lesson is presented.
3. The process of delivering a speech.
4. The process of delivering the learning activities to learners. *Also called* implementation.

delivery method
The means by which instruction is offered.

delivery system *basic term*
1. The media and other resources used to deliver instruction.
2. The equipment used to deliver a technology-based learning program.

delivery system selection
The procedure to determine the combination of media and resources that will be most useful in delivery of the instruction.

Delphi
A commercial information retrieval service that can be accessed by a computer over a telephone line. A large number of sub-locations exist based on user interest. *See also* America Online, Compuserve, DIALOG, ORBIT, and Prodigy.

Delphi technique *basic term*
A cyclic method of prediction, forecasting, or information collection that employs multiple experts, who respond individually to precisely formatted questions. The compiled responses are again presented to the experts, who further refine them. Repeated cycles of the process converge to a consensus. The process may be terminated after a fixed number of iterations or repeated until nothing additional is offered and general consensus is reached. The consensus produced is considered the most effective prediction of the variable being studied. The Delphi technique is useful in forecasting when no data are available.

Deming, W. Edwards
The quality philosopher who is credited with helping the Japanese improve quality. The Deming award is named after him. *See also* Deming cycle *and* total quality management (TQM).

Deming cycle
The steps in quality process—plan, do, check, and act (PDCA)—

Continued on next page

developed by Walter Shewhart. Japanese quality enthusiasts called it the Deming cycle, which stuck. *Also called* the Shewhart cycle. *See also* Deming, W. Edwards *and* total quality management (TQM).

Deming's 14 points
Fourteen steps for establishing a quality process, developed by W. Edwards Deming. These steps are (1) create constancy of purpose, (2) adopt the new philosophy, (3) cease dependance on inspection, (4) stop awarding business based on price, (5) improve constantly and forever, (6) institute training on the job, (7) institute leadership, (8) drive out fear, (9) break down barriers, (10) eliminate slogans, (11) eliminate work standards and management by objective, (12) remove barriers to hourly workers, (13) institute a vigorous program of education and self-improvement, and (14) put everybody in the company to work to accomplish the transformation.

demonstration *essential 100 term*
An instructional technique. A presentation shows a group how something works, how to perform an act, or how to use a procedure. Demonstration is an important technique in on-the-job training and behavior modeling technology. *See also* behavior modeling, four-step method, modeling display, and on-the-job training (OJT).

departmentalization
Grouping jobs together to match the organizational structure.

Department of Education, Employment and Training
An Australian government department responsible for the provision of advice and the implementation of government policies through programs aimed at improving the effectiveness of education, employment, and training systems.

dependent variable *basic term*
In research, the nonintervention. The dependent variable is the status with which treatment will be compared. *Compare with* independent variable.

descriptive research *basic term*
Research that describes things as they are. For example, the HRD practices in the aviation industry. *Compare with* experimental research.

descriptive statistics
Methods used to characterize or summarize entire data sets. *Compare with* inferential statistics.

design *basic term*
1. One of the phases in the ISD process. The others are analysis, development, implementation, and evaluation.
2. Preparation of a detailed plan for the learning activity. The information gathered in the analysis phase forms the basis of the design. Parts of the design process include completion of a work analysis, specification of learning objectives, definition of entry behaviors, grouping and sequencing of objectives, specification of learning activities and assessment and evaluation systems, and selection of existing materials.

designer
The member of an instructional development group who specializes in design activities. In small groups this may be only one of the tasks performed by a single person.

desktop job aids
Those job aids often found in an office environment. The format may vary, but often is the common 8 1/2 x 11 inch (or A4) size of paper. *See also* job aid.

detection
In quality programs, a strategy that attempts to identify unacceptable output after production and separate it from the good output. *Also called* inspection. *Compare with* prevention.

developer *basic term*
The member of an instructional development group who specializes in development activities. In small groups this may be only one of the tasks performed by a single person.

developer-instructor *basic term*
An HRD practitioner who primarily develops courseware and secondarily teaches courses. *Compare with* instructor-developer.

developing a curriculum (DACUM) *basic term*
See DACUM.

development *basic term*
1. When used as one of the activity areas of HRD, learning. *See also* human resource development.
2. Learning activities that are not job-focused. Development prepares an employee for future, often higher level, responsibilities in the organization.
3. One of the phases in the ISD process. The others are analysis, design, implementation, and evaluation.
4. Production of instructional materials ready for trial use. Materials are produced as specified in the design phase and in accordance with the design and development strategy specified in earlier phases.
5. The process of changing or adding personal knowledge, skills, and attitudes.

developmentalism
A theory of learning. Developmentalism stresses the importance to learning of the individual life cycle developmental stages.

developmental needs
The needs of an individual for general improvement over a long time period.

developmental testing
See evaluation.

developmental theory of career planning
In career planning, the view that individual's lifetime developmental stages are related to their careers.

development planning
In career planning, an evaluation of future career opportunities, options, and goals and a plan to achieve those goals. Developmental planning is usually accompanied by activities that prepare individuals for future jobs and career decisions. *See also* succession planning.

development roles
The HRD role cluster comprising evaluator, HRD materials developer, and program designer. *See also* HRD Roles and Competencies Study.

development station
See authoring station.

deviance *basic term*
Behavior of group members that

Continued on next page

is not in conformity with norms or expectations.

device-based game
An instructional game in which play is centered on a non-electronic device.

Dewey, John
An educator who is especially well known for emphasis on practical experience.

diagnosis *basic term*
1. A synonym for analysis. *See* analysis.
2. The third step in action research

DIALOG
A commercial information retrieval service that can be accessed by a computer over a telephone line. A large number of data bases may be searched. *See also* ORBIT *and* BRS.

dialogue *basic term*
1. In conferences, a session with a predesignated small group of people. Their function is to listen to a session and then engage in a conversation with the presenter in front of the audience.
2. In conferences, a conversation between two individuals in front of a large group. Dialogue presenters talk extemporaneously. Participants listen, but do not take part until after the dialogue is completed.

dial-up teleconferencing
Use of a public telephone line to connect with a teleconference. Dial-up may be either with or without operator assistance.

diaphragm
Muscular membrane between lungs and stomach area. Diaphragm breathing is important for presenters. Diaphragm breathing employs lower chest and stomach rather than upper chest.

dias
A synonym for podium. *See also* podium.

diazo (process)
One method used to produce overhead transparencies. Usually found in the reproduction department of large organizations.

dichotomy
A division of group that identifies two components or two individuals.

dictionary of permissible words
A list of words that may be included in courseware to be used with special population. Used frequently when courseware is being developed on a production basis for a large international project.

didactic *basic term*
Intended for instruction. Didactic instruction usually features one-way type methods such as lecture, video, and demonstration. *Compare with* experiential.

didactic learning *basic term*
Learning about the culture of an organization. *Compare with* instrumental learning *and* self-reflective learning.

Differentiation and Integration Model
An OD model of differentiation and integration and associated concepts used in dealing with management of intergroup conflict. The Differentiation and Integration Model was originated by P.R. Lawrence and J. W. Lorsch.

digital *basic term*
Pertains to equipment and processes that use binary numbers to accomplish their purpose. Digital devices are replacing analog devices in technology-based learning. *Compare with* analog.

Digital Video Interactive (DVI)
Usually called by its abbreviation, DVI is a compact disc format designed for interactive multimedia. A 12-cm DVI disc holds a comprehensive mix of up to one hour of video, 7,000 still images, audio, computer text and graphics, and interaction capabilities. One competitive format for interactive multimedia. *Compare with* CD-I, CD-ROM, and CD-ROM XA.

digitize
1. Converting analog information to digital information.
2. Conversion of a visual image or real object into a format that can be processed by a computer.

digitizer
An input device used to permit rapid input of graphics, normally on a tablet by use of a stylus. Can be used for authoring or student input. *See* tactile input. *Compare with* plotter.

dilemma intervention
In organizational development, an intervention based on a search for alternative solutions to the problem at hand.

dimensional theory of career planning
In career planning, the view that effective career planning is based on analysis of the individual's personality and occupations, then matching the two.

dimensions-viewpoints matrix
See Figure on next page.

direct cost *basic term*
An expenditure directly attributable to a specific program. For example, printed brochures.

direction
One of six gestalt principles about perception. *See* gestalt perception principles.

directive instructional style *basic term*
An instructional style based on expertise in the subject with concentration of content. *Compare with* facilitative, Socratic, disseminational, and balanced instructional styles.

direct mail *basic term*
The process of mailing advertisements for HRD products or services directly to potential customers.

direct manipulation laboratories
A laboratory setup with all of the tools for a particular job class. Direct manipulation laboratories allow individuals to manipulate the tools used on their own job for learning. Such labs are costly. For example, a hydraulics laboratory.

director
In video production, the person who controls the action and words spoken in front of the camera.

direct question *basic term*
1. Any question that requires a specific answer. Direct questions focus communication but may be threatening. *Compare with* clarifying question, indirect question, and open question.

Continued on next page

dimensions-viewpoints matrix
A problem-solving tool. The dimensions-viewpoints matrix has the dimensions of a problem defining one axis and viewpoints defining the other axis. Each cell represents the interaction of a particular dimension with a single viewpoint.

Dimensions	Viewpoints		
	Management	Technical	Sales
Difficulty			
Timing			
Risk			

2. Any question directed to one individual. *Compare with* overhead question.

disclaimer
A written or oral statement inserted in media. For example, a disclaimer may indicate that the organization observes equal opportunity policies.

discovery learning *essential 100 term*
A method of instruction in which students discern underlying principles by themselves. In discovery learning, learners have experiences designed to illustrate the wanted principles.

discovery method
See discovery learning.

discovery sequence
See Eg-Rul sequence.

discrepancy intervention
In organizational development, an intervention focused on a contradiction in action or attitudes.

discrete data
Information that has gaps. For example, the average size of all HRD staffs in a sample may be 8.73. Each of the actual staffs in the sample had whole numbers, for example 8 or 9 of employees. *Compare with* continuous data.

discrimination
The ability to make different responses to different stimuli. A discrimination requires a person to determine the differences among

inputs and to respond differently to each of them.

discussion *basic term*
Any exchange of ideas among members of a group. *Compare with* buzz session.

disengagement
In consulting, the process of ending the consultant's role in the client organization for the contracted project. *Also called* closure and termination.

display
General term for the visual output of technology-based learning equipment. May use CRT, LCD, or plasma panel technology. The preferred term is VDT. *See also* video display terminal (VDT).

display system
Any method of showing material using boards (such as magnetic, flannel, and Velcro) to hold items.

display type
Type used in headlines and titles. Display type is not well suited for continuous reading. *Compare with* text type.

disseminational instructional style
An instructional style based on providing information to be memorized by the learner. *Compare with* balanced, directive, facilitative, and Socratic instructional styles and expository mode.

dissolve
1. The video technique of slow fading from one image to another. Fade-out is a dissolve to black.
2. Smooth blending of two projectors so that the image from one is replaced by the other, using a dissolve control.

distance learning *essential 100 term*
An instructional method in which the instructor or facilitator is geographically separated from the learners. *Also called* distance education *and* distant learning. *See also* computer conferencing *and* videoconferencing.

distant learning
See distance learning.

distributed implementation
A self-directed learning implementation strategy. In distributed implementation no learning center is specified. The instructional materials are sent to the learner's job location. Learning is usually facilitated by the learner's supervisor.

distributed practice
During learning, the process of spacing numerous, relatively short, practice sessions throughout the learning period. *Compare with* massed practice.

distribution
Observations of the target population. The distribution may form statistically predictable patterns.

divergent thinking *basic term*
A nontraditional approach to problems that may produce original solutions. Divergent thinking has been described as the expansive, generative, exploratory, option-finding stage of problem solving, which seeks to understand the issue thoroughly and to identify options for solving it. *Compare with* convergent thinking.

diversity instruction
Instruction to increase the awareness of employees of the cultures represented by other members of

Continued on next page

the workforce. Topics may include differences in race, ethnicity, gender, and mental preferences. *Also called* workplace diversity training.

division of labor
Distribution of duties, responsibilities, and tasks among a group of people.

documentation *basic term*
Written information added to, or included in, technology-based programs or equipment. Documentation makes it possible or easier to understand how they were authored or are supposed to be used. Poor documentation makes later revision very difficult. Poor documentation is a major problem of technology-based learning.

dolly
In video, the physical movement of the camera toward or away from the subject. *Compare with* pan and zoom.

domain
In performance support systems, an area of expertise.

domains of learning *basic term*
The three domains into which instructional activities can be placed. They include cognitive, psychomotor, and affective. *See* affective, cognitive, cognitive domain, interpersonal domain, motor skill domain, and psychomotor.

do more/do less list
A technique of OD data gathering. *See also* OD data gathering.

do steps
Major actions the learner must perform.

do substeps
The components of the major actions the learner must perform.

dots per inch (dpi)
A measure of display or printer resolution.

double-check question
A question used to verify participant's progress and understanding. Sometimes called a progress check, especially in technology-based learning.

double interact
Three contiguous acts performed by group members.

double loop learning *basic term*
In-depth organizational learning that looks at organizational norms and structures that cause the organization to function in the way it does. Double loop learning, developed by Chris Argyris, questions the system itself and why errors or successes occurred in the first place. *Compare with* single loop learning.

doubling role plays
A role play technique permitting facilitators to become involved when necessary. In doubling, the facilitator steps behind the current player to become an alter ego.

download
Using one computer to get information from another.

downsizing *basic term*
Reductions in force. Downsizing is often to reduce the number of employees and layers of management in an organization. Resulting lessened management opportunities result in increased scope of responsibilities and attendant train-

ing and development needs. *Also called* rightsizing.

drill and practice
1. A series of questions used to review and practice previously learned material.
2. In technology-based learning, one of the most common techniques. One of the modes of CAI. The others are instructional game, modeling, tutorial, and simulation.

driving forces
Those forces that push toward change.

dropped ceiling
A type of ceiling that allows for air-handling ducts and equipment to be placed between the apparent ceiling and the floor above. Removable ceiling panels permit access to equipment and cables. *Also called* suspended ceiling.

Drucker, Peter
The developer of the management by objectives (MBO) concept and a key advocate of management as a value-adding practice. Peter Drucker is considered by many to be the founding father of modern business management theory.

dry erase board
See whiteboard.

dry erase marker
A special type marker required for use with whiteboards. *Compare with* Magic Marker™.

dry run *basic term*
A practice or rehearsal.

dual career ladder *basic term*
A common pattern in organizations. One career path advances through levels of technical expertise, the other through levels of management.

dubbing
Transfer of information from one audio or visual source to another.

duetero learning
An organization's or individual's learning from critical reflection on taken-for-granted assumptions.

dummy
The final layout of page elements to guide paste-up.

during think steps
The things the learner must weigh while doing the steps of a process. *Compare with* before think steps *and* after think steps.

Dutch Trainers Organization
A professional society for HRD practitioners in The Netherlands

duty
A large segment of the work done by the individual.

Dvorak keyboard
(Pronounced da-vor′-zsaahk. Rhymes with shock.)
A keyboard with keys placed in ergonomic relationship. Most often used keys are struck by the strongest fingers. Can be learned quickly and capable of greater speed than the qwerty keyboard. The Dvorak keyboard has not been widely accepted. *See also* qwerty keyboard.

dyad *basic term*
A group of two people. *Compare with* triad, triplet, and quad.

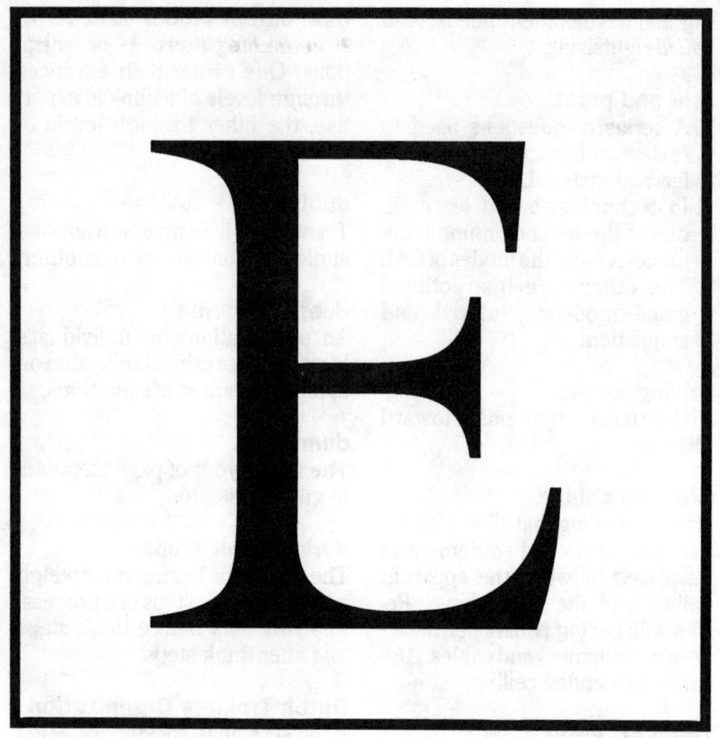

easel *basic term*
Equipment that holds flipcharts or posters. *Also called* a tripod.

economic theory of career planning
In career planning, the theory that assumes individuals choose their occupation based on its economic potential.

editing
Rearrangement of audio or visual elements in a medium for presentation.

education *basic term*

1. HRD activities designed to improve the performance of an employee in a specific direction beyond the current job. Education emphasizes far-transfer learning objectives and gives employees the broad knowledge and understanding needed to excel across a range of jobs. HRD use of the term does not try to account for the widespread use of the term in other contexts in public and higher formal education. *See also* adult education, human resource development (HRD). *Compare with* development *and* training.
2. The sixth and highest level of learning described by Benjamin Bloom. *See* Bloom, Benjamin *and* Bloom's taxonomy.

educational assistance
See employee educational assistance.

educational entitlement *basic term*
The practice of providing funds to employees so that they can study outside the company. The term "entitlement" implies that it is a regular right to which all workers are entitled. Most countries that have educational entitlement legislation insist that the employees should not study anything directly related to the job. *Compare with* levy system.

educational game
See instructional game

educational needs *basic term*
Learning needs intended to prepare individuals for possible future job requirements or for the realization of career plans.

educational outcome
See outcome.

Educational Technology
A periodical of interest to HRD practitioners involved in instructional technology. *Educational Technology* is published by Educational Technology Publications.

educational technology
A synonym for instructional technology. *See* instructional technology.

Educational Technology Research and Development
A periodical of interest to HRD practitioners involved in instructional technology. *Educational Technology Research and Development* is published by the Association for Educational Communications & Technology.

Education and Training Support Agency (ETSA)
A national inter-governmental agency established under the New Zealand industry Training Act to grant recognition to industry training organizations. Operates in conjunction with NZQA. *See also* New Zealand Qualifications Authority (NZQA).

effectiveness *basic term*
Achievement of the purpose of a procedure or action.

efficiency *basic term*
Timeliness and affordability of a procedure or action. A process described by Peter Drucker as, "Doing things right as opposed to doing the right things."

ego
A part of the personality described by Sigmund Freud. The ego is the part of the personality that interfaces with the world.

egogram
A diagram used in transactional analysis to explain the parent, child, and adult ego states.

Eg-Rul sequence
Eg-Rul is an abbreviation for "from example to rule." An instructional approach to the teaching of concepts developed by M. David Merrill and colleagues. *Also called* discovery sequence.

80-20 rule
See Pareto principle.

elaboration (strategy)
Any method used to make new information more memorable by imposing it on another memorable item. *See also* method of loci, mnemonics, and imagery.

electrical/mechanical simulation
See simulator, full scale.

electronic blackboard *basic term*
A special device resembling a chalkboard. The electronic blackboard is used to transmit a blackboard-like image drawn on the device through a standard phone line to a decoding device and onto a video monitor at the receiving end. A useful system for the exchange of simple, spontaneous graphics. One method of transmitting information in distance learning. *Also called* electronic chalkboard *and* electronic whiteboard.

electronic game
An instructional game that involves the use of an internal data-processing device or an external computer. *See also* self-contained electronic game and computer game.

Electronic Information Delivery System (EIDS)
Usually called by its acronym, EIDS is a particular interactive video format developed by the U.S. Army, using a unique form of videodisc. EIDS was selected as the IVD standard by some U.S. government agencies. *See* interaction *and* interactive video.

electronic mail
A means of sending text messages to individuals or groups of individuals using a computer network. The sender inputs a message to the computer via a terminal, and the receiver also uses a terminal to read and respond to messages. One method of transmitting information in distance learning. *Also called* E-Mail.

electronic performance support system
See performance support system.

electronic performance support tool
See performance support tool.

electronic publishing
Loosely, a synonym for desktop publishing.

electronic still camera
A camera that records images on a 2 x 2 inch disc for viewing on a video monitor. Often used to capture images for electronic publishing.

electronic-systems skill
The HRD competency of having knowledge of functions, features, and potential applications of electronic systems for the delivery and management of HRD, such as computer-based training, teleconferencing, expert systems, interactive video, and satellite networks. *See also* HRD Roles and Competencies Study.

electrostatic copier
Correct term for the xerographic process. Note: it is not correct practice to call any electrostatic copier a "xerox" machine or to use "xerox" as a verb. That is a protected trademark of the Xerox Corporation.

element
The smallest component of performing a task. *See also* task *and* task analysis.

Elmire effect
See keystone (effect).

embedded instruction
Instruction about one or more as-

pects of any technology-based system available to the user within the system itself. The distinction is that the user need not quit the work problem to seek the instruction. *Also called* embedded training.

embeddedness
One of six gestalt principles about perception. *See* gestalt perception principles.

emcee
Short word for M.C., the master of ceremonies at a formal meeting.

emergence
A gradual process of development of roles (including leader) and decisions in a leaderless group discussion.

emphasis
The principle of design related to a focus point within a visual. *Also called* center of interest.

empirical
Derived from experience or experiment rather than from theory.

employee assistance program (EAP) *basic term*
Programs conducted by employers to assist employees in overcoming difficulties that have an impact on how employees work. Examples include alcoholism, drug abuse, wellness, and fitness programs.

employee development
A process of strengthening employees' occupational skill for the betterment of themselves and the organization.

Employee Development and Training Program (EDTP)
A United Auto Workers-Ford project. EDTP addresses the needs of both active and laid-off U.S. hourly workers. EDTP is funded through company contributions.

employee educational assistance *basic term*
Programs that provide funding or reimbursement for employee's course or degree programs. Reimbursement ranges from partial to full and may be based on the grade earned or on the relevance of the degree work to the employee's work. A provision in the U.S. tax code under which employees are not taxed on *non* job related education tuition reimbursement. *See also* educational entitlement.

employee empowerment *basic term*
Giving employees the opportunity to manage themselves and make their own decisions.

employee involvement *basic term*
A process that involves employees in organization decision making. Employee involvement is based on the need of leaders of the organization to know the opinions and feelings of its members and on the positive benefits of getting employee input toward, and buy-in of, organizational decisions.

employee involvement group
A group of employees, selected from appropriate organizational units, formed to improve organizational effectiveness. Employee involvement group strategies include decision making, group cooperation, information sharing, and problem solving. *See also* employee involvement.

employee participation
See employee involvement.

empowerment *basic term*
The principle of investing managerial tasks or decision-making processes in the employee or employee group for the purpose of increasing corporate effectiveness and ability to react to problems.

empty chair technique
A spontaneous role play technique based on gestalt theory. For example, a learner says, "I wish I could tell Charlie how to run this project!" The instructor points to an empty chair and says, "Charlie is sitting right in this chair now. Go ahead and do just that!" *See also* gestalt *and* hot role play. *Compare with* magic wand technique.

emulative change
In organizational development, a change process characterized by identification with and emulation of power figures. *Compare with* indoctrination change, and planned change, coercive change, technocratic change, interactional change, socialization change, and natural change.

enabling objective *basic term*
A formal description of a skill or competence that contributes to the achievement of a larger or more complex competence called the terminal objective. *Also called* subordinate objective or en route objective. *See also* learning objective. *Compare with* terminal objective.

enactive model
A model involving a set of appropriate actions for achieving a specific result(s).

encapsulation
A method used for controlling social conflict through regulating conflict according to a set of rules agreed upon by all parties.

encoding/decoding
Structuring information into a suitable format for transmission, and then reconverting it after transmission.

encounter group
See sensitivity training.

end-of-course evaluation *basic term*
Any evaluation provided by the student near or at the end of the course. End-of-course evaluations sometimes provide useful feedback about the course, instructional materials, facilities, and instructor. *See also* reaction *and* summative evaluation. *Compare with* formative evaluation.

end product
Desired result of any process.

English as a second language (ESL) *basic term*
Programs aimed at employees with limited or no English language skills. ESL programs attempt to enable the employee to function effectively and productively at work and in the organization's normal HRD programs.

enhanced graphics adapter (EGA)
Medium resolution video signal used in VDTs. Considered inferior to VGA resolution for technology-based learning. *Compare with* color graphics adapter (CGA) *and* video graphics array (VGA).

enrichment
Supplementary material that aids the learner in progressing through the course but that is not considered crucial to learning.

enrollee
When learning is involved, the learner. *See also* learner.

entrepreneurial structure
An organizational design in which only one manager has decision-making authority.

entry
1. In consulting, the first stage of the project.
2. The first step in action research.

entry behavior
A formal statement of the prior knowledge and skills necessary for undertaking a particular instruction. *See also* target population description.

entry evaluation
A test given to students at the beginning of a course. Entry evaluation helps to determine the skills they bring to the course. Specifically the entry evaluation verifies knowledge skills identified as necessary prerequisites. *Also called* pretest.

entry level performance
See entry behavior.

entry level skills
See entry behavior.

entry skills
Skills a participant has before beginning an instructional exercise.

entry test
See entry evaluation.

enumeration
In presentations, the technique of listing points in a numbered sequence. For example, "the first point is . . ."

environment
See learning environment.

environmental variables
Any differences between individuals that are the result of culture, family, and social class.

environment analysis
1. In instruction, identification of both where the instruction will occur and how the instructional materials will be used.
2. In OD, identification of the characteristics of the environment most critical to the organization. Environment analysis also predicts how those characteristics are likely to change.

episodic memory
The memory of events, faces, smells, lights, sounds, emotions, etc. A form of long-term memory. *See also* long-term memory.

Equal Opportunities Commission (EOC)
An organization established by the British Government in 1975 to promote equality of opportunity for individuals, avoiding prejudice, and refraining from discrimination on ethnic origin, gender, marital status, and religion basis.

Equal Opportunity Statutes
A collective term for U.S. laws directed at equality in the workplace. For example, the Civil Rights Act of 1964 and Age Discrimination Act of 1975.

Equal Pay Act
Legislation in England and Wales beginning January 1, 1984, stating that when a woman is employed on work which is, in terms of the demands made upon her, of equal value to that of a man in the same

Continued on next page

employment, she is entitled to the same pay.

equipment-related job aids
A type of job aid. Equipment-related job aids should be physically attached to the equipment itself. The best-known example of this type job aid is the pilot's checklist. On simple aircraft the list is on a plate riveted to the airplane cockpit within the pilot's view.

equivalent comparison group design
In research, when two groups are established randomly, one receives the treatment the other does not. Both groups are measured in the same way. Compare with non-equivalent comparison group design.

ergonomics
See human factors.

error
In testing, effects that influence reliability. Error includes the alertness or mood of subjects, variations in conditions of administration, and differences in scoring or interpreting results.

error analysis
A process used to identify the frequency and form of mistakes committed by the target population. Error analysis may be included in a needs analysis. *See also* needs analysis.

esteem needs *basic term*
One of the levels of needs in Abraham Maslow's hierarchy of needs. *See* Maslow's hierarchy.

ethical issues
Moral problems of right and wrong. For example, HRD practitioners sometimes face situations where their action, choice, or decision might violate the rights of individuals, groups, or even the HRD field itself.

ethics
A system of moral values. Ethics provide a standard for attitudes, beliefs, and actions, and help individuals identify right from wrong according to that standard.

ethnocentrism *basic term*
A bias towards one's own culture and experience. People assume that the way something is done in their own country is the *right* way.

European Training & Development Organization (ETDO)
A professional organization launched in London in 1992 to be the European network of training organizations. ETDO urrently attracts members from Eire (Ireland), Finland, Germany, Portugal, Romania, Spain, and the U.K. In some countries, ETDO is known under its French name, *Organisation Europeenne pour la Formation et le Developpement* (OEFD).

evaluation *essential 100 term*
1. Evaluation can be considered as two separate steps. First, an important evaluation is conducted using learners before the general implementation of the program materials. It is called formative evaluation. Second, the measure of the effectiveness of the materials in solving the instructional problem identified in the analysis phase, called summative evaluation. Kirkpatrick's four level model of summative evaluation is often used. *See also* formative evaluation *and* summative evaluation.

2. One of the phases in the ISD process. The others are analysis, design, development, and implementation.
3. A systematic process to determine the worth, value, or meaning of something.
4. Techniques used to determine weak areas in a course and to improve the instruction. Can include entry evaluations, performance testing, and written tests.
5. Overall judgment of the value of a process, product, or event, taking into account all available evidence from various assessment measures.

evaluation, purpose
Activities conducted to decide whether to continue offering a program, to get ideas for improvement, and to justify the use of HRD to solve a performance problem. Evaluations often decide who should participate in future programs, determine the cost-benefit ratio of an HRD program, determine whether a program is accomplishing its objectives, gather data to assist in marketing future programs, identify the strengths and weaknesses in the HRD process, and reinforce major points made to the learner.

Evaluation Model, Four Level
A summative evaluation model developed by Donald L. Kirkpatrick. It distinguishes four levels of summative evaluation. They are reaction, learning, behavior, and results. This model is widely respected and used in HRD. *See also* behavior, evaluation, learning, reaction, and results.

evaluator
The HRD role of identifying the impact of an intervention on individual or organizational effectiveness. *See also* HRD Roles and Competencies Study.

evolution
In OD, the characteristic of a system embodying its history, that is, the enduring changes in the system's structure and function over an extended period of time.

excursion
See field trip.

executive development *essential 100 term*
A collective term for HRD programs designed and conducted for upper level managers of the organization to ensure they have the skills they need to excel in their jobs.

executive producer
In video, the client or the person in charge of the project for the organization. Day-to-day responsibility of the video project is assigned to the line producer.

executive summary
1. Normally an abstract of a document for the benefit of high-level managers who only wish to get a brief overview of it.
2. Concise summary of the presentation, given at the start.

exercise *basic term*
1. A generic term for participant activities of all types. *See also* experiential learning *and* structured experience.
2. A planned experience designed to allow participants to practice, repeat, and reinforce a previous learning or new learning, or to experience a problem.

existential theory of career planning
In career development, the theory that career decisions emanate solely from individual choice.

exordium
The introduction of a speech. A rhetorical term. The exordium is designed to awaken interest and give the audience a favorable impression of the speaker. It provides the audience with a glimpse of the subject and nature of the speech. The exordium is a key feature of a good speech.

expatriate
An employee who works for an extended time in a country other than the one in which citizenship is held.

Expectancy Model *basic term*
A model, originated by Victor H. Vroom. The Expectancy model suggests that motivation is related to how much something is wanted. The belief that one thing will lead to another thing is called an expectancy. The Expectancy Model principle has been applied in mental imagery for success in selling and athletics. *Also called* the self-fulfilling prophecy *and* the Pygmalion effect.

experience-based learning
See experiential learning.

experience-centered instruction *basic term*
A cognitivism-based theory of instruction focused on the learner's experience during instruction and production of fresh insights.

experienced worker standard (EWS)
A standard to which to compare graduates of instruction. Since instruction does not usually prepare learners to perform at the same level as experienced workers, learner ability is usually expressed as a percent of EWS. For example, 80 percent of EWS.

experiential learning *essential 100 term*
A collective term for HRD activities based on participants' reactions to the practical activities during an exercise, as opposed to passive learning. Based on the work of David Kolb, Pfeiffer and Jones' experiential learning design model portrays the process as a circle of five revolving steps: experiencing, publishing, processing, generalizing, and applying.

experimental group (E-group)
Subjects in an experiment who receive the experimental treatment. *Compare with* control group.

experimentalism
The willingness to expose ideas to procedures, empirical testing, and action.

experimental research
Research based on an experimental design. *Compare with* descriptive research.

experimental research design *basic term*
A type of research design involving a true experiment. Assignment of subjects to groups must be random. The experiment follows a treatment provided to one individual or group and compares changes with those of another individual or group that did not experience the treatment. *Compare with* quasi-experimental design.

experimentation intervention
In organizational development, an

intervention based on testing and comparing two or more courses of action before selecting one.

expert system *basic term*
Programs that offer on-the-job advice to a user. Named for the origin of their information, the collected knowledge of an expert. Expert systems assist the user with taking appropriate action exactly as does a job aid. Expert systems are the principle component of performance support systems. *Compare with* artificial intelligence *and* job aid.

expert system shell
Specialized software used specifically for the creation of expert systems.

explanation
In a presentation, the material that provides description, definition, and ground rules.

explicit norm
A norm that stems from formal policy or procedure. *Compare with* implicit norm.

expositive sequence
See Rul-Eg sequence.

expository mode (of instruction) *basic term*
An instructional style in which all decisions concerning the mode and pace are determined by the instructor. *Compare with* disseminational instructional style.

ex post facto research design
Research or evaluation conducted to determine the cause of change over time.

exposure
A stage in the concept life cycle model. *See also* concept life cycle.

extemporaneous
Speaking without fully written notes or memorization. Extemporaneous speaking is, however, organized and developed. Occasionally used when impromptu (unprepared) would be more appropriate. *Compare with* impromptu.

extension education
Educational experiences offered for adults by home or county extension agents, usually for rural populations. *See also* adult education.

external consultant *basic term*
A consultant who is not an employee of the client system organization. *See also* consultant. *Compare with* internal consultant.

extinction
The pattern a person followed when a person stops performing a given behavior. Basically, a behavior will gradually extinguish (stop occurring) if it is not followed by any reinforcement. *See also* Pavlovian conditioning.

extraversion (E)
One of the 8 basic predispositions included in the Myers-Briggs typology. Extraversion is often misspelled as extroversion. *See* Myers-Briggs Type Indicator (MBTI).

eye contact
In presentations, the technique of looking directly at members of the audience in order to increase their personal involvement in a presentation. Eye-contact technique is to scan the entire group slowly and maintain eye contact with individuals for at least a full sentence.

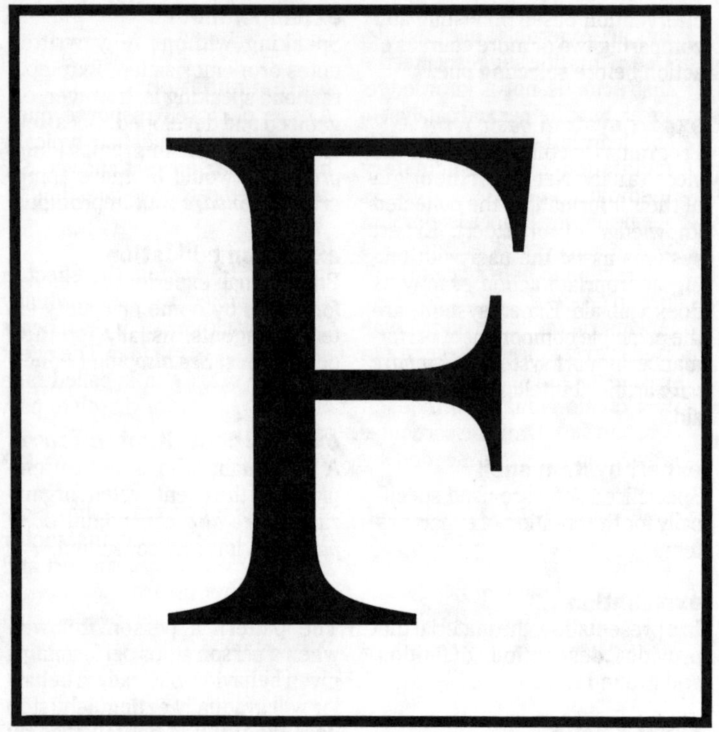

facilitation *basic term*
1. A process of guiding a group based on a learner-centered mode of instruction. The leader in this mode is called a facilitator. A facilitator may be considered a group member as well as leader. A facilitator contrasts with the image of a teacher as presenter of information. A technique associated with Carl Rogers. *See also* facilitator.
2. In organizational development, the process used by the OD practitioner to stimulate insight and learning.
3. Support of new learning by prior learning. Cues provided suggest a helpful connection with the new learning. *Compare with* negative transfer.

facilitative instructional style
An instructional style based on experience. The learner is free to explore areas of choice. *Compare with* balanced, directive, disseminational, and Socratic instructional styles.

facilitator *essential 100 term*
1. A leader of an instructional activity. Facilitator is a title for a person assisting in any learning, but is particularly applied to leaders of groups whose purpose is behavioral change. Instructors who favor the facilita-

tive instructional style advocated by Carl Rogers also use this title. Use of this title suggests that the instructor is not a knowledge-giver, but a helper and catalyst in the learning process. *See also* facilitation *and* participatory methods.
2. A person who is not a leader, but who is concerned with process interaction to help a group with group process.
3. An instructor in an individualized instruction setting such as a CAI laboratory. The facilitator works individually with each learner, supplying the particular advice and help as needed by that person.
4. In organizational development, the term applied to the OD practitioner.
5. Loosely, a synonym for trainer, moderator, discussion leader, or instructor.

facilities
Space and equipment set aside for HRD.

facilities skill
The HRD competency of planning and coordinating logistics in an efficient and cost-effective manner. *See also* HRD Roles and Competencies Study.

facsimile (fax)
The communications process in which graphics and text documents are scanned, transmitted via a telephone line, and reconstructed by a receiver. Fax can be used to for instructional communications and in distance learning classrooms.

factor analysis
A method for reducing large numbers of measures to fewer factors that can completely account for the results obtained, and for the correlations between them.

factual question
A type of closed response question. A factual question typically has only one correct answer. *See also* closed response question.

fade in
In video production, the effect in which a subject appears gradually from a black image or disappears in the opposite manner. The effect opposite of fade in is called fade out. *Compare with* dissolve, pan, and zoom.

fading
A cognitive apprenticeship technique whereby the instructor gradually withdraws support and transfers full control of a performance to the learner. *See also* cognitive apprenticeship.

family group
A group composed of the subordinates of a manager and that manager. Participants may include other key people in the manager's organization. Family group is a term borrowed from OD. *Compare with* strangers' group *and* cousins' group.

far transfer
The extent to which learners apply the learning to situations novel or different from the one(s) for which they were trained. *Compare with* near transfer. *See also* transfer of training.

fault tree analysis (FTA)
An instructional methodology based on charting a system or program with symbols that indicate failure events, to produce a fault tree chart. The tree identifies the

Continued on next page

weakest links in a program to permit taking steps to remedy them.

Federation of Human Resource Associations of Canada
A federation of professional HRD societies in Canada.

feedback *essential 100 term*
1. Information given to learners regarding their progress. Feedback may be immediate or delayed, oral or written, one-time or ongoing. It usually takes the form of simple information regarding knowledge of results or substantive information. Feedback helps learners to reinforce their learning and helps to adjust and perfect their behavior or response. The feedback does not *necessarily* indicate the rightness of an action. Rather, it relates the results of the action from which inferences about correctness can be drawn. Criteria suggested by David Nadler for effective feedback include relevant, understandable, descriptive, verifiable, limited, and impactable. *See also* confirmation, knowledge of results, negative feedback, positive feedback, and survey feedback. *Compare with* feedforward.
2. In technology-based learning, information presented to learners after they answer a question. Correct answers, incorrect answers, unexpected answers, and failure produce different feedback.
3. The process of verifying that communication has taken place between sender and receiver. The receiver tells the sender what is understood.
4. The fourth step in action research. *See also* action research.

feedback mechanism
Any method used to secure feedback. Feedback mechanisms should serve a specific purpose and offer the possibility of positive use of the information gathered.

feedback sessions
Meetings held to make learners more aware of what they do and how they do it.

feedback skill
The HRD competency of communicating information, opinions, observations, and conclusions so that they are understood and can be acted on. *See also* HRD Roles and Competencies Study.

fee determination
See fee negotiation.

feedforward
Information on what to do to improve performance on the job. *Compare with* feedback.

feeling (F)
One of the 8 basic predispositions included in the Myers-Briggs typology. *See* Myers-Briggs Type Indicator (MBTI).

fee negotiation
The process of reaching agreement on a fair and equitable fee for the services offered, whether internal or external.

felt board *basic term*
A flannel display board used to display small placards. The placards are backed with sandpaper. Such items can be rapidly placed and easily moved or removed. A felt board can be improvised anywhere by placing a blanket over a large board. *Also called* flannel board. Although manufactured

flannel and felt boards are now obsolete, the technique is still used in field situations. *Compare with* hook-and-loop. *See also* placard.

fidelity
The degree to which a training simulator approaches the actual job condition. Airline and nuclear plant simulators necessarily have very high fidelity.

field evaluation
See pilot test.

field experience *basic term*
A limited assignment under real conditions. A field experience should contain specific tasks for the learners to perform that focus the learner's attention on aspects of the job, the culture, or even the language that might otherwise be overlooked.

field game
A psychomotor skill game in which the players operate in or on a field that is big enough to accommodate the actual players. *See also* game. *Compare with* board game.

field test
See pilot test.

field trial
See pilot test.

field trip *basic term*
A carefully organized group visit for firsthand observation by participants. Field trips permit learners to experience impressions that could never happen in their classroom, but which are characteristic of the real world environment. Field trips can also let learners who work in one part of the organization see the impact and dependencies they have with other parts. *Also called* excursions, observations, or tours. A field trip should be preceded by expectations about what to look for, letting learners determine how the field trip will contribute to the course objectives. Specially planned questions to be answered on the trip focus the learning.

file drawer problem
In research, the tendency to not report studies with lower effect sizes or undesired outcomes.

film chain
In video production, the equipment used to transfer slide or film picture frames to video picture frames. The film chain consists of film and slide projectors, a multiplexer, and a television camera. *Also called* telecine.

filmograph
A sequence of still images on film or videotape.

filmstrip *basic term*
A medium based on a series of pictures on 35mm film. It displays the series of still frames one at a time, similar to 35mm slides. Audio can be coordinated with the film. The filmstrip is a disappearing medium.

finding metaphors
An exercise used in creativity training. For example, learners inscribe a book title, movie marquee, T-shirt, with a saying that captures their character or behavior. Pictorial metaphors can be made in collages assembled from newspaper and magazine photos by a team to capture an idea.

FIRO-B *basic term*
A well-known instrument used to establish the group members' interpersonal relations orientation.

Continued on next page

The scale measures six needs: (1) expressed affection, (2) wanted affection, (2) expressed control, (4) wanted control, (5) expressed inclusion, and (6) wanted inclusion.

fishbone diagram
See cause and effect diagram.

fishbowl *basic term*
A discussion group in which a few members of the group sit in the middle of the room while the others ring their chairs around the group. The inner circle (the fishbowl) has a meeting or a discussion and the outer group (observers) observes. After a certain time, some participants may exchange places or the discussion may be opened up for observations or questions from the observers. Various creative fishbowl variations are used.

Fitzgerald Act
A common name for the National Apprenticeship Act, passed in 1937 by the U.S. Congress and still in effect. *See also* apprenticeship.

fixed cost
An underlying cost that will be incurred regardless of other variables such as number of programs conducted. For example, rent and utilities.

flannel board
See felt board.

fleximode
Flexible arrangements for self-paced learning. Fleximode is based on a combination of pre-produced materials, instructional resources, and facilitator contact.

flight
The behavioral tendency of a group to stop considering their task. Flight serves to avoid an unpleasant situation such as social conflict.

flipchart *basic term*
A common training support device consisting of a large pad of paper. The pad is attached to a special stand called an easel. Both together are often called a flipchart. The flipchart paper may be plain (called newsprint), lined, or quadrille.

flow chart *basic term*
A graphic representation of the steps in a process, procedure, or algorithm. Widely used in technology development. Flow charting is also applicable to representing the path a product or service follows. For example, comparison charts can be drawn of both what happens and what should happen.

flush right (or left), (justification)
Compare with centered *and* ragged.

focus
Sharpness of any visual image.

focus clusters
A short course composed of clusters of related topics. Focus clusters are sometimes used in supervisory training.

focus group *basic term*
A facilitator-led group of six to twelve participants convened for a specific purpose, usually related to an organizational challenge, problem, or opportunity. Focus groups may meet only once or continually, depending on their charter.

foil
A synonym for transparency. *See* transparency.

follow-up evaluation
See evaluation.

font
1. A complete set of characters for one style of one typeface.
2. In incorrect but common nonprofessional usage, refers to one typeface.

forced choice index
An evaluation tool. The forced choice index causes the user to choose between two items. The user's score is based on the discrimination indexes (prepared in advance by experts) of the items checked.

force field analysis *essential 100 term*
See Figure.

foreign
A person or organization from outside the country in question.

formal
A term used to describe the communication networks, norms, and status hierarchy of a group that have been sanctioned or prescribed by a legitimate authority or source of power.

formal balance
Equal distribution of information on either side of the center of a visual. *Compare with* informal balance.

force field analysis *essential 100 term*
A technique developed by Kurt Lewin that analyzes the factors working for and against change to help understand which direction will prevail. Factors working for change are called driving forces. Those working against change are called restraining forces. Change can occur when the forces are not in balance. Force field analysis is widely used in HRD and OD. *See also* Lewin, Kurt, *and* organization development (OD).

Driving Forces	Restraining Forces
loss of needed people →	← lack of understanding
harm to reputation →	← limited interest
criminal charges →	← inconvenience
will cost more money later →	← will cost money now
lawsuit →	← bad advice

formal HRD programs
See structured HRD programs.

formal OJT
See on-the-job training (OJT).

formative evaluation *essential 100 term*
The evaluation of material conducted during its early developmental stages for the purpose of revising materials before widespread use. Formative evaluation is conducted during the development phase of ISD. *See also* evaluation. *Compare with* summative evaluation.

formula answer
Any oversimplified solution to a complex problem.

forum *basic term*
A period of open discussion by audience participants following a panel, debate, colloquy, or speech. In a forum, participants interact with presenters under the direction of a moderator. *See also* colloquy, debate, panel, and speech.

four step method
An instructional sequence used for training during World War I. The four steps are (1) show, (2) tell, (3) do, and (4) check. The four step method was the foundation of job instruction training (JIT) developed during World War II. It is still used in on-the-job training. *See also* job instruction training *and* on-the-job training (OJT).

four systems of learning
A comparison of organizational and performance characteristics developed by Rensis Likert. The four systems of learning are (1) exploitive-authoritative, (2) benevolent-authoritative, (3) consultative, and (4) participative-group.

four temperaments
A differentiation of human disposition used since ancient times. The four traditional temperaments are applied as the underlying concept of the Myers-Briggs Type Indicator. *See* Myers-Briggs Type Indicator (MBTI).

frame
1. The amount of graphic and text material that appears on the viewing screen at any one time. In computer-based learning, the concept can become slightly more difficult because the screen (the basic frame) can change greatly through addition or removal of overlays, while retaining the same general appearance and information.
2. In video, a frame consists of two interlaced fields of either NTSC, PAL, or SECAM standard.
3. Plastic or cardboard mount for transparencies.
4. The process of play composed of the game board and rules of play.

frame game
An instructional game deliberately designed for easy removal of old content and insertion of new content. For example, several versions of BINGO are used as frame games to teach any content that requires a matching response.

freeze frame
One frame of video displayed continuously on the monitor.

frequency distribution
A statistical table that presents a large volume of data so that the central tendency and distribution are clearly displayed.

front end analysis
A needs analysis method named by Joe Harless. *See* needs analysis.

front matter
A term for material that appears before the body of a document. For example, in a bid this may include cover, title page, proprietary statement, executive summary, response matrix, and letter of transmittal.

F test
A statistical method of determining the significance of the difference among the means of several groups.

full coverage marketing
A marketing method for HRD activities' offerings. *Compare with* market specialization, product concentration, product specialization, and selective specialization marketing.

full labor cost
An employee's salary plus benefits and overhead.

full mission simulator
A device that allows simulation of major tasks related to *all* crewmembers for a given aircraft-mission combination. It has the capability of simulating environmental conditions necessary for mission performance, including, but not limited to, motion and visual systems, flight characteristics, full instrumentation of sensors necessary to the mission, and simulation of environmental stimuli for their activation. A fully dynamic system. *See also* simulation *and* simulator.

functional context training
An instructional technique that works from simple, familiar tasks to more complex tasks. Functional context training also provides opportunity for practice.

functional illiteracy *basic term*
The lack of one or a combination of basic skills necessary to communicate or compute effectively in written or arithmetic forms. For example, the inability to read a job instruction.

functional job analysis
Interviews to determine what an employee actually does and to identify the necessary knowledge, skills, and abilities.

functional literacy
Possession of the minimal written and arithmetic skills required to function at work and in the normal HRD programs of the organization. *See also* literacy training.

futuring skill
The HRD competency of projecting trends and visualizing possible and probable futures and their implications. *See also* HRD Roles and Competencies Study.

Futurist
A periodical of general interest to HRD practitioners. *Futurist* is published by the World Future Society.

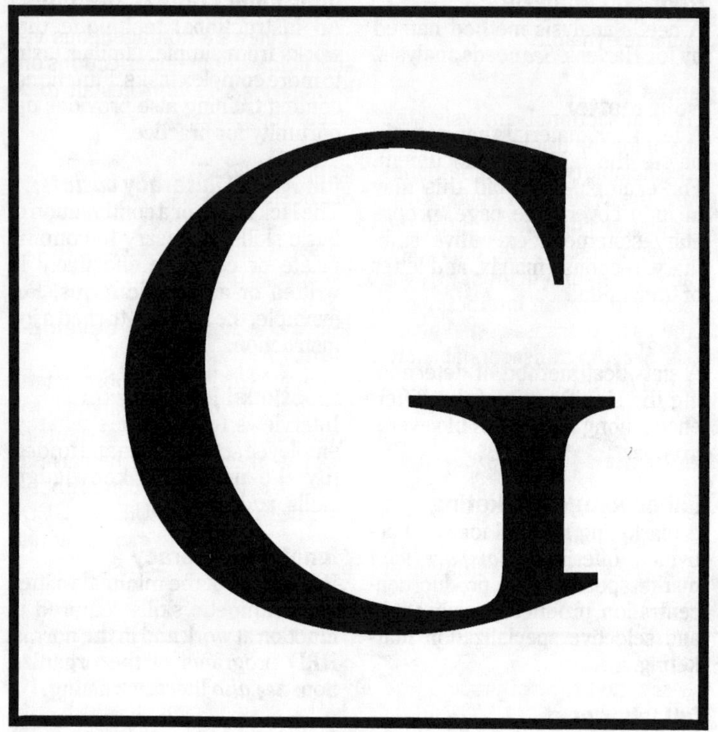

gaffer
In video production, the chief lighting person or electrician. The gaffer physically sets the lights under the direction of the director of photography.

Gagné, Robert M.
A researcher and psychologist whose work has impacted the development of criterion-referenced learning and ISD. He is best known for the research-based events of instruction. His published work includes *The Conditions of Learning*.

gainsharing
A formal method for sharing the financial benefits of service improvement with employees.

game
See instructional game.

game board
The surface upon which play takes place during a board game.

game dynamic
The environment established during a game play.

game organizer's guide
A document designed to assist the game controller in setting up, running, and debriefing a game.

game play
See game dynamic.

games
1. In transactional analysis, the term for the transactions with a predictable outcome. The games are the product of each of the potential combinations of the three states: parent, child, and adult. The combinations of these states in human interactions is the basis of transactional analysis. *See also* transactional analysis (TA).
2. *See* instructional game.

Gantt chart
See Figure.

ganzfeld
A Gestalt psychology technique of creating a situation in which the subject views a homogeneous visual field without imperfections or boundaries. *See also* gestalt *and* stress reduction.

gap analysis
See needs analysis.

general discussion
See topical discussion.

general educational development (GED)
Usually heard in its abbreviated form, the term GED is applied to tests and the high school equivalency degree that may be earned through a program of comprehensive testing in the U.S. A GED degree is often the goal of adult basic education systems.

Gantt chart
A method of planning and tracking project completion over time. The required start and end dates for each significant step is displayed to develop an overall plan. The strength of Gantt charts is display of the timing of steps. *Compare with* PERT chart.

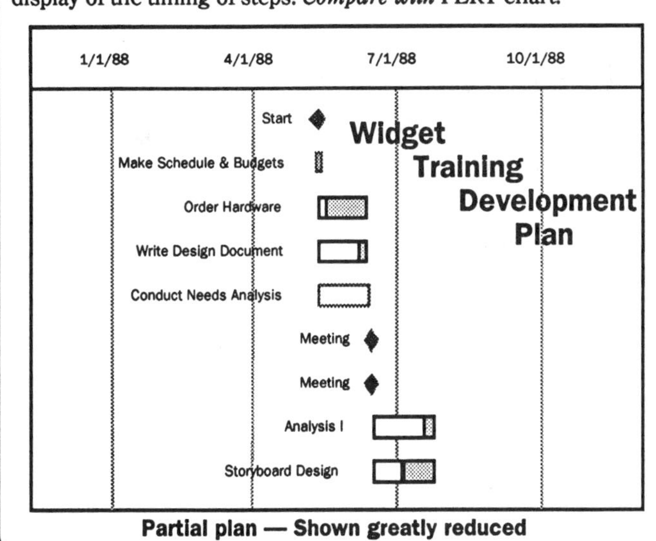

Partial plan — Shown greatly reduced

generalization
Learning to respond to a new stimulus similar, but not identical, to one that was present during original learning. For example, during learning a child calls a shepard and poodle by the term "dog." A child who has generalized would respond "dog" when presented with beagle as a stimulus.

general learning objective
See learning objective.

general session
Conference sessions intended for all participants. The general session usually relates directly to the theme of the conference or an aspect of it. Competing events are never scheduled at the same time as general sessions. *Compare with* breakout, concurrent, and track sessions.

generation
1. In technology-based learning hardware, reference to stages in product development usually incorporating significant improvements.
2. In all analog media, the number of times a copy is removed from the original. The first generation is made from the original. The second generation copy is made from a first-generation copy. Each generation results in a noticeable degradation of image quality. This applies to audiotape, videodisc, and videotape. The problem does not exist with digital media.

generational loss
The reduction in quality resulting from the copying of analog media. *See also* generation.

generative organizational learning
The learning that an organization generates or creates itself from its reflection, analysis, or creativity.

generic courseware *basic term*
Courseware that is not specific to one organization. Generic courseware may appeal to a broader market, as opposed to custom course-ware, which primarily meets the needs of one specific client or audience. *Also called* plain vanilla courseware. *Compare with* custom courseware *and* off-the-shelf materials.

GEnie
A commercial information retrieval service that can be accessed by a computer over a telephone line. A large number of sub-locations exist based on user interest. *See also* America Online, Compuserve, DIALOG, ORBIT, and Prodigy.

gestalt *basic term*
(Pronounced ge-shtalt′, rhymes with halt.)
1. A school of psychology originated in Germany by Max Wertheimer, Wolfgang Kohler, and Kurt Koffka. The gestalt view is to avoid breaking everything into categories. Gestalt focuses on considering the whole altogether. A figure ground example is the old woman/young woman exercise. *See also* holism, old woman/young woman, and synergy. *Compare with* behaviorism.
2. Loosely, any events, properties, characteristics, forms, or patterns that make up a unified whole.

gestalt perception principles
There are six gestalt principles of perception. They are (1) closure, (2) contiguity, (3) direction, (4) embeddedness, (5) joint destiny, and (6) likeness.

giga
Prefix meaning one billion. Often used in technology-based learning for comparison of size.

Gilbert, Thomas
A pioneer in concept of the study of human performance, developer of the performance improvement potential (PIP) concept, and the the Mathetics system of task analysis and design. He is the author of *Human Competence. See also* Mathetics *and* performance improvement potential (PIP).

globalization *basic term*
An all-encompassing concept that includes three ideas: international, multinational, and transnational. Globalization is considered the ultimate and most desirable phase in the series from domestic, export, international, multinational, transnational and global. It is generally considered to require a higher level of competence and commitment than lower states. *See also* global learning organization.

global learning audit
A comprehensive analysis of how effective an organization is relative to the learning capability of its various functions (finance, marketing, manufacturing, etc.) and its organization-wide systems.

global learning curve
A scale to determine to what stage an organization has advanced relative to corporate globalization.

global learning organization
Any organization that both operates in at least two countries and implements the activities associated with (domestic) learning organizations, while coping with the additional complexities of the international environment. *See also* globalization *and* learning organization.

goal *basic term*
1. An intended outcome. A goal is a broad statement of intent. *Compare with* objective.
2. The end-object of an expert system. The answer(s). *See also* expert system.

goal analysis
A process used to identify the important components of a performance. *See also* task analysis.

goal-oriented learner *basic term*
A learner who uses instruction to accomplish clear-cut objectives. *Compare with* activity- *and* learning-oriented learner.

goal statement
A broad description of the planned outcome of the HRD activity. The goal statement is a general expression of the expectations of the developers of the instruction.

good practice flyers
A technique to document the positive side of a training quality review. Good practice flyers are circulated company-wide. These flyers recognize exemplary training practices and share the knowledge gained.

gothic letters
A category of letter style typified by uniform weight of line and the absence of serifs. Gothic letters are sans serif.

Government Executive
A periodical of interest to HRD practitioners employed in the U.S. government, published by the National Journal Inc.

grade book
One of the typical record keeping features of CMI systems. *See* computer managed instruction (CMI).

graph
1. *See* chart.
2. A basic tool used in the quality process. *See also* seven quality process tools.

graphical user interface (GUI)
(Pronounced gooey.)
Uses of icons to represent actual objects, such as a trash can. The learner can access and manipulate these with a mouse. *See also* user interface.

graphics
Plotted points, drawn lines, and other pictures either in hard copy or on the display screen of a computer or a terminal. Graphics aid student understanding of complex items or processes, and can make an important contribution to the learning process. *Compare with* alphanumeric. *See also* animation.

graphics pad
See digitizer.

graphic symbol
A pictorial element that helps users to visualize concepts.

Grid
See Managerial Grid®.

grip
In video production, a person who performs physical tasks on the set, including moving furniture and bringing equipment.

group
Three or more learners whose behaviors are interrelated so that each exerts a mutual reciprocal influence on the others.

Group & Organization Management
A periodical of interest to HRD practitioners involved in organization development. *Government Executive* is published by Sage Publications.

group discussion *basic term*
A meeting among participants in a learning event. A group discussion is typically limited in length. It provides an opportunity for participants to share information and derive a group solution to an assigned problem.

group dynamics
The methods by which a group functions as a collective whole. The give and take that occurs in all groups.

group facilitator *basic term*
The HRD role of managing group discussions and group process so that individuals learn and group members feel the experience is positive. *See also* HRD Roles and Competencies Study.

group-lockstep
A form of group-pacing in which the instruction is locked into the time periods specified in the course chart. *See also* group-pacing *and* self-pacing.

group mind
The concept, no longer popular, that a group's manner of thinking and feeling is independent of its members. *See also* groupthink.

group-on-group meetings
A group technique in which the group is divided exactly in half. One group sits in the middle of the room and has a meeting or a discussion. The other half lines up one-on-one, each observing the behavior and contributions of a single participant in order to give that person helpful feedback about his or her style after the observation period is over. Then the groups reverse roles and positions. Similar to the fishbowl technique. *Compare with* fishbowl.

group-pacing
A procedure in which learners progress together toward the same objectives. Group-pacing is often employed where self-pacing is not practical for administrative reasons. *See also* group-lockstep *and* self-pacing.

group processing
In group facilitation, a technique in which the facilitator asks members of the group to express their feelings about the group's progress on tasks and each other.

group process skill
The HRD competency of influencing groups so that tasks, relationships, and individual needs are addressed. *See also* HRD Roles and Competencies Study.

groupthink
The situation in group facilitation, described by Irving Janis, in which group members think alike. Groupthink reinforces conformity and discourages innovation. It is caused by rigid adherence to group norms. *See also* group mind.

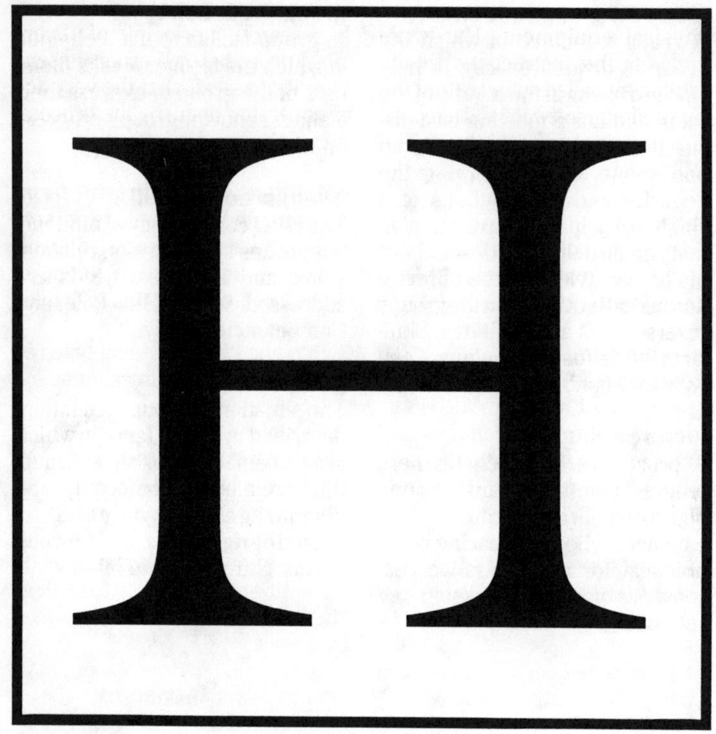

halo effect *basic term*
When one's general impression of a person biases ratings of that person's behavior. The halo effect can distrort evaluation or research.

hand-held microphone
A microphone carried in the presenter's hand. Hand-held microphones limit the ability to make gestures and operate media.

handout *essential 100 term*
Print material distributed to amplify, explain, supplement, or reinforce a specific learning activity.

hands-on
Learners operation or manipulation of equipment or other real objects.

haptic learning
A synonym for interactive learning.

haptic learning preference
An individual learning style based on preference for touch. *See also* aural, interactive, kinesthetic, olfactory, print, and visual learning styles.

haptics
One area of nonverbal communications.

hard copy
1. Piece of paper on which computer-based information has been printed.
2. Reproduced copies of visuals.

hardware
Physical equipment. Hardware excludes the instructions to the equipment called software and the instructional software and supporting physical materials called courseware.

harmony
The principle of design that relates to the compatible relationship among visual elements.

Harvard Business Review (HBR)
A periodical of interest to HRD practitioners involved in management. *Harvard Business Review* is published by Harvard Business School publication division.

Harvard case study
See case study.

Hawthorne effect *basic term*
Subjects' awareness that they are participating in an experiment, which effects their behavior. The Hawthorne effect may confound the results of the experiment. In simple terms, any newly introduced change may improve performance. The term evolved from many of what were initially puzzling results in Elton Mayo's experiments at Western Electric's Hawthorne plants. *See also* evaluation. *Compare with* Pygmalion effect *and* self-fulfilling prophecy.

Hawthorne studies
See Hawthorne effect.

head-mounted display (HMD)
A miniaturized video display used in virtual reality to permit the user to view only the display while maintaining freedom of motion for the head. *See also* virtual reality.

Heisenberg principle
In research, a principle of uncertainty proposed by Werner Heisenberg that asserts that the very act of observing disturbs the process being observed.

helping relationship *basic term*
1. A situation in which one person deploys special knowledge or skills to help another, often in the area of personal effectiveness.
2. In consulting, the ideal type relationship. *See also* client-centered relationship.

help system, on-line
See on-line help system.

hemisphericity
Recognition that different areas of the brain are specialized for different sensory, motor, and cognitive functions.

herringbone branching
Simple branching in a CAI program design. Herringbone branching is named for multiple dead-end branches. Herringbone branching is not a synonym for, and has nothing in common with, the fishbone technique.

Herrmann, Ned
Originator of the Herrmann Brain Dominance Instrument and author of *The Creative Brain*, Herrmann is best known as the popularizer of the whole brain concept.

Herrmann Brain Dominance Instrument
A questionnaire devised by Ned Herrmann. The instrument produces a brain dominance profile which provides a metaphor for the subject's brain quadrant preferences. *See also* whole brain learning.

Hertz (Hz.)
The frequency of a signal. Often in millions or MHz (pronounced mega-Hertz).

Herzberg, Frederick
Herzberg is a researcher known for his development of the motivation-hygiene theory. He identified satisfier and dissatisfier factors called motivators and hygiene factors respectively. He also developed the concept of job enrichment. His work is the basis for many organizations' management training. *See also* job enrichment *and* motivation-hygiene theory.

heterogeneous *essential 100 term*
Not alike, with dissimilar parts or elements. For example, learners with different work experience. *Compare with* homogeneous.

heuristic *basic term*
1. A rule of thumb, guideline, adaptive procedure, or practical knowledge. Heuristics are used to solve problems that may take on unanticipated forms within a range of possibilities.
2. Heuristic is also used by some practitioners to describe the discovery learning approach to teaching. *Compare with* algorithm.
3. In performance support systems, the trial-and-error problem solving to reach a final result.

hidden factory
A quality process concept, developed by Armand Feigenbaum. The concept is that organizations potentially have a hidden factory—one that has to deal with defects and rework. *See also* quality costs *and* total quality management (TQM).

HI8 Video
In video production, an 8-mm format combining high-quality with excellent portability.

hierarchical approach
An instructional technique based on learning of skills from the simplest level to the most complex.

hierarchy, objectives
See learning objectives.

Hierarchy of Needs
See Maslow's hierarchy.

high angle
In video production, a shot from any location higher than the subject. *Compare with* pan *and* zoom.

high-definition television (HDTV)
A new video format with resolution superior to NTSC, PAL, or SECAM broadcast standards.

high-level language
A computer language that permits an action which actually requires several steps inside the computer to be specified by a single command. An example is Tencore™. *See also* author language. *Compare with* authoring utility.

high resolution
1. Generally, true high resolution (2400 x 2400 pixels per inch) is used for computer-aided design and is beyond the needs of technology-based learning.
2. In industrial technology-based learning, resolution greater than the best television screen (such as 480 x 640 or 512 x 512 pixels per inch) is desirable. *See* resolution. *Compare with* NTSC.

hippocampal commissure
The bundle of axomic fibers connecting the left and right halves of the limbic system.

hippocampus
That part of the limbic system responsible for transferring memory and thus essential to learning.

histogram *basic term*
See Figure.

holism
(Not spelled wholism.)
A particular thinking style based on the concept that the whole is greater than the sum of its parts. Holistic refers to an entirety. For example, a holistic view of the company. *See also* gestalt.

holist
A learning style describing learners who tend to form complex analogies to learn. *Compare with* serialist.

holistic
See holism.

holistic learner
A person who learns by perceiving and understanding the "big picture" without dwelling on individual elements of an idea, concept, or situation. A holistic learner can see the forest as contrasted with the trees. *See also* learning style.

holograph
A three-dimensional image created through the process called holog-

Continued on next page

histogram *basic term*
1. In statistics, a type of column chart used to show the distribution of data. Histograms show the number of cases in each category.
2. A quality control chart that shows the distribution of a variance. *See also* seven quality process tools.
3. Any column chart.

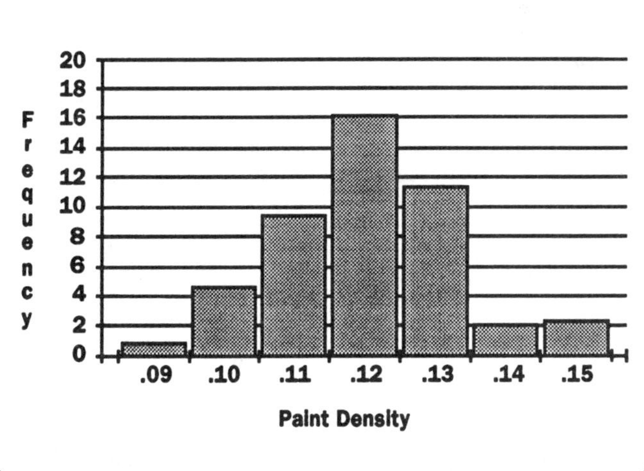

raphy. A technology that has been experimentally related to instruction. Future technological improvements may increase its practical use. *Also called* hologram.

home country
Any country from which the person or organization involved in the international HRD activity or project originates.

homogeneous *basic term*
Alike, with the same or similar parts or elements. For example, learners with identical work experience. *Compare with* heterogeneous.

Hong Kong Society for Training and Development
A professional society for HRD practitioners in Hong Kong

honorarium *basic term*
A token amount paid to a speaker or provider of a professional service when a market price is not feasible or appropriate. An honorarium is often a lower amount than would normally be charged for the time of the same person. Plural of honorarium is honoraria.

hook-and-loop (board)
A display board using small pieces of Velcro. The placards are backed with Velcro. Such items can be rapidly placed and easily moved or removed. Similar to a feltboard.

horizontal audience
Those learners who can participate in a program or currently do.

horizontal job loading
See job enlargement.

horizontal sensing
In organizational development, a small group diagnostic technique involving interviews of a horizontal slice of the organization.

horn effect
In research, when one negative observation distorts all subsequent observations.

horseshoe *basic term*
A style of room arrangement in which the table is in the shape of a U or horseshoe. *Also called* U-shaped.

hoshin planning
A disciplined form of strategic planning characterized by using data-based problem-solving tools and deploying the company's objectives throughout the organization. *See also* policy deployment *and* strategic planning.

host country
Any country where the international HRD activity or project will be carried out.

hot role play
A role play technique used to immediately resolve classroom issues. The participants are not given prepared instructions. The instructor reacts spontaneously to the immediate classroom dynamics. Any situation can become the content of a extemporaneous "hot" role play. *See also* empty chair technique *and* magic wand technique. *Compare with* structured role plays.

Hotel Sales and Marketing Association International
A professional society of interest to hospitality industry sales training professionals.

HR Canada
An umbrella organization consisting of representatives from the Provincial HRD Associations.

HRD activity *basic term*
1. HRD activities are training, education and development. *See also* education, development, HRD, and training.
2. Any intervention that is intended to develop an individual's or team's work-related capacity.

HRD consultant *basic term*
A consultant who serves as a partner with management to link HRD efforts to the organization's strategic direction and to provide various HRD services. For example, needs analysis.

HRD cost
Any expenditure assigned to an HRD program.

HRD department
The department which has responsibility for directing and coordinating HRD in an organization. Traditionally, *also called* training department.

HRD effort
Any HRD activity at any level.

HRD function
All instructional and administrative activities related to HRD that occur in an organization. Also, instructional activities are considered part of the HRD function, whether conducted by the HRD department or others.

HRD manager
The person responsible for the HRD unit within an organization.

HRD materials developer
The HRD role of producing written or electronically mediated instructional materials. *See also* HRD Roles and Competencies Study.

HRD Partnership
An organization formed in the U.K. in 1989 and comprising the British Association for Commercial and Industrial Education, the British Institute of Management, the Department of Employment, the Industrial Society, the Institute of Personnel Management, the Institute of Training & Development, and the National Economic development Office. The partners are committed to the development of cultures and processes which encourage and integrate organizational and people development (HRD) to achieve corporate objectives.

HRD practitioner
Anyone who works in the field of HRD. *See also* human resource development (HRD).

HRD Review
A newsletter of general interest to HRD practitioners. *HRD Review* is published by George F. Khoury.

HRD Roles and Competencies Study
General reference to two studies conducted by the American Society for Training and Development. The studies were led by volunteer Patricia McLagan to identify roles, outputs, and competencies for HRD professionals. *See also: Models for Excellence* (1983)/*Models for HRD Practice* (1989).

HR Focus
A periodical of interest to HRD practitioners involved in the HR field. *HR Focus* is published by the American Management Association.

HR Horizons
A periodical of interest to HRD practitioners involved in the HR

Continued on next page

field. *HR Horizons* is published by Business & Legal Reports.

HRMagazine
A periodical of interest to HRD practitioners involved in the HR field. *HRMagazine* is published by the Society for Human Resource Management.

HR Reporter
A newsletter of interest to HRD practitioners involved in the HR field. *HR Reporter* is published by Buraff Publications.

human factors *basic term*
1. The design of equipment or processes based on the human body, so that people are comfortable working. *Also called* ergonomics.
2. Those aspects of technology-based learning courseware that were included to make it easy for learners to use.

humanism
1. A philosophical viewpoint that stresses human reason as a source of authority. Humanism strives for good in the present world.
2. The "fourth" dimension of the International HRD SUCCESS Model.

humanistic psychology *basic term*
A relatively recent school founded by Abraham Maslow and Carl Rogers, among others. Humanistic psychology opposes the dehumanizing Freudian and behaviorist schools and encourages attention to the individual rather than the universal. *See also* behaviorism; hierarchy of needs; Maslow, Abraham; Rogers, Carl; and self-actualization.

human potential movement *basic term*
The human relations training popular in the 1960s. The human potential movement produced encounter groups and sensitivity training. *See also* sensitivity training *and* T-groups.

human relations training *basic term*
Programs designed to help people interact more effectively. Human relations training includes communications training, team building, and participative management. The term itself is less used today. *See also* sensitivity training *and* T-groups.

human resource accounting *basic term*
Measurement of the cost and value of an organization's employees. Human resource asset accounting views people as capital assets.

human resource development (HRD) *essential 100 term*
1. A concept developed by Leonard Nadler and published in *Developing Human Resources.* Nadler defines human resource development as organized learning experiences provided by employers within a specified period of time to bring about the possibility of performance improvement or personal growth. HRD activities are training, education, and development. HRD is differentiated from adult education in that it is focused on learning activities provided by organizations to their employees. *See also* development; Nadler, Leonard; and training. *Compare with* adult education.
2. The name of the profession.
3. The name of the field loosely

called training or training and development in some organizations.

Human Resource Development Quarterly
A research journal of general interest to HRD practitioners. *Human Resource Development Quarterly* is published by the American Society for Training and Development/Jossey-Bass Inc.

human resource environment (HRE)
The quality of work life.

human resource information system (HRIS)
Software designed to assist with HRD functions.

Human Resource Management
A periodical of interest to HRD practitioners involved in management. *Human Resource Management* is published by John Wiley & Sons.

human resource management (HRM)
A synonym for the personnel function and industrial relations.

Human Resource Planning
A periodical of interest to HRD practitioners involved in planning. *Human Resource Planning* is published by the Human Resource Planning Society.

human resource planning (HRP)
Determining the organization's human resource needs under changing conditions and developing the activities necessary to satisfy those needs. HRP integrates and coordinates hiring, promoting, training, and other activities.

Human Resource Planning Society
A professional society of interest to some HR professionals.

human resource practice
Nine areas specified in the ASTD competency study. The human resource practice areas are (1) compensation/benefits, (2) employee assistance, (3) human resource planning, (4) organization development, (5) organization/job design, (6) personnel research and information systems, (7) selection and staffing, (8) training and development, and (9) union/labor relations. *See also* human resource development (HRD) *and* organization development (OD).

human resources concept
The philosophy that people are assets. The human resources concept maintains that the development of employees represents an investment rather than an expense.

human resource utilization (HRU)
The traditional functions of personnel. *See also* human resource management (HRM).

human resource wheel
A graphic depiction of human resource areas originating in the *Models for Excellence* study. *See also* HRD Roles and Competencies Study.

hygiene factors
See motivation-hygiene theory.

hypermedia *basic term*
A program that links different media under learner control in a way similar to hypertext linkage of text. Hypermedia links media such as text, graphics, video, voice, and

Continued on next page

animation. For example, the learner can choose video when available, see a related video sequence, and then return to the program. *See also* hypertext *and* multimedia.

hypertext
A program that links nonlinear text. Hypertext allows flexible, learner-directed browsing to seek additional information by moving between related documents along thematic lines without losing the context of the original inquiry. For example, the learner chooses a word such as *gear*. The program links to text that says, "This equipment has *helical* gears." Further exploration of *helical* is possible.

hypnopedia
A synonym for sleep learning emphasizing stimulus properties, suggestibility, set, and training. Hypnopedia is a term used particularly by Russian researchers.

hypotheses
See hypothesis.

hypothesis *basic term*
A proposed explanation of the relationship between two or more variables. A hypothesis differs from a problem statement or objective in that it offers a tentative answer to the problem. The plural is hypotheses. *See also* experimental group (E-group), experimental research design, and null hypothesis.

hypothetical mode (of instruction)
An instructional style in which the instructor and students cooperate in reaching decisions concerning the mode and pace of instruction. *Compare with* disseminational instructional style.

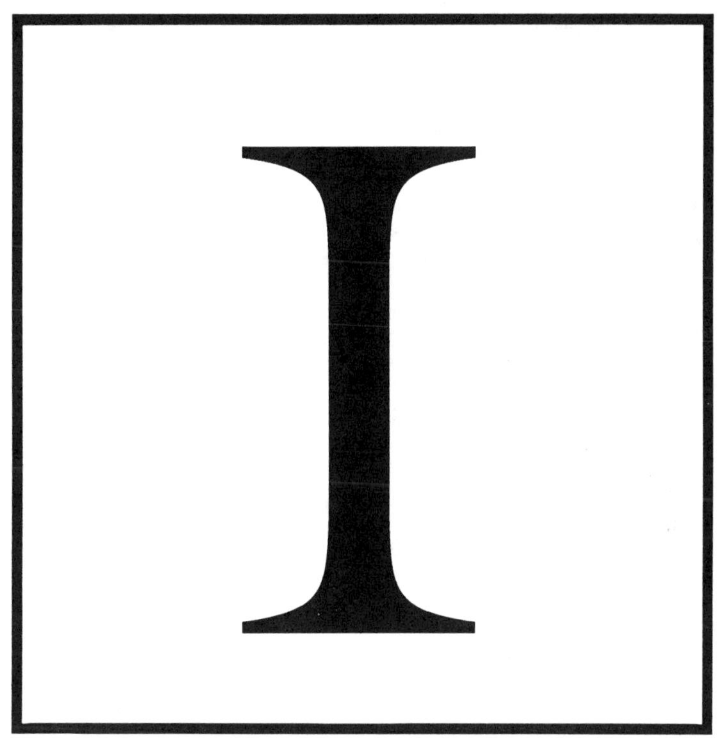

Icebreaker *basic term*
A climate-setting activity designed specifically to facilitate people getting to know each other and to place a group at ease for instruction. *Also called* a warm up or mixer.

Icon
A symbol that looks like an object. An icon can represent any function or task. In icon-driven systems, the learner chooses the icon with a tactile device, such as a mouse, instead of pressing function keys or typing commands.

Iconic model
A model involving a set of summary images or graphics that stand for a concept.

Id
A part of the personality described by Sigmund Freud. The id is the repository of instincts.

Ideal model
In model-building, an ideal model exaggerates certain features of what it represents, usually for comparative purposes.

Identical elements approach
In transfer of training, the facilitation of transfer through making the training experience closely similar in nature to the task demands of the job.

Illiteracy *basic term*
The lack of fundamental reading

Continued on next page

and writing skills. *Compare with* basic skills.

imagery *basic term*
A method of storing information in long-term memory by generation of vivid mental visualizations. Imagery includes mental images formed from memories of sounds, touch, muscle activity, emotion, or abstract concepts. *See also* creativity training *and* long-term memory. *Compare with* mnemonics.

imaginative learner
A person who learns by forming mental images of things not immediately available to the senses or never wholly perceived in reality. An imaginative learner is able to confront and deal with a problem in a new way. *See also* learning style.

imaging *basic term*
Imprinting in one's own mind a mental picture of improved behavior and using that vision to stimulate appropriate behaviors.

imaging style
A preferred dimension in individual imaging. Imaging styles include imagers, nonimagers, and occasional imagers. Types of imagery include visual and kinesthetic.

impact
See results.

implementation *basic term*
One of the phases in the ISD process. The others are analysis, design, implementation, and evaluation. Delivering the learning activities to the target population of learners in the intended environment. All instructional materials are reproduced and distributed during the implementation phase. *Also called* delivery.

implementive evaluation
See evaluation.

implicit norm
A norm that arises informally, and remains unstated, between individuals. *Compare with* explicit norm.

impromptu
Speaking with little advance notice or preparation. *Compare with* extemporaneous.

improvement
1. In career development, a concept used to describe the establishment of a relationship with another individual for mutual advantage.
2. Keeping instructional content and techniques up-to-date.

in-basket exercise *essential 100 term*
1. A simple simulation technique that places the learner at a desk with realistic documents in an in-basket. The learner must process the documents, which include, but are not limited to, letters, memos, notes from the boss, records of telephone calls, appraisal forms, and routine reports which create realistic conditions. Sometimes not all documents have relevance to the goal. The participant must decide what to do with each item while taking into consideration the principles taught in the HRD program. In-basket exercises can measure decision-making or technical competence. Variations may stress wise use of time, decision-making ability, telephone calls, and instructor-simulated emergencies. *Also called* in-basket technique. *See also* simulation.
2. Loosely, a method of instruc-

tion in which an individual is called upon to respond to hypothetical situations as they are provided.

Inches per second (ips)
The standard for measuring audio and videotape speed.

Incident process *basic term*
A role play technique developed by Paul Pigors, used to help learners acquire skill in knowing what questions to ask, how to phrase them, how to draw inferences from the data gathered. The instructor presents a brief problem situation. The case used lacks sufficient detail to reach any decision. Pertinent facts are only provided in response to the group's specific questions. The learners question the instructor to find the information needed to resolve the case. The incident process teaches skills of interrogation, analysis, and synthesis. It is often used in courses in labor relations, grievance handling, investigative techniques, and problem solving. *See also* case study *and* action maze.

Incubation
A key concept in creativity training. Incubation is the period during which one's attention is deliberately shifted away from the problem or task at hand. Solutions typically come as insight or sudden inspiration. *See also* creativity training.

Independent variable
The experimental treatment or intervention. *Compare with* dependent variable.

Indian Society for Training and Development
A professional society for HRD practitioners in India.

Indigenous
Occurring or living naturally. Indigenous is a descriptor usually applied to a person with origin in the country in which currently found. *Compare with* native.

Indirect cost
A cost associated with keeping the HRD department operating. Indirect costs are not chargeable to a specific program. For example, telephone and copier costs.

Indirect question
A question directed to the entire group. *Also called* an overhead question. *Compare with* direct question.

Indirect time
See unapplied billing entry.

Individual career development advisor
The HRD role of helping individuals to assess personal competencies, values, and goals and to identify, plan, and implement development and career actions. *See also* HRD Roles and Competencies Study.

Individual career plan (ICP)
A synonym for individual development plan. *See* individual development plan (IDP).

Individual development *basic term*
Planned learning efforts that help the individual in the development of the essential competencies needed to grow and prepare for potential futures.

Individual development plan (IDP)
In career planning, a component of succession planning. The individual development plan becomes

Continued on next page

an action plan to prepare the identified successor with the knowledge, skills, and experience needed to perform competently. The IDP is usually executed on a prepared form.

individual education
See individualized learning.

individualization
1. Development of any instructional package for individualized study.
2. The degree to which courseware has been individualized.

individualized instruction
essential 100 term
An instructional technique in which the instruction is designed to be used by individual learners. The learner is taught only the material that is not already known, instead of taught everything in a specified curriculum as is true with traditional instruction. This is more than learners simply working on materials without regard to the activities of other learners in the same class. All individualized instruction is self-paced instruction. But not all self-paced instruction is individualized. *Compare with* self-directed learning, self-instruction, and self-paced instruction.

individually-initiated developmental experiences
Any development activity commenced by an individual without prompting from others.

individual reports
Learner-presented reports on any aspect of an HRD activity, delivered to the other learners and to the instructor.

individual/work profile
In career planning, a component of succession planning. The individual/work profile is usually executed on a prepared form.

indoctrination *basic term*
In organizational development, a change process characterized by mutual goal-setting and imbalanced power. *Compare with* planned change, coercive change, technocratic change, interactional change, socialization change, emulative change, and natural change.

induced forces
Those forces that act on an individual from the surrounding environment.

induction
The process of generating a system from data through the use of software rather than analysis. *See also* performance support system.

inductive approach
Moving from specific observations of parts to generalize the whole. The inductive approach is prefered by some individuals. *Compare with* deductive approach.

Industrial Relations Research Association
A professional society of interest to some HR professionals.

industry understanding
The HRD competency of knowing the key concepts and variables that define an industry or sector, such as critical issues, economic vulnerabilities, measurements, distribution channels, inputs, outputs, and information sources. *See also* HRD Roles and Competencies Study.

inert knowledge
The knowledge a learner has acquired but fails to activate in appro-

priate situations.

Inference engine
The processing portion of expert systems and performance support systems. It contains the priorities, strategies, and rules used in problem solving. *See also* knowledge base.

Inferential statistics
Methods used to generalize characteristics of a large group based on characteristics of a small group. *Compare with* descriptive statistics.

Infobase
A database concept extended to include the means to gather information appropriate to performing tasks.

Informal
A term used to describe the communication networks, norms, and status hierarchy of a group that are developed through natural processes and not necessarily sanctioned by any source of authority.

Informal balance
Equal distribution of information on both sides of the center of a visual, where one side of the visual does not identically duplicate the other side. Informal balance effectively employs the use of white space. *Compare with* formal balance.

Informal HRD programs
See unstructured HRD programs.

Information
1. Facts, ideas, and figures that relate to a need.
2. The goal of some presentations. *Compare with* learning.

Information for bid and award (IFB)
A term used in procurement. *See also* two-step procurement.

Information load
The amount of information a person receives in a given situation. Information load may be overload or underload compared with the amount of information needed to function effectively.

Information Mapping®
A method of structuring complex information developed by Robert Horn. Material is rendered in consistent formats from memos to manuals.

Information processing model
A representation of learning as a system. The information processing model links the environment to long-term memory through receptors, a sensory register, and short-term memory. Long- and short-term memories are linked back to the environment through a response generator and effectors. Contributions were made to the information processing model by many people, including Georg von Békésy and Robert Gagné. *See also* short-term memory *and* long-term memory.

Information retrieval service
A computer-based service that can be accessed by a computer over a telephone line. A large number of data bases may be searched. Examples include DIALOG, ORBIT, and BRS.

Information search skill
The HRD competency of skill in gathering information from printed and other recorded sources, and identifying and using information specialists, reference services, and

Continued on next page

reference aids. *See also* HRD Roles and Competencies Study.

InfoWindow
A widely applied display system standard in common use for interactive video. The InfoWindow standard is derived from hardware that is no longer produced.

in-house *basic term*
Literally, anything that takes place within the organization. In-house is distinct from external, which is anything that occurs outside the organization. The term "out-house" is not used.

in-house education
See in-service programs.

in-house HRD programs
Those HRD programs sponsored by an organization. HRD activities are considered in-house whether conducted by the in-house staff or external individuals or organizations.

in-house HRD staff
HRD practitioners employed by the organization. *Compare with* consultant *and* vendor.

initialism
Initial letters of a term verbalized letter by letter, such as OJT. *Compare with* acronym.

input *basic term*
1. *See* stimulus.
2. Originally a computer term. Today, a shorthand way of referring to any information, in whatever form, that is presented for consideration and later processing. *Compare with* output.

in-service programs
HRD activities designed for employees and provided by the organization. *Also called* in-house education or training.

inspection
See detection.

institute *basic term*
1. A learning event sponsored by an authoritative organization and conducted with greater formality than a seminar. Institutes may qualify participants to work in a specific field. *Compare with* seminar.
2. A learning event characterized by a series of meetings that may extend over weeks, months, or years.

Institute for International Human Resources (IIHR)
A division of the Society for Human Resource Management intended to provide a forum for the development of global human resource professionals. *See also* Society for Human Resource Management (SHRM).

Institute of Personnel Management (IPM)
An institute in the United Kingdom for personnel professionals and of interest to HR practitioners, many of whom are members of both the IPM and the ITD. *See also* Institute of Training & Development (ITD).

Institute of Personnel Management New Zealand (IPMNZ)
An institute for personnel professionals and of interest to HR practitioners.

Institute of Training & Development (ITD)
A professional society for HRD practitioners in the U.K., committed to serving the professional in-

terests of members and upholding the highest ideals in HRD. *See also* Institute of Personnel Management (IPM).

Instructional aid
Auxiliary items to support instructor-led instruction. Instructional aids stand in contrast to instructional media which present instruction. Examples of instructional aids include chalkboard, flipchart, and slides. Loosely, *also called* little media. *See also* media. *Compare with* big media.

Instructional analysis
A process that is carried out during the design of instruction to identify the presentational components necessary for the learner's mastery of complete skills. Sometimes confused with needs analysis, which is carried out during the analysis phase. *Compare with* needs analysis.

Instructional climate *basic term*
The state of relative readiness to learn. Climate setting is closely aligned with adult learning. The two components of climate are organizational climate and instructional climate. *See also* climate setting *and* organizational climate.

Instructional design *basic term*
1. The activity of planning and designing for instruction. Also, a discipline associated with the activity. *See also* instructional technology
2. Related to the design phase of ISD. *See also* instructional systems development (ISD).
3. Loosely, a synonym for instructional development. Some practitioners prefer to use one of these terms, while other practitioners strictly use the other term.

Instructional developer
A practitioner of instructional development.

Instructional development *basic term*
1. The process of producing learning activities. *See also* instructional technology *and* instructional systems development (ISD).
2. Related to the development phase of ISD. *See also* instructional systems development (ISD).
3. Loosely, a synonym for instructional design. Some practitioners prefer to use one of these terms, while other practitioners strictly use the other term.

Instructional experience
1. The result of participation in an instructional program.
2. The learning activity itself.

Instructional game *essential 100 term*
1. A rule-governed activity involving some conflict that obstructs the players from reaching a specific goal. Instructional games usually, but not always, include some form of competition. *See also* simulation *and* simulation game.
2. Any game from which participants can learn something of value.
3. One of the modes of CAI. The others are drill and practice, modeling, simulation, and tutorial. The dividing line between amusement and education is not always easily discernible since learning by playing is still learning. Despite the instructional legitimacy and value of instructional gaming, it has not been well accepted by some organizations.

Continued on next page

4. Loosely, any variety of experiential learning activity. *See also* connect the dots, experiential learning, method, and old woman/young woman. *Compare with* game (transactional analysis usage).

instructional hour
A measure of instructional time typically calculated based on a formula. Used in many organizations, but particularly important in formal instructional settings to determine instructional costs and loads. *Also called* clock hour.

instructional materials
Any materials provided to the learner before, during, or after instruction to assist in learning.

instructional materials package
See learning activities package.

instructional media
See media.

instructional need
Any need that should properly be addressed by an HRD effort. Distinct from both noninstructional need and a want. *See* needs analysis.

instructional objective
See learning objective.

instructional prerequisites
See prerequisite.

instructional prescription
An assignment given to a learner in individualized learning situations to provide needed learning. Instructional prescriptions are often based on a pretest given to participants to determine what level of knowledge, skill, or aptitude they bring to the instruction. *See also* criterion-referenced instruction *and* pretest. *Compare with* post test.

instructional resource
See learning resource.

instructional strategy *basic term*
The methods and media to be used in a particular HRD activity.

instructional style *basic term*
An approach to instruction that varies with individual instructors. Experts do not agree on categories for instructional styles. Styles include, but are not limited to, facilitative, directive, Socratic, disseminational, and balanced.

instructional system *basic term*
An integrated combination of resources including students, instructors, materials, equipment, and facilities; techniques; and procedures performing efficiently the functions required to achieve specified learning objectives. *See also* instructional systems development (ISD).

instructional systems design
See instructional systems development (ISD).

instructional systems development (ISD) *essential 100 term*
Usually heard in abbreviated form, ISD is a term for a variety of related systems that organize the development of instruction. ISD should be a deliberate and orderly, but flexible, process for planning and developing instructional programs that ensure personnel are taught in a cost-effective way the knowledge, skills, and attitudes essential for successful job performance.

The phases of ISD are analysis, design, development, implementation, and evaluation. ISD depends on a description and analysis of several integral instructional factors, such as the tasks necessary for performing the job, and learning objectives. Tests are clearly stated before instruction begins, evaluation procedures are carried out to determine whether or not the objectives have been reached, and methods for revising the process are based on empirical data. *See also* analysis, design, development, implementation, and evaluation.

Instructional technology *basic term*
The systematic practice of designing, carrying out, and evaluating the total learning process, employing a combination of human and nonhuman resources to bring about more effective instruction.

Instructional television (ITV) *basic term*
1. Any use of video, in any format, for learning. *Also called* instructional video.
2. Broadcast television intended for learning.

Instructional triad
The concordance of an employee's on-the-job performance, with the instruction to enable it, and the test to ensure that it is learned.

Instructional video
See instructional television.

Instruction Delivery Systems
A periodical of interest to HRD practitioners involved in technology-based learning. *Instruction Delivery Systems* is published by Communicative Technology.

Instructor *basic term*
1. The HRD role of presenting information and directing structured learning experiences so that individuals learn. *See also* HRD Roles and Competencies Study.
2. A synonym for trainer, facilitator, and group leader.
3. Loosely, anyone in charge of a class of learners.

Instructor-dependent
Instruction that depends on the instructor for delivery.

Instructor-dependent outline
A general outline that lists each topic with a few key words. Only the person who prepared it or a skilled instructor who is also a subject matter expert (SME) can interpret and use it. *Compare with* instructor-independent outline.

Instructor-developer
An HRD practitioner who primarily instructs in the classroom and secondarily develops courseware for the courses he or she teaches. *See also* developer-instructor.

Instructor guide *basic term*
A publication prepared by many organizations that sponsor instruction designed to provide the instructors with information about the objectives of the materials, the procedures involved in their development, suggestions for their best use, and descriptions of what might be expected from the materials based on their previous effectiveness.

Instructor-independent
Courseware that does not depend on an instructor for delivery. *See also* learning activity package *and* self-directed learning. *Compare with* instructor-led.

Instructor-independent outline
A detailed outline that lists topics, subtopics, key points, and explanations. The format may be specified by the organization responsible for the instruction. Any qualified instructor can interpret and use it. An instructor-independent outline is more specific than a script. *Compare with* instructor-dependent outline *and* script.

Instructor-led
Courseware that depends on an instructor for delivery. *Compare with* instructor-independent *and* self-directed learning.

Instructor-led training *basic term*
Any learning activity dependent on an instructor or facilitator. Instructor-led training is a relatively new term for an old activity occasioned by the development of alternatives such as CAI.

Instructor of instructors
The consistent HRD term for trainer of trainers. A person who conducts train-the-trainer sessions.

Instructor/student ratio
See student/instructor ratio.

Instrument *essential 100 term*
Paper and pencil devices used in HRD to gather information about individual, group, or organizational attitudes, values, behavior, and so forth. A wide variety of instruments have been developed. For example, checklists, inventories, opinion-rating scales, questionnaires, reaction forms, surveys, tests.

Instrumental learning *basic term*
Informal learning that takes place when people learn how to do their jobs better. *Compare with* didactic *and* self-reflective learning.

Instrumentation
See instrument.

Instrumented training
The use of instruments to accomplish specific learning objectives.

Intangible benefit
Outcomes of HRD that cannot be measured easily, such as improved customer satisfaction and better decision making.

Integrated service-digital network (ISDN)
A digital telecommunications channel that allows for the integrated transmission of voice, video, and data. ISDNs will become increasingly important in distance learning.

Integrated training
Instruction covering the mix of skills required by the job itself.

Intellectual competencies
Competencies described in the HRD Roles and Competencies Study as knowledge and skills related to thinking. These competencies include data-reduction skill, information search skill, intellectual versatility, model-building skill, observing skill, self-knowledge, and visioning skill. *See also* HRD Roles and Competencies Study.

Intellectual versatility
The HRD competency of recognizing, exploring, and using a broad range of ideas and practices; thinking logically and creatively without undue influence from personal biases. *See also* HRD Roles and Competencies Study.

Intelligence
The ability to learn and to deal with problems, new situations, and abstract concepts. No one definition of intelligence is sufficient since intelligence can be revealed in many different ways.

Interaction *basic term*
1. A reciprocal interchange between the learner and the instructional medium. In CAI an interaction is never simply pressing a key to advance the display. A complete interaction is a question or problem, directions, expected correct and incorrect answers, and feedback for each possible answer. The interaction may be followed by branching, contributing to individualized instruction. The interactivity of courseware is sometimes judged by counting the frequency of interactions. *See also* branching, individualized instruction, and levels of interaction.
2. The give-and-take between participants in learning activities.
3. The give-and-take between teleconferencing participants in different locations.

Interactional change
In organizational development, a change process characterized by mutual goal-setting and equal power without deliberateness on either side. *Compare with* coercive change, emulative change, indoctrination, natural change, planned change, socialized change, and technocratic change.

Interaction Process Analysis (IPA) *basic term*
The system of interaction analysis developed by Robert F. Bales.

Interactive *basic term*
1. The quality of an exercise that involves participants in communicating with one another or with a computer.
2. In distance learning, communications with either two-way audio and video, or two-way audio and one-way video. This provides for question-and-answer interactivity.
3. In instructional games, the involvement of players with the material of the game as well as with each other.

Interactive demonstrations *basic term*
Demonstrations that allow learner-watchers to participate instead of merely observe. Learners may move objects in purposeful ways, move around, ask questions, and interact. Job instruction training (JIT) is a perfect format for this. Once the climate is set, the instructor tells and shows the first step of the task, as learners *do* that first step right along with the instructor. This permits cumulative repetition and the practice that makes perfect.

Interactive drawing
A creativity training method developed by Betty Edwards to help access the right side of the brain, gain confidence in creative abilities, and support creative problem solving. *See also* brain lateralization *and* creativity training.

Interactive learning preference *basic term*
An individual learning style based on preference for verbalization. *See also* aural, haptic, kinesthetic, olfactory, print, and visual learning styles.

Interactive lecture
A presentation that encourages and facilitates communication between

Continued on next page

the instructor and the learner or among the learners. Most interactive lectures incorporate game-like elements. *Compare with* lecture.

interactive media *basic term*
1. Instructional hardware that involves the viewer as a source of input to determine the content and duration of a message. Interactive media permit program material to be individualized.
2. Telecommunication channels that allow the two-way exchange of information.

interactive modeling
See behavior modeling.

interactive multimedia (IM) *basic term*
Essentially, CAI carried to its logical conclusion. IM is a somewhat redundant term that has grown in popularity primarily because of marketing efforts. *See also* interactive video *and* multimedia.

Interactive Multimedia Association
A professional society of interest to some HRD professionals.

interactive video
See interactive videodisc (IVD).

interactive videodisc (IVD) *basic term*
Video images linked with a computerized learning program that are learner-controlled through the use of a computer. Depending on the learner's response to a question, the learner may be shown any one of several video sequences. Technically, IVD is CAI controlling an added 12-inch laser-read player. IVD usually includes motion video, audio, and a touch panel. Sequences can be still, regular, slow, or fast motion. Videodiscs hold 54,000 video images or about one hour. *Also called* interactive video. Never spelled videodisk. *See also* auxiliary device, Electronic Information Delivery System (EIDS), optical media, and multimedia.

interactive video instruction (IVI)
See interactive videodisc (IVD).

interactivity
The degree to which a technology-based or other HRD activity responds to the actions of the learner.

Intercollegiate Case Clearing House
A clearing house established by the American Association of Collegiate Schools of Business and Harvard University's Graduate School of Business. The clearinghouse is a source for cases. Case length and content vary widely.

intercultural
A synonym for cross-cultural.

interdisciplinary *basic term*
Anything that involves aspects of a number of subject areas.

interface
The link between two pieces of equipment.

interface cluster
Four roles concerned with the relationship between the HRD department and its environment. These roles are marketer, group facilitator, instructor, and transfer agent. *See also* HRD Roles and Competencies Study.

intergroup meeting
In organizational development, a problem-solving meeting held for frank discussion and airing of prob-

lems that have become acute.

Intern
Any person serving an internship. *See also* internship.

Internal appraisal
A strategic planning step to assess the success with which the organization is realizing its purpose. Internal appraisal includes analysis of organizational strengths and weaknesses.

Internal consultant *basic term*
A consultant who is an employee of the client system organization. *Compare with* external consultant.

Internal customer
People or groups within the organization who receive services from another group in order to accomplish their own missions.

Internal evaluation
The acquisition and analysis of internal feedback and management data from within the formal instructional environment to assess the effectiveness of the instructional process.

Internal service
The idea that everyone in the organization has a customer. Internal service implies that each person who is not serving a customer should serve someone who is.

International
A person or organization with origins in one country, intent on achieving personal and business success in at least one other country.

International Congress on the Assessment Center Method
A group formed to develop standards for assessment centers. *See also* assessment center method.

International Federation of Training and Development Organizations (IFTDO) *basic term*
The international HRD organization. IFTDO members are national HRD organizations. Individuals are members through their national organizations.

International HRD
Programs that involve people from more than one country. The actual venue can be in any country.

International HRD practitioner
A person who engages in HRD activities in a country other than his or her own. Loosely, *also called* international trainer.

International Interactive Communications Society
A professional society of interest to some HRD professionals.

International Labor Organization (ILO) *basic term*
An agency of the United Nations that conducts training programs throughout the world. The ILO includes unions, employers, and government.

International Society for Intercultural Education Training and Research
A professional society of interest to HRD professionals interested in global HRD. Formerly known as Society for Intercultural Education Training and Research (SIETAR).

International trainer
See international HRD practitioner.

Internship *basic term*
Programs conducted by many organizations to provide opportuni-

Continued on next page

ties for graduate and undergraduate students to gain practical experience while contributing to the organization. Participants are called interns.

Interpersonal competencies
Competencies described in HRD Roles and Competencies Study as having a strong communication base. These competencies include coaching skill, feedback skill, group-process skill, negotiation skill, presentation skill, questioning skill, relationship-building skill, and writing skill. *See also* HRD Roles and Competencies Study.

Interpersonal domain
See affective domain.

Interpersonal skills *basic term*
Those skills associated with dealing and working with other members of a group.

Interpretive title
A title that concisely explains the essence of the visual. *Also called* action title.

Interrelationship digraph
A quality process management and planning tool used to identify causal relationships between language data. The interrelationship digraph is useful to find root causes, relationships, and critical items among qualitative data.

Interrupted time series design
In research, when measurement is conducted repeatedly or continuously before, during, and after treatment. *Compare with* multiple baseline design.

Intervention *essential 100 term*
1. Any course of action taken by a change agent. Intervention is most often associated with OD. *See also* organization development (OD).
2. Loosely, any planned change effort undertaken by HRD or activity.

Interview *basic term*
1. A session between an individual and one or more interviewers held for the purpose of collecting information.
2. A presentation in which a resource person is questioned by one or more interviewers. The interview can be followed by a forum or work groups. *See also* panel.

Intragroup
Within a group.

Intraorganization
Within the organization.

Intra-organizer
Small amounts of information presented to learners periodically during a learning activity. Intra-organizers assist the learner to understand how the current topic fits in relation to the entire activity.

In-tray technique
See in-basket technique.

Introduction
The first part of a presentation or the lead-in comments by the program chairperson. The introduction often includes a brief overview of the presentation. *Compare with* body and conclusion.

Introversion (I)
In the Myers-Briggs typology, one of the eight basic predispositions included. *See* Myers-Briggs Type Indicator (MBTI).

Intuiting (N)
In the Myers-Briggs typology, one

of the eight basic predispositions included. *See* Myers-Briggs Type Indicator. (MBTI)

investigation
Any planned approach to discover, test, and apply new knowledge. Investigation is generally used to describe the activites of research. *See* research.

Ishikawa diagram
A synonym for cause and effect diagram named after Kaoru Ishikawa. *See* cause and effect diagram.

ISO 9000
A set of international quality standards originated by the desire for quality standardization within the ECC.

italic (type)
Type slanted to the right, similar to handwriting. *Compare with* roman.

item analysis
Statistical method for comparison of how respondents performed on individual items within the instrument as a whole.

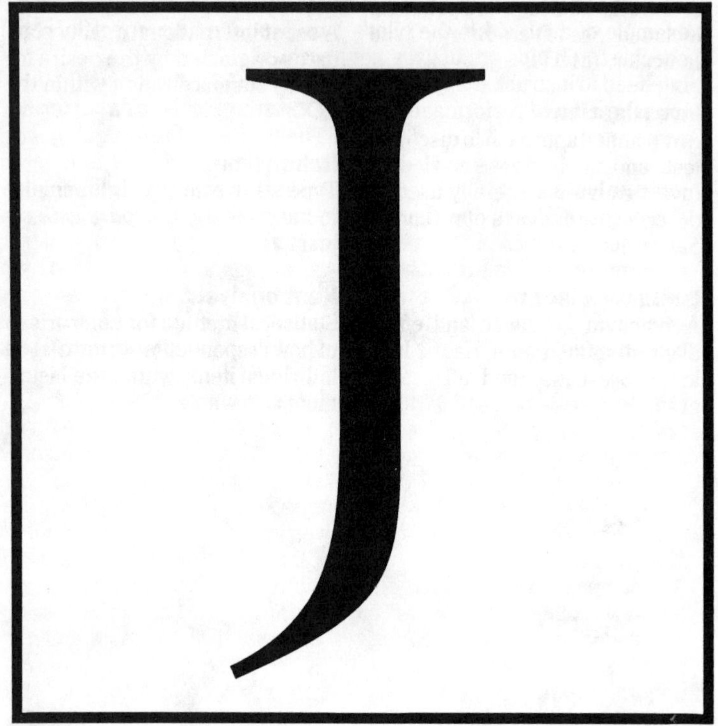

Jigsaw
An instructional technique in which learners or groups are given elements of a system, plan, or chart. They assemble these elements until a complete result is achieved. Variations include only one way to assemble the pieces properly, and a variety of individualized or creative results. In the latter case, the group then discusses the relative qualities of each result. Jigsaws are used to teach synthesizing skills, problem-solving skills, or organizational skills.

Job
The composite of duties and tasks performed by an individual.

Job aid *essential 100 term*
Any device, simple, or complex, that an employee uses on the job to perform reliably. Job aids reduce the amount of information the performer must recall or retain in order to successfully carry out a task and are usually employed to increase the likelihood of high fidelity performance. In some cases the employee may depend completely on the job aid for correct performance. The person often needs less training to perform reliably. Job aids are appropriate when tasks are infrequent or complex, there are high negative consequences for error, or training to perform the task

would be expensive. The classic example of a job aid is the pilot's checklist. Job aids are usually not intended to instruct. *Compare with* learning aid *and* performance support system.

Job analysis
A process of identifying the complete set of duties that a person performs on the job. Job analysis is often combined with task analysis when instruction is needed. *See* task analysis.

Job competency assessment (JCA)
Any of several formal processes used to determine the effectiveness of a job incumbent.

Job Corps
A U.S. government-sponsored nationwide training program. Particular attention was focused on assistance to poor, disadvantaged, and minority group members.

Job description
A formal explanation of the activities job incumbents perform at work.

Job design
The process of designing how tasks will be carried out, and the authority and systems to be utilized in individual jobs.

Job Development Program
A U.S. government-sponsored nationwide training program established in 1965. Particular attention was focused on assistance to poor, disadvantaged, and minority group members.

Job-duty-task method
In task analysis, a method of gathering data based on describing, in detail, what must be done in order to produce the specific result wanted.

Job enlargement *basic term*
The process of redesigning work which increases the number of tasks. Job enlargement is an older term, now considered a less satisfactory concept because it merely conveys increasing the number of tasks. Job enlargement is sometimes called horizontal job loading. *Compare with* job enrichment.

Job enrichment *basic term*
The process of redesigning work to build in motivators and incorporate more positive challenges. Job enrichment is sometimes called vertical job loading. For example, it may involve changes in how the job is done, when or where one works, or with whom one works. *Compare with* job enlargement.

Job instruction training (JIT) *basic term*
The classic four-step learning process developed during World War II to train a worker to do a job. JIT stressed tell, show, do, and review and follow-up. JIT instruction used lecture, demonstration, performance tryout, and critiques. JIT is still used in business and industry. *See also* four step method, on-the-job training (OJT), and vestibule training.

Job inventory
An instrument used for conducting an occupational survey. A job inventory consists of items for identification and background information, and a list of appropriate duty and task statements. It does not include standards of performance for the duties and tasks listed.

job model

1. Specific positions that represent other jobs and that are used to determine needed HRD activities for all the inclusive jobs. *Also called* benchmark position.
2. A profile of the work (outputs and tasks) and conditions associated with a job.

job performance aids
See job aids.

job performance measure (JPM) *basic term*
A test or other measurement to assess an individual's proficiency in a specific job task.

job performance requirements (JPR)
The tasks required of the job incumbent, the conditions under which these tasks must be performed, and the quality standards for acceptable performance. JPRs describe what people must do to perform their jobs.

job profile
The competencies, outputs, and major ethical issues for a job. The job profile may include relevant issues, future demands, roles, and quality requirements. A job profile may also be prepared for a team.

job progression ladder
In career planning, career paths in which progressively higher positions in the organizational hierarchy are clearly linked and the education and experience needed to progress are stated unambiguously. *See also* management career ladder *and* technical career ladder.

job qualification standard (JQS)
A list of tasks an individual is required to perform in his or her current job. Job qualification standard lists contain day-to-day production, contingency, and mandatory requirements.

job rotation *basic term*

1. In general, the practice of moving employees to various positions for a period of time. Job rotation may be motivated by many reasons. For example, to reduce boredom.
2. In service training, a method of making employees more aware of service problems by rotating them into positions that interface with customers.
3. In career development, a general strategy for exposing employees to jobs in different parts of the organization as a way of helping them explore new options or maintain challenge and learning.

job specification
A written description of the knowledge, skills, and abilities job incumbents need. Job specifications for a position are presumed to be required to meet the responsibilities or to carry out the activities for which the incumbent is responsible.

job study
See task analysis.

job task analysis (JTA)
See task analysis.

Job Training Partnership Act (JTPA)
Legislation enacted by the U.S. Congress in 1982 which provides funding for job training and related employment services to economically disadvantaged persons who lack job skills and to "dislo-

cated," "displaced" workers who possess outdated skills for jobs that are fast disappearing. The JTPA program is operated through local Private Industry Councils (PICs) composed of representatives from business, education, labor, etc.

Johari window *basic term*
See Figure.

joint destiny
One of six gestalt principles about perception. *See* gestalt perception principles.

joint presentation *basic term*
Presentation with two or more presenters. *Also called* team presentation.

Jones, John E.
Co-developer, with William Pfeiffer, of the *Handbook of Structured Experiences for Human Relations Training* and *The Annual Handbook for Group Facilitators* used for small-group theory and methods.

Journal for Quality and Participation
A periodical of interest to HRD practitioners involved in the quality process. *Journal for Quality and Participation* is published by the Association for Quality and Participation.

Journal of Applied Behavioral Science
A periodical of general interest to

Continued on next page

Johari window *basic term*
(Pronounced joe′-haarie.)
A graphic representation of potential states of understanding. The Johari window is a square composed of four cells. The cells are defined by two conditions on each of two axes. The intersections of the axes in the cells result in four different combinations that produce unique conditions described by each cell. The Johari window was named after its creators Joseph Luft and Harry Ingham. The Johari window has been adapted to widely varying concepts.

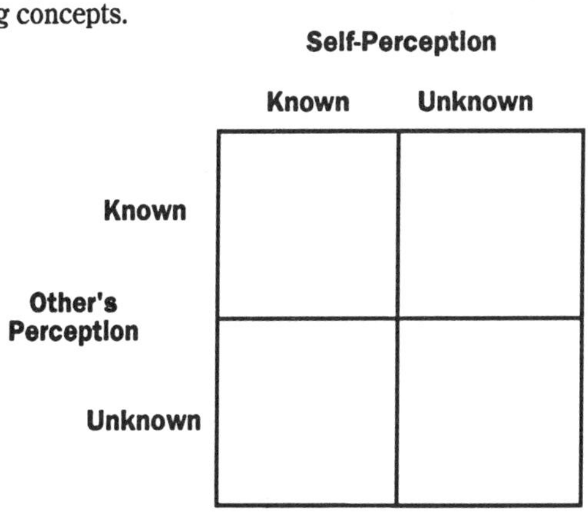

		Self-Perception: Known	Self-Perception: Unknown
Other's Perception	Known		
	Unknown		

HRD practitioners published by Sage Publications.

Journal of Applied Psychology
A periodical of interest to HRD practitioners interested in psychology. *Journal of Applied Behavioral Science* is published by the American Psychological Association.

Journal of Career Development
A periodical of interest to HRD practitioners involved in career development. *Journal of Career Development* is published by Human Sciences Press Inc.

Journal of Computer-Based Instruction
A periodical of interest to HRD practitioners involved in technology-based learning. *Journal of Computer-Based Instruction* is published by the Association for Development of Computer-Based Instructional Systems.

Journal of Educational Technology Systems
A periodical of interest to HRD practitioners involved in systematic instructional design. *Journal of Educational Technology Systems* is published by Baywood Publishing Company Inc.

Journal of Experiential Education
A periodical of interest to HRD practitioners involved in experiential learning. *Journal of Experiential Education* is published by the Association for Experiential Education.

Journal of Healthcare Education & Training
A periodical of interest to HRD practitioners in the healthcare field. *Journal of Healthcare Education & Training* is published by the American Society for Healthcare Education and Training

Journal of Interactive Instruction Development
A periodical of interest to HRD practitioners involved in systematic design of interactive instruction. *Journal of Interactive Instruction Development* is published by Communicative Technology Corporation.

Journal of Management
A periodical of interest to HRD practitioners involved in management. *Journal of Management* is published by the Southern Management Association.

joy sheet
A derogatory synonym for reaction sheet. *See also* reaction sheet.

Judging (J)
In the Myers-Briggs typology, one of the eight basic predispositions included. *See* Myers-Briggs Type Indicator (MBTI).

Jung, Carl
A Swiss psychologist who described personality in ways that are still used in HRD. Some of his ideas are incorporated in the Myers-Briggs Type Indicator. For example, he identified thinking, feeling, sensing, and intuition as the four psychological functions. *See also* Myers-Briggs Type Indicator (MBTI).

Juran, J. M.
Joseph M. Juran is a statistician who instructed that massive training is a prerequisite of quality. He is the author of the *Quality Control*

Handbook. *See also* total quality management (TQM).

Justification

1. A description of type margins. *See also* centered, flush right (or left), and ragged.
2. An explanation or defense of planned expenditures in a budget analysis.

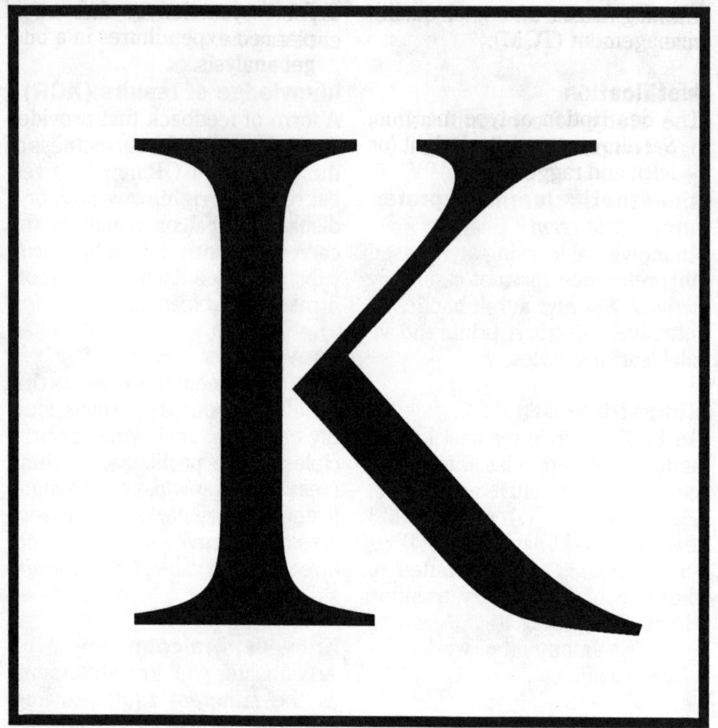

kaizen
A pragmatic approach to organizational improvement. Kaizen is a Japanese word that means improvement. Kaizen was introduced to the English speaking world by Masaaki Imai.

key questions
See open-ended key questions.

key results area (KRA)
Job duties. In some organizations these are *also called* areas of responsibility, important areas of responsibility, or job segments.

keystone
See keystone effect.

keystone effect *basic term*
Refers to the distortion of an image projected on a surface at an angle. The keystone effect is frequently seen with an overhead projector. The shape is wider at the top than at the bottom and resembles the keystone of an arch. *Also called* Elmire effect.

key-word visual
A slide or overhead transparency that displays only the most memorable words of each point to be covered.

kilo (K)
Commonly used as a prefix meaning thousand. The abbreviation K is often used in technology-based

learning to used for comparison of size.

kinesics
The study of communications based on posture and gesture.

kinesthetic learning preference *basic term*
An individual learning style based on preference for motor-sensory activity. *See also* aural, haptic, interactive, olfactory, print, and visual learning styles.

Kirkpatrick, Donald L.
An HRD practitioner best known as developer of the classic four level model of summative evaluation. The levels are (1) reaction, (2) learning, (3) behavior, and (4) results. Kirkpatrick contributed to the area of supervisory training. He is the author of *Supervising Training*, among other works. *See also* evaluation.

knowledge architecture
The repository for shared knowledge and collective intelligence that is organized for easy access by any staff member, at any time, and from anywhere. For example, a data base that collects key learning of individuals or an on-line newsletter that systematically gathers, organizes, and disseminates the collective knowledge of the organization members. *Compare with* social architecture *and* technological architecture.

knowledge base *basic term*
A structured representation of the information used by experts in solving a particular problem used in expert systems and performance support systems. *See also* inference engine.

knowledge of results (KOR)
A form of feedback that provides the learner with the correctness of the response. KOR may be a verbal report of right or wrong, or a display (verbal or visual) of the correct response. *Compare with* substantive feedback. *See also* confirmation *and* feedback.

knowledges
The use of mental processes that enable a person to recall facts, identify concepts, apply rules or principles, solve problems, or think creatively. Knowledges are manifested through performing associated overt activities. They are not directly observable. *Compare with* skills.

Knowles, Malcolm
An educator well known to many as the father of adult learning. Knowles popularized the concept of andragogy worldwide. He is the author of *The Adult Learner*, among other books. *See also* andragogy.

Kroy™
The Kroy™ machine is used to produce high quality, professional lettering. It cuts letters from plastic film. The film may then be applied to a paste-up board to create a mechanical for printing. *See also* mechanical. *Compare with* Merlin™.

kurtosis
A statistical term referring to the peak or flatness of the plotted curve of a frequency distribution as compared to the normal curve.

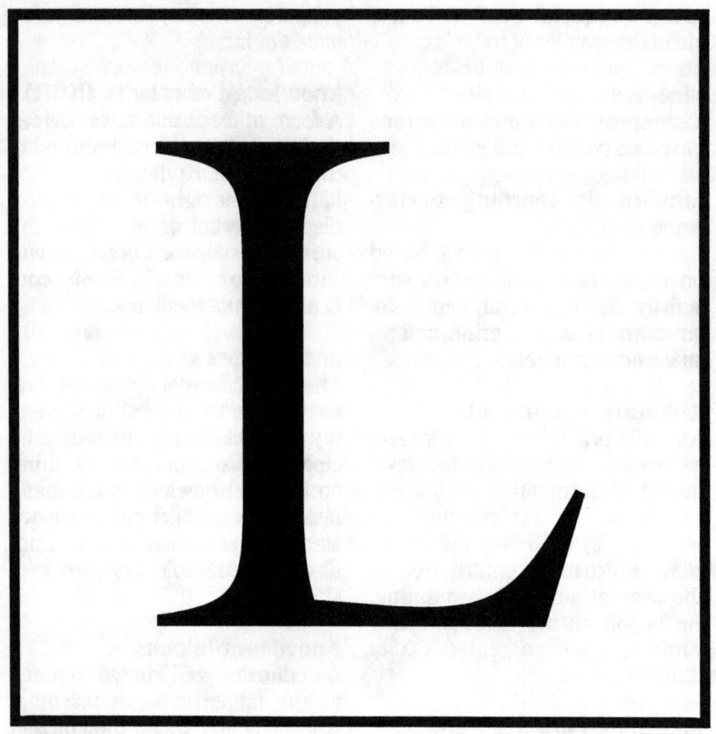

laboratory education
See laboratory training.

laboratory training *basic term*
A method used to increase individuals' sensitivity to their own and others' behavior. Laboratory training was widely applied in the 1960s and has declined since that time. Also known as laboratory education, sensitivity training, and T group experiences. *See also* sensitivity training.

landscape
Horizontal orientation of a display. *Compare with* portrait.

lane training
A technique for training company/team-level and smaller units on a series of selected soldier, leader, and collective tasks using specific terrain.

language laboratory *basic term*
A special learning center with capability of playing selected tapes from a library on demand by individual learners. The laboratory may also feature other materials such as workbooks and CAI. Learners study in carrels to hear and practice copying the foreign language.

lantern slide
A photographic transparency for projecting images. Lantern slide image area is 3 x 2 in. rather than 35 mm.

laptop computer
One of the smaller of today's computers. Includes a subcategory called "notebook computer." Microcomputers somewhat larger than laptop are often called "totable" and "lugable." Even smaller ones are called palmtop. *See* personal computer (PC).

larynx
The area of the throat (esophagus) containing the vocal cords. The larynx is commonly called the "voice box." References to the larynx are often made in presentation skills instruction.

laser holography
See holography.

laser pointer
A hand-held, battery-powered projection pointer that uses a laser beam.

laser rot
The degradation of a video or compact disc due to improper process control or raw material contamination. A common phenomenon of early videodiscs and CDs.

lateral communication
Any messages directed to persons of equal authority or status.

lateral thinking *basic term*
A concept developed by Edward de Bono to demystify the process of creative problem solving. Lateral thinking is a process of abandoning current vertical or linear progression of ideas and jumping laterally to a different starting point. Lateral thinking calls on characteristics associated with right brain hemispheric functions. *See also* brain lateralization *and* creativity training. *Compare with* vertical thinking.

lavaliere microphone *basic term*
A small microphone normally attached to a presenter's lapel. A lavaliere microphone is *not* cordless. A cordless microphone is a separate specific type.

Laws of Learning
One of seven "laws" proposed by Edward Thorndike. The laws are (1) analogy, (2) associative shifting, (3) effect, (4) exercise, (5) multiple response, (6) prepotency, and (7) readiness.

layers of necessity model
A model of instructional design and development that prioritizes the needs of a project into layers. The layers of necessity are each self-contained models.

layout
Arrangement of parts of a document for eventual printing.

LCD
The display technology commonly used in wristwatches, calculators, and laptop computer terminals. An important use is in panels ultimately used with overhead projectors. LCD is an abbreviation for liquid crystal diode. *Compare with* CRT, VDT, and plasma panel.

LCD panel
See liquid crystal display panel.

LCD projector
See liquid crystal video projector.

leader book
A leader tool maintained at crew level and above for recording and tracking soldier proficiency on mission-oriented tasks.

leaderless group discussion (LGD)
A task-oriented group whose members do not require a leader because they possess the capacity to determine the group's structure, function, and behavior for themselves.

leadership *basic term*
1. The active process through which an individual seeks to identify courses of action and to guide and stimulate the actions of others toward goals desired by the leader. Leadership my be exhibited by any person at any level, with or without formal authority. It compares with management, which may or may not be accompanied by leadership and is applied from a position of formal authority.
2. In LGD, a high-status position achieved by performing leadership acts recognized by other group members as helping the group perform its task.

leadership cluster
Consists of two related roles of the HRD practitioner, those of strategist and of manager of training and development. *See also* HRD Roles and Competencies Study.

Leadex
A self-assessing, multi-level leadership evaluation instrument, based on Karl Albrecht's six dimensional service leadership model. The dimensions are (1) vision and values, (2) direction, (3) persuasion, (4) support, (5) development, and (6) appreciation.

lean instruction
The development of the minimum instruction needed to achieve the objective. Lean instruction is achieved by developing less instruction than needed and adding clarifications and amplifications based on trial use of the materials. A concept popularized by Geary Rummler. *See also* Rummler, Geary; instructional systems development (ISD); and performance-based instruction (PBI).

learner *essential 100 term*
The preferred term for anyone who is acquiring new skills, attitudes, or knowledge through HRD. Learner includes such terms as student, participant, and trainee. "Learner" is widely used in adult learning settings.

learner-centered instruction *basic term*
An instructional climate in which learners set their own goals. *Also called* learner controlled instruction. *See also* individualized learning. *Compare with* self-directed learning.

learner-controlled instruction
An instructional setting or activity where learners determine the sequence of activities. *See also* individualized learning. *Compare with* self-directed learning.

learner-defined objectives
Objectives that are developed at the beginning of an instructional experience by asking learners to identify what outcomes they desire from instruction.

learning *basic term*
1. A change in attitudes, knowledge, or skill. The change can be physical and overt, or it can be intellectual or attitudinal. *See also* long-term memory. *Compare with* information.
2. In evaluation, the second level of summative evaluation proposed by Donald Kirkpatrick.

Learning involves the testing of the learners' knowledge after instruction. Used in a majority of HRD situations. *See* reaction, behavior, and results.
3. Loosely, the purpose of instruction.

learning activities description
A statement describing activities that the learner must perform in order to reach the learning objective(s). *See also* criterion-referenced instruction (CRI).

learning activity package (LAP)
An organized sequence of activities which the learner undertakes alone. Usually based on a booklet that gives directions and states what materials are to be used and which activities are to be done in what sequence. When organized for use by both learners and instructor it is called an instructional materials package.

learning aid *basic term*
Any device, tool, or written aid that can be used in the classroom to make the learning of knowledge or skills easier. A learning aid can often be used as a job aid. *See* job aid.

learning center *basic term*
A special location for learning, usually staffed by one or more facilitators. A learning center often has been specifically developed to foster individualized instruction and contains individualized, self-paced, or self-directed learning packages geared to adult learning styles. A learning center often emphasizes use of media to augment print resources.

learning-centered
Interest in learning and knowledge for its own sake.

learner-centered instruction (LCI)
An instructional process in which the content is determined by the learner's needs, the instructional materials are geared to the learner's abilities, and the instructional design makes the learners active participants. The ISD process produces learner-centered instruction.

learner-controlled instruction
An instructional environment in which the student can choose from a variety of instructional options for achievement of the terminal objectives. Students can vary their rate of learning, the media used, etc.

learning community *basic term*
1. A special group atmosphere in which all participants share responsibility for supporting one another's learning and performance improvement and contribute actively to it.
2. All types of gatherings in which learning is the main objective.
3. A euphemism for classroom.

learning contract *basic term*
A written agreement between the learner and instructor (or others). The basis of the contract is the new knowledge or skill the learner seeks. Factors in the contract include timing or schedule, method for learning acquisition, resources to be used, support to be provided, and method of demonstrating that the goal has been achieved. *See also* self-directed learning.

learning design *basic term*
People, methods, equipment, location and timings intended to achieve learning objectives in the most effective way.

learning environment *basic term*
The setting in which learning is expected to occur.

learning hierarchy *basic term*
A representation of skills arranged from simple to complex. In the hierarchy developed by Robert Gagne, they are identified as follows: stimulus recognizing, response generating, procedure following, terminology using, discrimination making, concept forming, rule applying, and problem solving.

learning methods
See instructional strategy.

learning moment
See teachable moment.

learning need
See needs analysis.

learning objective *essential 100 term*

1. Learning objectives are the key part of the instructional system. Carefully written objectives will identify the sought-after behavior for trainers as well as for learners. They must communicate in clear and precise language. In the system developed by Robert Mager, a well-written objective contains three elements: (1) the condition, (2) performance, and (3) the criterion. *Also called* instructional objective. *See also* behavioral objective; enabling objective; Mager, Robert F.; and terminal objective. *Compare with* performance objective.
2. A hierarchy of objectives includes enabling and terminal objectives. Two or more enabling objectives, taken together, form the component parts of the terminal objective.
3. Loosely, a statement of the desired changes in learner's attitude, knowledge, or skills.

learning organization *basic term*
Any organization that has a climate that acceleratres individual and group learning. This concept regards the organization as a living organism, existing in its environment and having good feedback mechanisms and the ability to adapt to changes by taking timely action. Learning organizations teach their employees the critical thinking process for understanding what their organization does and why it does it. These individuals help the organization itself to learn from its mistakes as well as its success. As a result, the organization recognizes changes in its environment and adapts effectively. Research in the late 1980s, particularly the work of Richard Pascale, introduced the concept of the learning organization. *See also* global learning organization.

learning-oriented learner *basic term*
A learner who seeks knowledge for its own sake. *Compare with* goal- *and* activity-oriented learner.

learning point
An element of a learning module that must be delivered in a whole brain way in order for the integrated learning to be conveyed to a mentally diverse learning group.

learning pyramid
A graphic depiction, developed by National Training Laboratories, of the relative retention rate of information presented by methods that range from lecture to immediate use of learning.

learning requirement *basic term*
Instructional equivalents of job requirements. Criteria called job requirements are described in instructional analysis. Learning requirements must be established to form the basis for learning activities to teach them.

learning resource *basic term*
Anything from which a learner might learn. Learning resources may be in text, audio, video, film, or computer form.

learning resource center
See learning center.

learning specialist
See HRD practitioner.

learning station
A location for a person to study. A learning station may feature a video player, computer, and any associated input or output devices based on the particular learning need. *Compare with* authoring station *and* workstation.

learning strategies
See instructional strategy.

learning style *basic term*
Each individual's unique approach to learning. The learner's psychological traits determine how that person will perceive, interact with, and respond to any environment. Specifically, the ways an individual behaves, feels, and processes information in learning situations. Experts do not agree how to categorize these styles.

learning styles inventory
Any of several instruments that identify a learner's learning style. *See also* learning style.

learning technology
See instructional technology.

learning to learn *basic term*
A general term applied to programs conducted to enable learners to improve their personal learning skills and strategies.

leasing
One method for obtaining instructional materials for extended use. Often, a choice of lease or purchase exists, but some materials are not offered for sale by the vendor. Purchase of others may be too costly. *See also* rental.

lectern *basic term*
A stand or desk behind which speaker stands and on which are placed notes or manuscript. Not to be confused with podium, a platform. A lectern often contains a microphone. It may contain other room controls.

lecture *basic term*
1. A structured oral presentation intended for instruction. A lecture is distinguished from a speech in that it has an instructional intent rather than an informative or persuasive intent. A lecture has little or no learner participation. Can be coupled with forum, audience reaction team, and other strategies. *See also* discussion *and* lecturette.
2. Loosely, any oral presentation.

lecture notes
See speaker's notes.

lecturette
Any short lecture. *See also* lecture.

left brain
See brain lateralization and whole brain learning.

left brain/right brain theory
See brain lateralization and creativity training.

left mode thinking processes
One of four whole brain learning descriptors. It includes cerebral and limbic left quadrants. *Compare with* right mode thinking processes. *See also* whole brain learning.

legitimacy
Norms, values, roles, or other standards imposed on a group by some person or source outside the group. That person or source's authority over the group must be recognized by the members.

lesson *basic term*
Any block of learning designed around a specific skill. A lesson may be made up of a number of modules, each covering one learning objective.

lesson design system (LDS)
Called more than an authoring system, LDS is an advisor. LDS is the implementation of M. David Merrill's component display theory. *See also* component display theory.

lesson objective
The terminal objective for any lesson. *See also* outcome.

lesson plan *essential 100 term*
A document, often formal, that identifies the basic information related to a unit of instruction and contains an outline of important points of a lesson arranged in the order in which they are to be presented. Organizations often specify the specific content and format of the lesson plan. *See also* learning design.

levels, interactive systems
Three standards of videodisc system interactivity proposed by the Nebraska Videodisc Design/Production Group have been widely accepted. They are

1. Level One system: Usually a consumer-model videodisc player with still/freeze frame, picture stop, chapter stop, frame address, and dual-channel audio, but with limited memory and limited processing power.
2. Level Two system: An industrial-model videodisc player with the capabilities of Level One, plus on-board programmable memory and improved access time.
3. Level Three system: Level One or Two players interfaced to an external computer and/or other peripheral processing devices.

levels of interactivity
Derived from interactive systems levels. Does not relate to the quality, relative value, or degree of sophistication.

levels of prerequisite
See prerequisite levels.

leveraged training
The improvement return received by the organization from the design, implementation, and use of programs increasing the learner's full application or transfer of training to the job.

levy system
A system used in many countries of the world which mandates that employers with over a certain num-

ber of employees (usually 20) spend at least some percentage of payroll on training (usually 1.5%). In levy systems, the government taxes employers to the extent not spent and then uses the money for HRD programs. The levy system does not currently exist in the United States, although it was proposed by a number of commissions and reports and proposed in legislation in the 1991 Congress.

Lewin, Kurt
A social psychologist associated with experiential learning and OD methods and models. Lewin developed the force field concept. *See also* action research, change agent, force field analysis, organization development (OD).

L group
See sensitivity training.

library, the
A technique of OD data gathering. *See also* OD data gathering.

library skill
The HRD competency of gathering information from printed and other recorded sources. Identifying and using information specialists and reference services and aids. *See also* HRD Roles and Competencies Study.

licensure
A required process administered by a governmental body or other governing group. *Compare with* certification *and* accreditation.

life cycle costs
The costs of an HRD project over its entire lifetime. *See* life cycle model.

life cycle model
A cost-benefit analysis model that identifies the costs of a project over its entire lifetime. In this model, phases of the life cycle are R&D, start up, operational period, and termination period. *Compare with* resource requirements model, benefits model, and productivity model.

life cycle theory *basic term*
The conviction that individuals, groups, departments, and organizations progress through stages of development. Life cycle theory proposes that each stage is characterized by a central crisis that must be resolved before the individual may progress to the next stage. *See also* life stages.

life-long learning *basic term*
The concept of continual learning in order to stay current with one's job.

life planning *basic term*
A process of establishing goals and directions for one's entire life. These include education, family, leisure activities, spiritual development, and work. An ingredient of life planning is career planning.

life stages *basic term*
1. Stable periods of six to eight years interspersed with difficult transitional periods of four to five years, described by Daniel Levinson in *The Seasons of a Man's Life*.
2. The successive phases of individual maturation.

light pen
A device that can be pressed against a display that will inform the computer system of the selected location. *See also* tactile in-

Continued on next page

put. *Compare with* touch panel and mouse.

likeness
One of six gestalt principles about perception. *See* gestalt perception principles.

Likert, Rensis
A social psychologist, Likert is widely known as the originator of opinion and attitude measurement scales that bear his name and the linking-pin concept. *See* Likert scale.

Likert scale *essential 100 term*
(Pronounced lick'-ert.)
A type of instrument commonly constructed and used to measure opinion. It is characterized by requiring the participant to answer questions by selecting from among choices that range from strongly agree to strongly disagree.

limbic left quadrant
The quadrant of the brain associated with planned, organized, detailed, sequential functions. *Compare with* limbic right quadrant. *See also* whole brain learning.

limbic mode thinking processes
One of four whole brain learning descriptors. It includes limbic left and right quadrants. *Compare with* cerebral mode thinking processes. *See also* whole brain learning.

limbic right quadrant
The quadrant of the brain associated with emotional, interpersonal, feeling-based, kinesthetic functions. *Compare with* limbic left quadrant. *See also* whole brain learning.

limited-scope curriculum
One part of an organizational curriculum. A limited-scope curriculum is intended for learners in a specific job class, job progression ladder, or occupation.

limited-scope curriculum objective
A learning objective used in a limited-scope curriculum.

line
A design element that assists eye movement throughout a visual.

linear *basic term*
1. In technology-based learning, a program that progresses through a sequence of frames without being affected by the responses of the learner. A linear program offers far less potential for effective learning than a branching program. *Compare with* branching.
2. In instructional games, a structure involving specified sequential stages. Before going on to the next stage, participants must have successfully completed the previous stage.

line producer
In video production, the person in charge of all aspects of the shoot.

linking pin
See Figure on next page.

Link trainer
A simulator (originally developed during the Second World War) designed to teach basic flying skills. It was the first well-known simulator.

Lippitt, Gordon
A psychologist who developed the organization renewal model. Author of *Organizational Renewal.*

linking pin
The notion that individuals are tied to tasks that are grouped and tied upward to organizational units. Each unit has an integrated relationship to the other units. The linking pin idea was originated by Rensis Likert in *The Human Organization.*

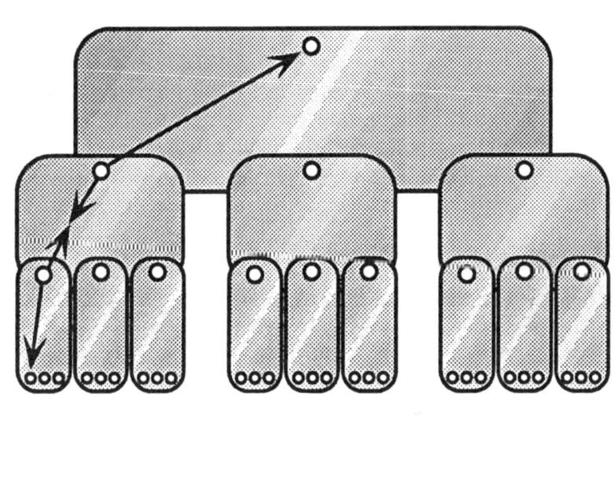

liquid crystal diode
See LCD.

liquid crystal display panel
An electronic panel placed over an overhead projector used to project a computer image. A video image is transferred from a computer to the device's transparent panel. LCDs in the display panel create the display. More powerful overhead projectors have emerged to increase the image brightness. *Compare with* CRT, liquid crystal video projector, plasma panel, and VDT.

liquid crystal video projector
A display device that projects video information onto a screen. The projector uses a high-intensity lamp and lens system to focus and project the video image. *Compare with* liquid crystal display panel.

listening, active
See active listening.

listening groups *basic term*
A technique used in general sessions. Groups of participants each listen for a different element in the presentation. The listening groups then serve as a resource for work groups, breakout sessions, or questions to presenters.

literacy support group
Instructor and counselor-led groups formed to provide practice and support in literacy skills for those employees without immediate job-related reading needs.

literacy training *basic term*
Programs, similar to ESL (English as a second language), aimed at improving language skills of employees whose native language is English. These programs attempt to enable the employee to function at work and in the normal HRD programs of the organization. *See also* functional illiteracy.

little media
A synonym for instructional aids, used to describe auxiliary supports for instruction, such as chalkboard, flipchart, and slides. *See also* media. *Compare with* big media.

live (presentation)
A personally delivered presentation, as opposed to one with a taped soundtrack.

local area network (LAN)
A LAN is a small computer network. In technology-based learning it is typically in one location, such as a classroom. *Compare with* wide area network (WAN).

Local Enterprise Council (LEC)
Set up in Scotland in 1991 to link public and private resources in developing enterprise and training services to meet local needs. LECs are independent companies directed by business leaders and include local authority, trade union, and Employment Service representation. *See also* Training & Enterprise Councils.

log-in
Process that must be performed in order for a computer system to recognize an authorized user. In technology-based learning this is termed "sign-on" or "log-on." *See* sign-on.

logistics *basic term*
The planning of details and materials or supplies needed to carry out the operational requirements of any activity. HRD logistics include scheduling events, arranging facilities, obtaining needed equipment, notifying participants, reproducing instructional materials, and selecting instructors.

long-range HRD planning
See strategic HRD planning.

long shot
In video production, a general view of the subject. *Compare with* high-angle *and* low-angle shot.

long-term memory (LTM)
Information that is encoded, stored, and retained in the brain. Memories are stored in LTM. Some information may be passed from short-term memory to long-term memory for later retrieval and use, but the rate of transfer is limited. Human beings use long-term memories unconsciously every day. *Compare with* short-term memory. *See also* information processing model.

looping
Repeating short sound samples to create a longer sound.

lost opportunity costs
The cost of failure to conduct an HRD program. For example, the lesser amount of future revenue derived when a sales training program is not conducted.

low-angle shot
In video production, a view with the camera lower than the subject. *Compare with* high-angle *and* long shot.

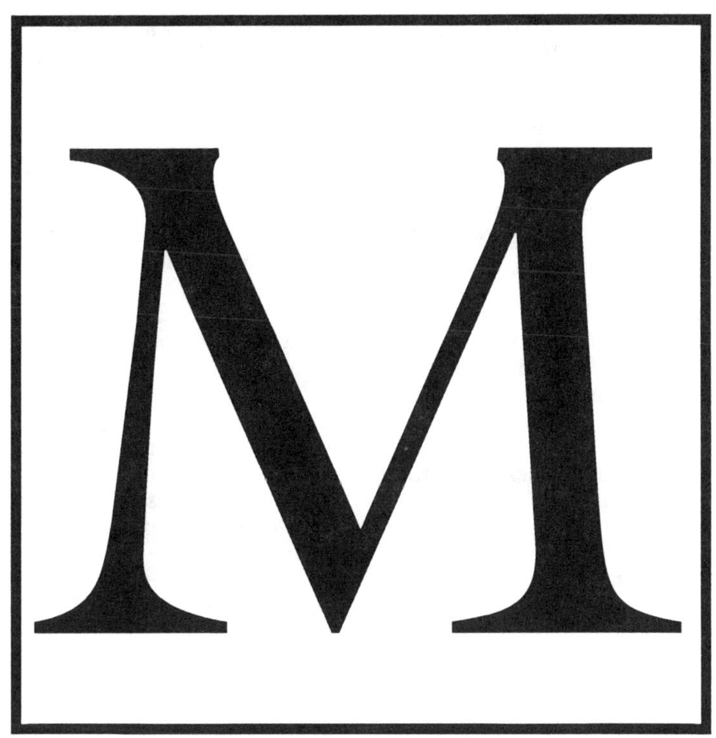

machine lettering
Lettering produced on a Kroy™ or Merlin™ machine. Such machines use pressure on a special film to cut and transfer lettering to paper or film. *See also* Kroy™, mechanical, and Merlin™.

machine mediated learning
Learning provided through standalone devices. For example, a video disc player.

Mager, Robert F.
The author of several influential books on instructional design who made behaviorism useful to millions of HRD practitioners. His *Preparing Instructional Objectives* may be the most influential HRD-related book. Many HRD practitioners who apply his widely used practical methods are unaware of the source.

Magerian
Related to the work and ideas of Robert Mager. *See also* Mager, Robert.

Magic Marker™
A brand of permanent or water-soluble markers. The term "magic marker" is loosely (and improperly) used as a generic reference for all. Most HRD practitioners are careful to say dry erase marker when they mean the special marker for a whiteboard. *Compare with* dry erase marker.

magic wand technique
A spontaneous role play technique. For example, a learner says, "I wish I could tell Charlie how to run this project!" The instructor simply hands the participant a pencil and says, "This is a magic wand. Now you have the power to do just that. I'm Charlie. Tell me now!" *See also* hot role play.

magnetic board
A metal board on which material can be mounted, using magnets or various other magnetic materials. Magnetic boards are useful for messages and permit illustration of the changing position or movement of material. *Compare with* whiteboard.

main message
The core of an informational presentation. For example, always wear your safety glasses!

maintenance
The continued use, and sometimes upgrade, of newly acquired knowledge and skills over an extended period. *See also* maintenance of behavior.

Maintenance Assistance and Instruction Team (MAIT)
A U.S. military mobile training team specialized in maintenance subjects.

maintenance costs (of instruction)
The sum of administrative costs, consumable materials, and costs of revisions to instruction. Maintenance costs are one of several types of costs used in calculating instructional cost. The instructional cost is a component needed for cost-benefit analysis. *See also* cost-benefit analysis.

maintenance of behavior
The continued change in behavior by an individual on the job after the instruction is completed.

maintenance skills and behaviors
Those actions performed to enable a group to work and function effectively together as a team. Effective teamwork requires attention to both task and maintenance behaviors. *See also* task skills *and* behaviors.

major course objective
An objective that defines the expected outcome of a complete course. Sometimes called course objective or terminal objective for the instruction.

Major Training Area (MTA)
The U.S. military designation for the largest size areas reserved for training use.

makeup person
In video, the person responsible for putting makeup on the cast.

Manage
A periodical of interest to HRD practitioners involved in management. *Manage* is published by the National Management Association.

management by objectives (MBO) *basic term*
A method of articulating goals to achieve results. Tasks are resolved into smaller objectives. These add up to the whole task when completed. Management may then concentrate on the objectives to complete the larger task. The process has been called the application of the general systems theory to management. MBO was one of the mainstays of management prac-

tice in the 1970s but has faded from popularity due to sometimes over-structured application. However, the basic precepts of MBO are still widely accepted in Western management. Peter Drucker is often credited with evolving MBO. It was popularized by George Odiorne in the USA and by John Humble in Europe. *See* Drucker, Peter *and* Odiorne, George.

management by objectives and results (MBOR)
The same as management by objectives. *See* management by objectives.

management by walking around (MBWA) *basic term*
A method of managing (improving) organizational performance. It is based on the concept that a manager who walks around the organization will learn of problems and therefore be able to resolve them. MBWA is a subject in many management development programs.

management career ladder
A career ladder describing conditions in which progress is associated with increasing responsibility. *Compare with* technical career ladder.

management career track
See management career ladder.

management commitment
basic term
Management commitment is support of the top management group, stronger than a pledge or promise. It includes the actions of top management to allocate resources and lend support to the HRD effort in the organization.

management consultant
basic term
A person primarily engaged in advising on the most effective business strategies and organizational processes. This activity often includes HRD or HRD-related activities. For example, activities may include delivering time management or performance appraisal sessions.

management consulting firm
A firm that performs the activities described under management consultant. *See* management consultant.

Management Contents
A commercial data base supplying references and abstracts to business and management topics from conference proceedings, journals, newsletters, and other publications. Available on BRS and DIALOG.

management development
essential 100 term
The various HRD activities to assist managers in acquiring or enhancing the knowledge, skills, and values needed to be effective in their current and future managerial or supervisory leadership roles. Management development usually includes activities for employees down to first level supervisor. For example, time management sessions. This term is sometimes preferred over management training for prestige reasons. *Compare with* executive development, leadership development, supervisory development, teambuilding, technical and skills training.

Management Development Report
A newsletter of interest to HRD practitioners involved in manage-

Continued on next page

ment development. *Management Development Report* is published by the American Society for Training and Development.

management game
See business game. *See also* games.

management involvement
basic term

1. The extensive involvement on the part of all levels of management in the HRD process. Management involvement includes taking part in the programs.
2. The extent to which management and other professionals outside the HRD department are actively engaged in the HRD process in addition to participating in programs.

Management Review
A periodical of interest to HRD practitioners involved in management. *Management Review* is published by the American Management Association.

management skills
The competencies necessary for carrying out management functions such as planning, organizing, staffing, delegating, controlling, organizing, and budgeting.

management style
See Managerial Grid®.

management support *basic term*

1. Supportive actions of the entire management group for HRD, including top, middle, and first-line management.
2. In learning transfer, the wide range of actions critical to the success of most HRD programs. Part of a series of actions by managers, instructors, and learners involved in a specific HRD program, to support the full transfer of learning from that program to the job. *See also* transfer of learning.

Management To-day
The monthly publication of the British Institute of Management, covering a broad range of subjects, many of which are of interest to management trainers.

Managerial Grid® *basic term*
A technique popularized in the mid-60s by Robert Blake and Jane Mouton. The grid is used to plot production vs. people concerns on a two-dimensional 9-point scale. The same "grid" principle has been applied to other subjects.

manager of HRD
See manager of training and development.

manager of training and development *basic term*
The HRD role of planning, organizing, staffing, controlling training and development operations or training and development projects and of linking training and development operations with other organization units. *See also* HRD Roles and Competencies Study.

manager of transfer of training
The HRD role, identified by Mary Broad and John Newstrom, of serving as an organization's expert on, and advocate for, transfer of training.

mandatory continuing education
See continuing education.

mandatory training *basic term*
Training required by the organization for one or more groups of

employees. Mandatory training is appropriate for newly hired employees and others who must apply certain knowledge necessary to the proper functioning of the organization.

manipulation
1. In CAI, manipulation refers to the learner moving objects on the screen through tactile interaction.
2. In the psychomotor sense, manipulation refers to individuals physically moving, placing, or changing objects for the purpose of learning.

Manitoba Society for Training & Development (MSTD)
A professional society for HRD practitioners in the Province of Manitoba. *See also* HR Canada.

Mann, Horace
An educator who taught that useful knowledge is more important than theoretical.

mannerisms
1. Unconscious and repeated movements of an instructor or presenter that detract from the message being communicated.
2. In presentations, unconscious and repeated speech patterns. For example: y'know, for sure, uh huh, hadda, and fantastic. They can be distracting to an audience, just as are physical mannerisms.

manpower development
See human resource development (HRD).

Manpower Development and Training Act (MDTA)
A U.S. government-sponsored nationwide training program. Particular attention was focused on assistance to poor, disadvantaged, and minority group members.

manpower planning
See human resource planning (HRP).

manual *basic term*
1. By hand, manually.
2. One form of the print medium. Manuals are used to provide reference information to users. They are sometimes used to aid learning, but are used more frequently for supplemental information, rather than directly for instruction.

manual exercise *basic term*
1. Exercises requiring only paper and pencil.
2. A game simulation or case study that does not make use of a computer. Also, nonelectronic instructional games that do not depend primarily on psychomotor skill.

manual game
See manual exercise.

manual job aids
Three general types of job aid that are used or manipulated by hand: desktop, pocket, and equipment-related. *See* desktop job aids, pocket job aids, and equipment-related job aids.

manuscript
A fully typed text or speech.

map exercise (MAPEX)
A low cost, low overhead training exercise that portrays military situations on maps. Sometimes supplemented by terrain models and sand tables. *See also* terrain models *and* sand tables.

mapping, information
See Information Mapping®.

mapping, mind
See mindmapping™.

maps
One of the several standardized template formats used in structured writing. Maps each serve clearly defined purposes. For example, concept, classification, and procedure.

marginal costs
The change in outlay that occurs when one minor element is changed. For example, when one additional participant is added to a class roster.

marker
Ink pen or crayon for writing on visuals or boards. Ordinary markers must not be used on dry erase boards because they will leave permanent marks.

market analysis *basic term*
The study of the extent to which HRD activities are useful to, or desired by, various constituencies within or outside the sponsoring organization. Markets can be analyzed through market research and market testing. *See also* market research *and* market testing.

marketeer
See marketer.

marketer
The HRD role of marketing and contracting for HRD viewpoints, programs, and services. *See also* HRD Roles and Competencies Study.

marketing methods
Patterns of publicizing HRD activities offerings. There are several marketing methods: full coverage, market specialization, product concentration, product specialization, and selective specialization.

marketing mix
The combination of HRD activities, price, promotion, and location offered by an HRD department.

marketing plan (strategic)
A long-range plan to achieve marketplace success. *Compare with* strategic plan.

marketing training
See sales training.

market research *basic term*
This activity is comprehensive study of the HRD consumers, providers, and others who make decisions to allow instruction to be conducted.

market specialization marketing
A marketing method for HRD activity offerings focused on a particular market. *Compare with* full coverage, product concentration, product specialization, and selective specialization marketing.

market testing
The limited trial of the HRD product or service in the marketplace.

marking question
Questions that require the learner to answer by marking part of the display in technology-based learning.

markup, answer
Graphic feedback used when the learner's answer is partly correct.

Maslow, Abraham
A psychologist and author; one of

the founders of humanistic psychology, best known for the theory of self-actualization most often called Maslow's hierarchy. *See also* Maslow's hierarchy.

Maslow's hierarchy *essential 100 term*
See Figure.

massed practice
During learning, the process of providing all practice sessions at a specific point in the learning period (usually at the end of instruction). Massed practice is generally considered inferior to distributed practice. *Compare with* distributed practice.

mass marketing
See mass selling.

mass selling
Communicating information promoting HRD offerings to large numbers of potential users at one time. *Compare with* public relations, sales promotions, and personal selling.

master (copy)
Art or tapes that are of best quality. Masters are used to make duplicates for general use.

master performer
An employee who has the highest skill level. In the analysis phase of instructional development, this person is observed to determine how the task(s) should be done.

Maslow's hierarchy *essential 100 term*
A classic theory of motivation developed by Abraham Maslow and often used in management development. The theory names five specific needs, arranged in priority order: (1) physiological, (2) safety, (3) love and belongingness, (4) esteem, and (5) self-actualization. They are often represented as successive levels of a pyramid. The theory suggests that until lower needs are satisfied, higher needs cannot be addressed, and that a satisfied need no longer is a motivator. *See also* hierarchy of needs; humanistic psychology; Maslow, Abraham; and self-actualization.

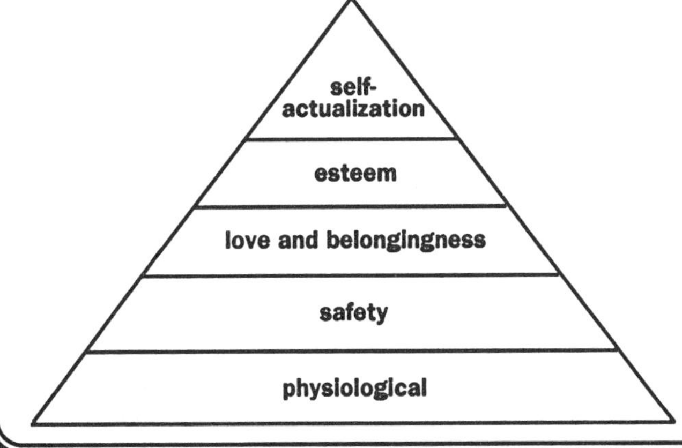

master performer model
Instruction based on a model of desired on-the-job behavior exemplified by a master performer.

master program of instruction (MPOI)
The controlling version of a U.S. military curriculum document.

master sheet
In instructional games, the camera-ready copy of material prepared for print or photocopy.

mastery learning *essential 100 term*
A principle of evaluating learning based on mastery of material according to a predetermined criterion. *Also called* criterion-referenced instruction (CRI) or preformance-based instruction. This is in contrast to norm-referenced learning, in which the learner is compared to other learners instead of to a fixed standard. *See also* performance-based instruction.

mastery learning concept
See mastery learning.

mastery learning system
See mastery learning.

Mathetics *basic term*
A system of task analysis and design introduced by Tom Gilbert in *Mathetics: The Technology of Education*. It is a more elaborate approach to task analysis than that in common use. Development includes making a map of behavior called a prescription.

matrix diagram
A quality process management and planning tool used to compare one set of items against another set and identify the strength of their relationship. The matrix diagram is useful when needing to show logical connecting points between items and to identify related items.

matrix-managed organization
An organizational structure in which ad hoc project teams are created. Project managers use the services of employees who are regularly assigned to other divisions of the organization. Employees are commonly assigned to one or more short- or long-term projects at a time.

matrix management
See matrix-managed organization.

matrix structure *basic term*
An organizational form in which project managers function at the same level as divisional managers. *See also* divisional structure *and* project structure.

mature worker
See older worker.

maturity
A stage in the concept life cycle model. *See also* concept life cycle.

Mayo, Elton
Director of the famous Hawthorne productivity studies. *See* Hawthorne studies.

maze technique case study
A case study is divided into several short episodes, calling for a multiple-choice decision at each step of the way, leading, as in a maze, to the culmination. Only two or three of the alternatives lead to a successful final result.

McClelland, David
A theorist in the field of motivation, especially in the study of the need for achievement. *See also* achievement motivation.

McGregor, Douglas
Known for a management model called Theory X and Theory Y. These represent descriptions of two extremes incorporating often seen management styles. They appeared in his book *The Human Side of Enterprise.*

McGuigan's Ratio
A formula for calculating the ratio of what the students have actually learned to what they could have learned.

McLagan, Patricia
Volunteer director, and author of the *Models for Excellence* studies of HRD roles, outputs, and competencies sponsored by the American Society for Training and Development. There were two studies. *See: Models for Excellence* (1983)/*Models for HRD Practice* (1989).

McLuhan, (Herbert) Marshall
A Canadian author and educator who wrote about the impact of the media on our methods of perceiving. Although mainly interested in mass communication, his ideas are relevant to instructional media development. His publications include *The Medium Is the Message.*

mean (M) *essential 100 term*
The most common measure of central tendency. The arithmetic average of a group of numbers, often test scores. The one score that most typifies an entire set of scores. The mean is calculated by adding the values and dividing by the number of items in the group. It is the most common measure of central tendency. Usually it is also the most meaningful, because it includes every value in the data. The symbol for the mean is M. *See also* central tendency and frequency distribution. *Compare with* median and mode.

meaningful learning
Anchoring new learning in already-acquired cognitive structures. A term coined by David Ausabel. *Compare with* rote learning.

measurement
See evaluation.

measurement error
Error that is inevitable in measuring the performance of individual human beings based on mass standards.

measuring return on investment
See return on investment (ROI).

mechanical
See mechanical art.

mechanical art
Board(s) used in the production of printed media. The designer pastes the type in position on the mechanical and indicates where the photos will be placed. This board is then given to the printer who photographs it to make the printing negative. *Also called* mechanical.

mechanical arts, schools of
In the mid-19th century so-called schools of mechanical arts were established to help workers cope with the introduction of new machinery. New York's Cooper Union is an example of a mechanical arts institution that has survived to the present day.

mechanical simulator
A non-computer simulator that appears like a real environment. The mechanical simulator can be simple, but is often very complex.

Continued on next page

See also computer simulator and part-task simulator.

mechanical spacing
Letter-spacing technique allowing for an equal amount of space between individual letters.

mechanistic theories
See behaviorist theories.

media *basic term*
(Singular form: medium.)
1. In the learning sense, the delivery modes for instruction and learning. For example: text, film, audio or videotape, or CAI. Media is sometimes called AV materials. *See also* big media, little media, and media selection chart. *Compare with* instructional aid.
2. In the technology sense, material that holds data. For example, magnetic media.
3. Loosely, all forms and channels used in the transmission of information.

media classification table
A table that groups media into distinct categories for choosing media for instruction. *Compare with* media selection chart.

media mix
Any combination of media used for a particular instructional activity.

media model
A simplified representation of the decision steps used by an HRD practitioner to select, develop, apply, and evaluate media.

median *basic term*
A measure of central tendency. The median is the middle value of a group of values, the score that divides the set of scores into upper and lower halves. There are an equal number of values above and below the median. The median is preferable to the mean as a measure of central tendency when the distribution of the data is skewed. *See also* central tendency and frequency distribution. *Compare with* mean *and* mode.

media selection
The processes of choosing one or more media for a planned instructional design. The strengths and weakness of each media are considered and weighed against the requirements of the learner and instructional objective. A media selection chart and media classification table may be used by those new to the process. *See also* media selection chart.

media selection chart
A chart that aids in the choice of media for instruction. The chart serves as a performance aid, presenting a series of decisions leading to the choice of the medium.

media specialist
The HRD role of producing software for and using audio, visual, computer and other hardware-based technologies for training and development. *See also* HRD Roles and Competencies Study.

medium
Singular form of media. *See* media.

meeting
See conference, workshop, and seminar.

meeting planner *basic term*
A person who plans meetings. Broadly, includes meeting planners, meeting consultants, and the

suppliers of goods and services for meetings.

meeting room *basic term*
Synonymous with function room. Meetings have requirements different from both large conferences and instruction. A variety of room arrangements are appropriate depending on the nature of the meeting. *Compare with* conference and learning center.

meet-me bridge
An audioconferencing bridge. A meet-me bridge permits participants to call a common telephone number. When automatically connected, multiple participants are able to hear each other.

meg
Oral abbreviation for mega or million. *See* mega.

mega (M)
Commonly used prefix meaning one million (in computer terms 1,048,576, or 2 to the 20th power). Often used in technology-based learning for comparison of size.

memory
1. An organized collection of storage elements in a technology-based instructional device into which instructions and data can be deposited and from which information can be retrieved.
2. A human being's storage mechanism for information. *See also* information processing model, long-term memory, and short-term memory.

mental diversity
Mental differences in peoples of all ethnic and cultural groups.

mental practice
The symbolic rehearsal of physical activity in the absence of any gross muscular movements. For example, when a golfer closes his or her eyes and imagines going through the motions of putting.

mental set
A mental picture provided to learners before instruction. The mental set is typically brief and includes the overall structure of the information to be learned.

mentofacturing
The production of products and services through the efforts of the mind, through brainpower. Mentofacturing stands in contrast to manufacturing, which is derived from the Latin *manus* meaning hand.

mentor *basic term*
A person, usually older or more experienced, who guides and supports another. Another label for mentor is coach. Not a formally identified HRD role. *Compare with* protégé.

mentoring *essential 100 term*
1. A process to help people with their career development. Experienced and successful employees are matched with newer or junior employees to provide useful job and career guidance. Mentoring is often informal, but formal programs also exist.
2. A formalized process to introduce selected employees to the inner network of the organization to aid them in their career advancement.

mentoring system (program)
See mentoring.

menu
1. In technology-based learning, a list of choices available for a learner.

Continued on next page

2. In an authoring system, utilities available for an author.
3. In the HRD Roles and Competencies Study, one of six menus: future forces, HRD outputs, quality requirements, ethical issues, HRD competencies, and HRD roles. These lists reflect the breadth of HRD, establish common terms, and can be used for various personal and organizational applications. *See also* HRD Roles and Competencies Study.

menu-driven
The types of authoring or learning systems in which actions or topics are selected from a list of choices. *Also called* prompted systems.

Merlin™ machine
The Merlin™ machine is used to produce high quality, professional lettering. It cuts letters from plastic film. The film may then be applied to a paste-up board to create a mechanical for printing. *See also* mechanical. *Compare with* Kroy™.

message, main
See main message.

message, nonverbal
See nonverbal message.

message board
See message center.

message center
A facility at meetings and conferences for the exchange of various information among participants. Also, provides a method of contacting individual participants on routine matters that do not merit a public announcement.

meta-analysis
Statistically analyzing the findings of many individual analyses. Meta-analysis is especially appropriate for integrating a group of studies related by a common conceptual hypothesis or common operational definitions of dependent and independent variables.

metacognition
A synonym for learning to learn. Knowledge of the human cognitive process.

metalanguage
See paralanguage.

metaphor *basic term*
In general HRD, a term that implies a different meaning than the one which it ordinarily signifies. For example, the Macintosh computer operating system uses a desktop metaphor to enable users to refer to familiar objects such as "folders" when directing the computer to carry out functions.

meta strategies
Groupings of types of methods used to improve instruction. Meta strategies are usually arranged in a taxonomy. For example, methods to improve: the learner, instructor, improve the context or setting in which learning occurs, and the content.

method *basic term*
Any one of many instructional approaches or combinations of approaches to achieve learning. Methods, combined with media, form the instructional strategy. *See also* experiential learning, instructional strategy, and participatory methods. *Compare with* media.

method, scientific
See scientific method.

method of loci
A method of placing needed information in long-term memory by

associating the information in an already-remembered mental route or edifice. The items may then be recalled by mentally retracing the route. *See also* imagery *and* mnemonic.

methodology
See method.

methods of evaluation
See evaluation, methods.

methods of observation
See observation, methods.

microcomputer
A desktop computer, laptop computer, personal computer, or standalone computer. *Compare with* palmtop computer.

Microcomputer Index
A commercial data base supplying references and abstracts for articles, book, hardware, and software reviews, and product information from microcomputer-related journals. Available on DIALOG.

microphone, lavaliere
See lavaliere microphone.

microphone (mic) (mike) *basic term*
Microphones commonly seen in HRD activities include *fixed* microphones mounted to a stand and immovable and *hand-held* microphones held near the mouth by hand and movable. *See also* lavaliere microphone.

micro-teaching *basic term*
Instruction focused on a very small task or sub-task in order to facilitate learning. The learner then performs this task under the instructor's observation. Video is often used to record micro-teaching sessions for immediate review and critique.

microworld
A computer-based simulation that provides opportunity for manipulation of content and skill practice.

mid-range planning *basic term*
The middle range of the planning processes used by organizations. May involve reorganization, expansion, contraction, and development of new products and services. Mid-range planning is often defined as planning for the period 2-5 years in the future. *Compare with* long- *and* short-range planning.

millisecond
One-thousandth of a second.

mimeograph
The type of machine used for reproduction of paper handouts and other materials. Formerly popular due to low cost, the simplicity, quality, and low cost of the electrostatic copier has made the mimeograph obsolete.

mind calming
Physical exercises designed to enhance concentration by decreasing external pressure and increasing awareness of self.

Mindex
A self-assessment thinking style instrument developed by Karl Albrecht. Identifies the user's characteristic ways of organizing and processing ideas.

mindmapping™ *basic term*
An information recording technique using branching lines to relate connections of topics to one another. The format does not conform to normal paragraph construction. Adherents claim mind-

Continued on next page

mapping™ coincides better than traditional techniques with the way people associate ideas. Mind-mapping™ is a much-used tool for many people involved in creative work, problem solving, and instruction.

mindset
A predisposition to hold a given opinion. Sometimes the term "mindset" suggests inflexibility.

minimal training
An instructional approach that seeks to provide the least instruction needed to help the learner master a skill. Based on minimalist theory developed by John M. Carroll, minimalist training emphasizes active learning and meaningful learning tasks.

minisummary
In information presentations, to restate the key points before transitioning to the next point. *Compare with* transition.

mirror (technique)
A one-sided intergroup activity used to discover how a group is seen by others outside the group.

mission
The purpose and goals of an organization. Missions are often formal, derived with care, and referenced frequently. *See also* mission statement.

mission essential task
A collective task in which an organization must be proficient to accomplish an appropriate portion of its wartime mission. *Compare with* METL.

mission essential task list (METL)
A compilation of mission essential tasks in which a U.S. military organization must be proficient to accomplish its wartime mission.

mission statement *basic term*
1. A formal declaration of the overall goals of an organization.
2. In HRD organizations, a statement that identifies the reason for the existence of the HRD function. The mission statement should be linked to the overall mission, operations, and business of the organization.
3. *See* service strategy.
4. *Compare with* vision statement.

mission training plan (MTP)
A U.S. military document that describes what and how to train to achieve wartime mission proficiency. The MTP usually provides comprehensive training and evaluation outlines to assist field commanders in planning training.

mixer *basic term*
1. Activities designed to permit participants to get to know one another and legitimize strangers speaking to one another. Also known as warm ups, ice-breakers, and openers.
2. A device or system that combines two or more signals to feed another device or part of the audio system.

mnemonic *essential 100 term*
Memory prompt useful for learning lists. Mnemonic devices include rhymes, peg-word systems, and visual imagery. For example, the mnemonic HOMES cues the first letters of the Great Lakes (Huron, Ontario, Michigan, Erie, and Superior). *See also* imagery *and* method of loci.

mobile training team (MTT)
A type of training unit used by military organizations to provide

specialized training to field organizations.

mobilization and training equipment site (MATES)
A location used specifically for military mobilization training.

mock-up *basic term*
A simple form of simulation device. A mock-up has the appearance of the object simulated but not its capabilities.

mode *basic term*
1. A measure of central tendency. The value that occurs most frequently in a set of numbers. The mode is the most common value. It is a quick measure, but is not used as often as the median or mean. *See also* central tendency *and* frequency distribution. *Compare with* mean *and* median.
2. In CAI, drill and practice, instructional games, simulation, and tutorial.
3. In CMI, testing, prescription generation, and record keeping.
4. In CSLR, data base, communications, hypermedia, and performance support systems.
5. Loosely, an overall system of instruction such as instructor-led or CAI.

model *basic term*
1. A representation of an object, process, or phenomenon without regard to realistic appearance. *See also* ideal model.
2. A standard to guide thinking and practice.
3. A full-size or scaled representation of an idea, object, process, or phenomenon. A working model has moving parts.
4. A person who helps show the product.

model-building skill
The HRD competency of conceptualizing and developing theoretical and practical frameworks that describe complex ideas in understandable, usable ways. *See also* HRD Roles and Competencies Study.

modeling
One of the modes of CAI. The others are drill and practice, instructional games, simulation, and tutorial. Use of the CBL system to represent a system or process, permitting the learner to change values and observe the effects of the change on the system. An example is a model of population.

modeling, behavior (modeling, behavioral)
See behavior modeling and social learning theory.

modeling display
A demonstration of the exact behaviors wanted in the learner. Used in behavior modeling to change behavior. Usually shown in video or film format, but may be modeled live. *See also* behavior modeling *and* demonstration.

Models *basic term*
Models are a popular and useful way of describing ideas and processes in the HRD field. They present theoretical or practical frameworks to describe complex ideas in understandable and usable ways. The list below provides a sample of the number and variety of models in common use.
1. Andragogical Model. Malcolm Knowles. Adult learning.
2. Benefits Model. Greg Kearsley. HRD benefits.
3. Change Model. Kurt Lewin. Group modification.

Continued on next page

4. Change Process Model. Charles Reiner & Harvey Morris. Used in OD.
5. Component Display. M. David Merrill. Instructional design.
6. Concept Life Cycle. Jerry Gilley. Shows growth stages of HRD concepts.
7. Contingency Model. Fred Fiedler. Group leadership.
8. Critical Events Model. Leonard Nadler. Instructional design.
9. Differentiation and Integration Model. P. R. Lawrence and J. W. Lorsch. Management of inter-group conflict.
10. Dimensional Model. Robert Lefton and Victor Buzotta. Sales, sales management, and management training.
11. Distance Learning Model. Angus Reynolds. Distance learning.
12. Elaboration Model. Charles Reigeluth. Instruction in discrete levels.
13. Evaluation Model, Four Level. Donald L. Kirkpatrick. Four levels of summative evaluation.
14. Expectancy Model. Victor H. Vroom. Motivation. (*Also called* the self-fulfilling prophecy *and* the Pygmalion effect.)
15. Experiential exercise. Jerry Gilley & R. Dean. Selection, design, and use of experiential exercises.
16. Experiential Learning Model. David Kolb. Manager's learning styles.
17. Force Field Analysis Model. Kurt Lewin. Problem analysis.
18. Global Learning Organization Model. Michael Marquardt and Angus Reynolds. International HRD.
19. Hexagonal Model of Occupational Personality Types. John Holland. Personality types.
20. Hierarchy of Learning Model. Robert Gagne. Learning hierarchies
21. HRD Competency Model. Patricia A. McLagan.
22. HRD Model. Leonard Nadler. Human resource development.
23. Independent Study Model. Michael Moore. Classifies programs for autonomy and distance.
24. International HRD SUCCESS Model. Angus Reynolds. International HRD.
25. Minimalism Model. John M. Carroll. Instructional delivery.
26. Nadler Systems Model. David Nadler. Used in OD.
27. Organization Renewal Model. Gordon Lippitt. Organizational renewal.
28. PCDA Model. W. Edwards Deming. Quality process.
29. Performance-based Planning Model. C. Crumb. Planning supervisory training.
30. Rockham Model. Neal Rockham. Graphically shows transfer of learning.
31. Schema of Knowledge Model. Alex Romiszowski. Schema of knowledge.
32. Service Leadership Model. Karl Albrecht. Service.
33. Six-Box Model. Marvin Weisbord. Used in OD.
34. Structure of the Intellect Model. J. Guilford. A three-dimensional representation of intersecting categories.
35. Systems Approach Model (the ISD Model). Center for Educational Technology, FSU. Systematic design of instruction.
36. Training Cost Model. Glenn Head. Cost benefit.
37. Training Cost Model. Office of Personnel Management Training Cost Model. HRD cost.

38. Training Transfer Model. Mary Broad and John Newstrom. Transfer of training
39. Whole Brain Model. Ned Herrmann. Physiological brain metaphor.

***Models for Excellence* (1983) /*Models for HRD Practice* (1989)** *basic term*
Studies conducted by the American Society for Training and Development. There were two studies. The studies identified roles, outputs, and competencies for HRD professionals. The later study also provided application guides for HRD managers and HRD practitioners. The studies were led by volunteer Patricia McLagan.

Models for HRD Practice
See: Models for Excellence (1983)/ *Models for HRD Practice* (1989).

modem
Contraction for modulator-demodulator. Permits computer-to-computer transfer of data over common telephone or special data lines. The modem provides the connection between the computer and the communication (telephone) line.

moderator
See chairperson.

modern symposium
A program composed solely of lecturettes.

modification, behavior
See behavior modification.

modularization *basic term*
Organization of the instruction developed into units called modules. A selection of modules can be assembled in different combinations to create distinct courses and curricula.

modular principle
Offering learners a choice of units in a course. Learners build their own course from modules of the course or from among courses. From the German *baukasten prinzip*, the "box of bricks" principle. *See also* modularization.

modular scheduling
Assignment of learners to only those modules that pretesting and counseling indicate they need. In modular scheduling a course is divided into small units of instruction called modules. Each module supports one or more training objectives. The learners are pretested and counseled on objectives to determine which modules of instruction they require. *Compare with* block scheduling.

module *basic term*
An arbitrary unit of instruction. Usually, a module is constructed to teach one specific thing and can be taught, measured, evaluated for change, or bypassed as a whole. Modules can be assembled to form complete courses and curricula. *See also* modularization *and* modular scheduling.

moment of truth
1. Any episode in which a customer comes in contact with the organization and gets an impression of the quality of its service. It is a phrase taken from SAS President Jan Carlzon's recognition that SAS (the Scandinavian airline) had 50,000 "moments of truth" every day; originally contributed by Swedish consultant Richard Normann.
2. A metaphor for the interface between the organization's front

Continued on next page

line representative and a customer.

Moment of Truth Impact Analysis®
A process, developed by Ron Zemke, to closely analyze a particular moment of truth to redesign a part of a service delivery system.

monitor *basic term*
1. Room monitor. A person at meetings and conferences who performs functions related to meeting rooms. For example, seating latecomers and distributing evaluation forms.
2. Test monitor. A person who ensures that tests are conducted ethically. This function is required for certain promotion and certification tests. This technique is counter to principles of trust when not required.
3. Video or computer monitor. *See* display.

monotone
Voice of nearly constant pitch. An undesirable trait in a speaker.

montage
1. A series of short video scenes to condense time, distance, or action.
2. An image made of composite graphic elements overlaid and superimposed.

Monthly Labor Review
A periodical of business and economic of interest to some HRD practitioners. *Monthly Labor Review* is published by the U.S. Department of Labor.

Moore, Michael
Author of the theory of independent study. Education programs are classified based on the two dimensions of autonomy and distance.

mortality
The loss of one or more participants from the population sample of an evaluation. This makes it more difficult to compare sets of scores.

motion picture
See film.

motion stimuli
A prompt that activates a learner in a particular situation. For example, a motion visual showing a product moving through a mechanical process, to teach the process or a moving visual of a part's alignment to teach the proper alignment.

motion video
A group of graphic images which create the impression of motion when displayed in rapid sequence.

motion visuals
1. Those visuals that present movement. For example, film, video, and computer graphics.
2. Media that involve images in motion without audio. *Compare with* audio motion visual.

motivation *essential 100 term*
1. Encouragement to act in a particular manner.
2. Anything that acts to impel behavior.
3. The actuator of human behavior. The need for motivation is sometimes confused with the need for instruction because people may not be sufficiently motivated to perform a task that they actually know how to do.

motivational variables
Differences between an individ-

ual's reasons for action. Motivational variables are the differences in values that individuals assign to rewards.

motivation-hygiene theory
essential 100 term
A theory developed by the behavioral scientist Frederick Herzberg. The theory is based on the concept that job satisfaction has two independent sources: motivator factors and hygiene factors. *See also* Herzberg, Fredrick *and* satisfiers.

motivation theories
Includes Herzberg's theory of personality and motivation and Vroom's theory of work motivation. *See also* Herzberg, Fredrick *and* Vroom, Victor.

motor skills *basic term*
The psychomotor domain of learning. For example, writing, and aligning a control knob. *Compare with* cognitive *and* affective.

motor skills domain
See psychomotor domain.

mouse
In technology-based learning, a hand-held device moved on a desktop or special surface. As a result, the cursor moves in a like manner on the VDT. Pushing a button informs the computer system of the chosen location. *See also* tactile input. *Compare with* light pen, touch panel, and trackball.

Mouton, Jane Srygley
Co-developer, with Robert R. Blake, of the *Managerial Grid®* and grid theory concept. *See also* Blake, Robert R. *and* Managerial Grid®.

movement
Principle of design that determines the sequence of eye movements as the visual is reviewed.

movie projector
See projector, film.

moving agenda chart
A visual used to periodically show how the topic ties into the overall presentation. Used to help the audience or learners keep on track.

multi-disciplinary *basic term*
Involving a number of different subject areas.

multiechelon training
1. Simultaneous training of more than one military echelon on different tasks.
2. The simultaneous conduct of different exercises by a unit, or the training of different tasks by elements of a unit. Multi-echelon training occurs whenever collective training is being conducted. Typically, anytime training above soldier level is conducted, multiech-elon training is involved.

multi-image
Image simultaneously projected by two or more projectors to create a sophisticated presentation. Some multi-image presentations can involve six projectors.

multimedia *essential 100 term*
Use of any two or more instructional media together. Multimedia usually simulates person-to-person or person-to-machine dialogue. Technically, examples include any two media, such as tape-slide. In practice, this term has come to represent optical disk technology combined with computer power.

Multimedia & Videodisc Monitor
A periodical of interest to HRD practitioners involved in technology-based learning. *Multimedia & Videodisc Monitor* is published by Future Systems Inc.

multimedia approach
The correlated use of more than one type of instructional medium as a vehicle for presenting the instructional materials. Characteristically, an instructional package that employs a multimedia approach may use textbooks, films, slides, etc., to present various segments of the entire package.

multimedia performance support system
Any performance support system that uses more than one type medium in support of the system's purpose. Multimedia performance support systems may employ graphics, hypertext, and sound to support various segments of the system.

multimedia platform
Integrated computer and audiovisual technologies that provide access to multimedia content formats.

multinational
An organization, product, or service with origins in one country, but operating or available in many countries.

multiple-attack case study
A case study technique designed to give learners experience in thinking on their feet and in developing an offensive movement out of a defensive position. In multiple-attack case study, a document that outlines the conditions of the problem is given to each learner. Each learner is asked to write a brief reaction specifying what to do to solve the problem as stated. Responses are thrown into a hat, and each member draws out an answer, reads it aloud, and then defends it before the group, as if it were the learner's own answer.

multiple baseline design
In research, an evaluation strategy when instruction is introduced to different groups at different times. Early groups may be compared to later groups that have not yet received the treatment. *Compare with* interrupted time series design.

multiple career ladders
Different paths, progressions, or tracks available to employees in an organization. Often established to broaden options for advancement of upward mobility beyond the traditional management track.

multiple choice question
basic term
The most popular form of alternate-response question. Used to test learner's mastery of an objective.

multiple group presentations
An instructional technique in which the learners are divided into several smaller groups. Each group develops the same topic in either visual presentation, panel discussion, debate, spontaneous role play, or planned skit.

multiple integrated laser engagement system (MILES)
Almost always heard in its acronym form, MILES is a simulation system used by the U.S. Army for tactical training. MILES uses eye-safe lasers and laser detectors to simulate weapons fire in military battle training. Detectors, located

on troops or equipment, provide instant audiovisual indications of a hit, kill, or near miss.

multiple role play
A role play technique in which a large group divides into smaller groups so that each can enact the same role play simultaneously.

multiple screen images
See multiscreen.

multiple selection answer
Situation where learners must make more than one selection to answer an alternate-response question correctly.

multiscreen
Two or more screens used with multi-image projection presentations.

multi-standard decoder
A device that converts NTSC, PAL, SECAM, or NTSC video to RGB video.

multitrack course
Instruction that employs more than one delivery track or channel. Course goals are the same on all channels, but course content, degree of instruction, and presentation all vary to accommodate students of different aptitudes and levels of previously acquired skills and knowledges.

MURDER
A six-step learning strategy. The steps are (1) set the study Method, (2) read for Understanding, (3) attempt Recall, (4) Digest, (5) Expand knowledge by self-inquiry and amplification, and (6) Review mistakes. *Compare with* SQ3R.

Murphy's Law
General term to describe the rule "Whatever can go wrong will go wrong." Often used in specific ways within organizations to describe their business or function. For example, when the audiovisual expert assures you that you don't need to check it because it'll work fine, it won't. Not a special HRD term, but part of the vocabulary.

musical instrument digital interface (MIDI)
Almost always heard in its acronym form, MIDI is a standard protocol that allows computers and digital musical instruments to communicate.

mutual introduction
Each person introduces another person to the rest of the group.

Myers-Briggs, Isabel
Collected data on psychological type over many years. She developed what has evolved into the modern Myers-Briggs Type Indicator. *See also* Myers-Briggs Type Indicator (MBTI).

Myers-Briggs Type Indicator (MBTI) *essential 100 term*
See Figure on next page.

Myers-Briggs Type Indicator (MBTI) *essential 100 term*
A popular instrument used in teambuilding. The Myers-Briggs type indicator is based on categorizations of human beings devised by the Swiss psychologist, Carl Jung. The MBTI identifies 16 types of personality based on extroversion (called extraversion in the MBTI) or introversion, intuiting or sensing, thinking or feeling, and judging or perceiving. A group which works together may use the MBTI to help members see that others in the group have various styles. By learning that each style has something to contribute, the group is expected to work together more productively. MBTI is available in French and Spanish, but validation has been with predominantly North American sub-jects. *See also* Myers-Briggs, Isabel.

	Sensing Types		Intuitive Types	
Introverts	ISTJ	ISFJ	INFJ	INTJ
	ISTP	ISFP	INFP	INTP
Extraverts	ESTP	ESFP	ENFP	ENTP
	ESTJ	ESFJ	ENFJ	ENTJ

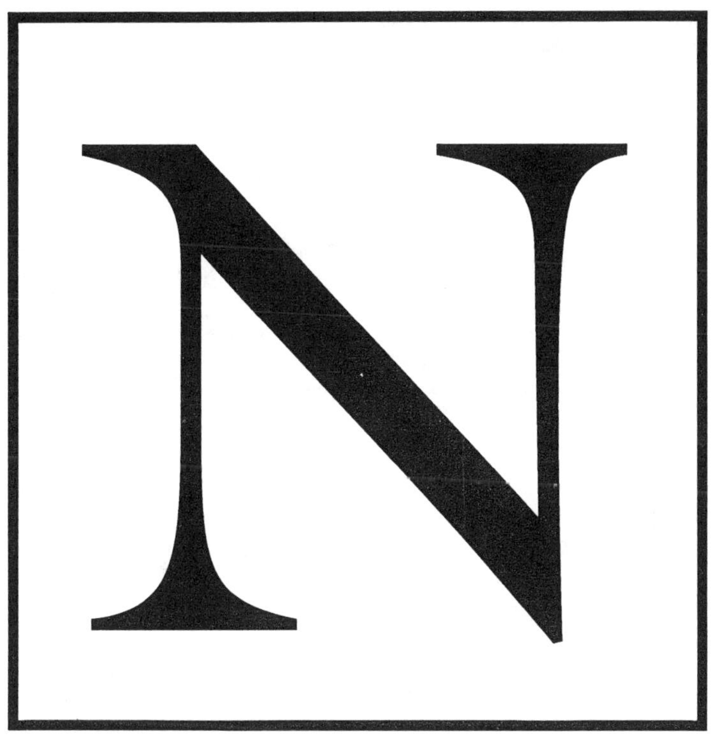

Nadler, David
An OD practitioner who developed the organizational architecture concept of autonomous work teams and high performance work systems.

Nadler, Leonard
Known to many as the father of HRD, Nadler developed the HRD concept, introduced the term HRD, wrote the first HRD book *Developing Human Resources*, and founded the first HRD doctoral program in HRD at the George Washington University. He is also author or coauthor, with his wife, Zeace, of many books and articles. *See also* human resource development (HRD).

Nadlerian
Related to the work and ideas of Leonard Nadler. Applied particularly to the HRD concept.

name card
Any card or device placed on tables to help meeting participants (or learners) and instructor meet and identify one another. *Also called* tent cards when constructed of stiff paper folded to sit upright.

nanosecond
One-billionth of a second.

narratio
The subject of a speech. It can take the form of a description or a nar-

Continued on next page

rative. A rhetorical term. A key feature of a good speech.

narrative appraisal
An appraisal technique based on open-ended descriptions of individual performance.

national
1. Any person who retains original citizenship despite working or residing in a different country. Time involved does not alter the status. *See also* culture, native, and third country national.
2. An organization with the origin, focus, and behavior of one country.

National Apprenticeship Act
Legislation passed in 1937 by the U.S. Congress to establish a uniform national apprenticeship system. The National Apprenticeship Act is still in effect. *Also called* Fitzgerald Act. *See also* apprenticeship *and* Bureau of Apprenticeship and Training.

National Association for State Training & Development Directors
A professional society of interest to HRD professionals who work in state government.

National Board of Education, Employment and Training
Provides advice to the Australian government on employment, education, and training policies, including those relating to technical and further education, skills formation, and the promotion of effective training through business and industry.

National Centre for Vocational Education Research (NCVER)
An Australian national vocational training research and development organization established as the result of a decision by government ministers.

National Council for Vocational Qualifications (NCVQ)
A body established by the British Government in the late 1980s and operating in England and Wales in order to reorganize the U.K.'s vocational education and training system. *See also* national vocational qualifications (NVQ) *and* Scottish Vocational Education Council (SCOTVEC).

National Office of Overseas Skills Recognition (NOOSR)
A national intergovernmental agency in Australia that provides expert advice to Australian registration authorities, professional and paraprofessional associations, employers, and educational institutions relating to the assessment of overseas qualifications.

National Pilot Program
A joint project of General Electric, U.S. Department of Labor, and the Greater Cincinnati Industrial Training Corporation. The project was planned to produce and sell technical training courseware to vocational schools, colleges, and business.

National Productivity Review
A periodical of interest to HRD practitioners involved in the quality process, published by Executive Enterprises.

National Report On Human Resources
A periodical of interest to HRD practitioners involved in the HR field. *National Report On Human Resources* is published by the

American Society for Training and Development.

National Society for Performance and Instruction (NSPI)
A professional organization comprised mainly of practitioners of instructional design and performance technology.

National Society of Sales Training Executives (NSSTE)
A professional society of interest to sales-related HRD professionals.

National Technological University (NTU)
A consortium of over 20 U.S. universities that delivers part-time advanced instruction for professionals via satellite.

National Television Standards Committee (NTSC)
See NTSC video.

National Training Board (NTB)
A national intergovernmental agency in Australia formed as an outcome of Australian government-sponsored conferences of ministers. Helps industry develop national competency standards for occupations and classifications in industry or enterprise industrial awards or agreements.

National Training Laboratories (NTL)
An organization that focused early on developing better diagnosticians of human behavior. NTL played a central role in the development of laboratory training. *See also* laboratory training.

national vocational qualifications (NVQ)
In the U.K., employment-led standards across all areas of work which identify, at five levels, qualifications applicable to the world of work and nationally recognized. The levels range from basic through graduate/post-graduate. *See also* National Council for Vocational Qualifications (NCVQ) *and* Scottish Vocational Education Council (SCOTVEC).

native
A person with origins in the country in which currently located. This is not a degrading term or "natives in grass huts." An American in downtown New York City is a native. *See also* culture, national, and third country national.

natural change
In organizational development, a change process characterized by no goal-setting. *Compare with* coercive change, emulative change, indoctrination, interactional change, planned change, socialization change, and technocratic change.

naturalistic observation
An evaluation in which the evaluator takes part in the planned learning experience. In naturalistic observation the evaluator observes and evaluates the experience as it happens as opposed to before or after.

natural process
The group development process that will occur naturally.

near letter quality (NLQ)
The name is an accurate description. An NLQ printer produces documents significantly less good than the quality produced by laser printers.

near transfer
The extent to which learners apply

Continued on next page

the learning to situations similar to or the same as the one(s) for which they were trained. *Compare with* far transfer. *See also* transfer of training.

need *basic term*

1. In HRD, a gap between actual and desired job performance, or what is and what should be, resulting from insufficient or inappropriate attitude, knowledge, or skill. *See also* needs analysis. *Compare with* want.
2. The gap between actual job performance and what job performance should be in the future.
3. *See* hierarchy of needs.

need for achievement (nAch)
Focus of studies by David McClelland, who employed the abbreviated form "nAch." *See also* achievement motivation *and* McClelland, David.

needs analysis *essential 100 term*

1. A step in the analysis phase of ISD. Needs analysis is a methodical process of collecting and evaluating information about on-the-job performance to determine the learning needs of the organization's employees. Procedures used include critical incident analysis, data analysis, interviews, nominal group techniques, and questionnaires. Often, a needs analysis is limited to a specific department or job, or related to a new work practice or technology. Because the performance deficiency is often related to equipment or procedures, most HRD practitioners insist on conducting a needs analysis to confirm the existence of a learning need. *Also called* competency assessment, competency modeling, front-end analysis, job analysis, needs determination, performance analysis, and needs assessment, although some of these are meant to specify particular approaches to needs analysis. *See also* instructional systems development (ISD), learning, noninstructional need, and task analysis.
2. Loosely, the process of identifying learning needs, universally acknowledged as the first stage in the development of any HRD program.

needs analyst
The HRD role of identifying ideal and actual performance and performance conditions and determining causes of discrepancies. *See also* HRD Roles and Competencies Study.

needs assessment
See needs analysis.

need-to-know material
Information related directly to learning objectives. Need-to-know material must be learned in order to master the objectives.

negative feedback
A response to a deviant act or event that serves to discontinue that act. *See also* positive feedback.

negative reinforcement *basic term*
According to operant conditioning, negative reinforcement does not equal punishment. It is rewarding a learner by reducing or removing adverse stimuli. *Compare with* positive reinforcement.

negative skew
When scores are grouped near the *high* end of the scale. For example, if the value plotted was quality, it

reflects a tendency for *all* units to have high quality.

negative transfer
In training transfer, a situation in which prior learning interferes with the acquisition of new knowledge or skills. *Also called* proactive interference. *Compare with* positive transfer.

negotiation skill
The HRD competency of securing win-win agreements while successfully representing a special interest in a decision. *See also* HRD Roles and Competencies Study.

network
1. A pattern of linkages among group members.
2. A group discussion in which participants are given advance assignments.
3. *See also* local area network (LAN) *and* wide area network (WAN).

networking *basic term*
Individual activities to build informal resources and communications with others. The networking resources may then be called upon to support a specific current or undefined future goal.

neurolinguistic programming (NLP)
1. Originally, a methodology for communication and behavior change developed by Richard Bandler and John Grinder. NLP is based on observations and analyses of eye movement, grammatical structure, speech tempo, use of metaphor, vocal tone, word choice, and other unconscious physical behaviors to identify patterns of thought and feeling.
2. Loosely, communication strategies based on the concept that people have preferred modes of taking information in and processing it.

New Directions for Adult and Continuing Education
A periodical of interest to HRD practitioners involved in adult learning. *New Directions for Adult and Continuing Education* is published by Jossey-Bass.

newsprint *basic term*
Any blank paper normally placed on an easel to create a flipchart. Newsprint is one of the most versatile and useful resources for small group work. *Also called* artists' paper, butcher paper, and wrapping paper.

New Zealand Association for Training & Development (NZATD)
A professional society for HRD practitioners.

New Zealand Institute of Management (NZIM)
A professional society of interest to some HR professionals.

New Zealand Qualifications Authority (NZQA)
A national intergovernmental agency created by an act of parliament to maintain and enhance the quality of education and training in New Zealand by establishing and coordinating a framework of education and training qualifications.

nice-to-know material
Information that during the development process is determined to be unnecessary for the mastery of the objectives. Nice-to-know material may be included in the instruction to exemplify or augment other information.

nine dot metaphor
See connect the dots.

noise
In the communication process, anything that interferes with the transmission of a message.

nominal group technique
essential 100 term
An idea-generating procedure developed by Andre Delbecq, commonly used in HRD. The nominal group technique has certain advantages over other techniques: every member becomes involved; issues are weighted and ranked; the problem selected is truly the choice of the group. First, the facilitator provides a statement of the issues. Group members then write down their ideas. In the next step each person states their ideas, and all ideas generated are recorded. Then each idea is discussed in order. Finally, the group ranks all of the ideas. *See also* brainstorming.

noncognitive
A purpose relating to activities other than the acquisition or processing of knowledge.

nonconformity
In quality, a specific occurrence of a condition that does not conform to specifications or other inspection standards. *Also called* discrepancy or defect.

noncontiguous communication
In distance learning, interaction between learner and facilitator at different locations. Can include correspondence, telephone, audiocassette, and computer exchange.

nonequivalent comparison group design
In research, when two groups are established nonrandomly, one receives the treatment the other does not. Both groups are measured in the same way. Nonequivalent comparison group design is less reliable and valid than a true research design. *Compare with* equivalent comparison group design.

nonexamples
An instructional method for teaching concepts. A nonexample is a closely related concept that could be confused with the concept being taught. The instruction explains why it is not an example of the concept.

noninstructional human technology
The systematic application of human-performance improvement methods that do not include instruction directed toward employee selection, discipline, incentives, or motivation.

noninstructional need
A need that cannot or should not be addressed through instruction. *See also* needs analysis.

nonparametric statistics
In research, statistics used to compare groups where it is assumed that samples come from populations that are normally distributed. *Compare with* parametric statistics.

nonstarter
In distance learning, students who are registered for a course but have not submitted assignments or otherwise used the system.

nonsummativity
The principle that the whole is

greater than or different from the sum of its parts.

nonverbal communication *basic term*
Communication based on a person's appearance, posture, style, or mannerisms. Nonverbal messages are a powerful factor in communication, especially with members of another culture. *Also called* body language and nonverbal message. *See also* culture.

nonverbal exercises *basic term*
A small group instructional technique used to assist physical release of emotion, allow expression of feelings, reduce inhibitions, or break down barriers to participation.

nonverbal message
See nonverbal communication.

norm *basic term*
An acceptable way of behaving in a group or organization. Norms may be explicit or implicit. *See also* culture, explicit norm, implicit norm, and organization development (OD).

normal curve *basic term*
See Figure on next page.

normal distribution *basic term*
In research, when the greatest number of observations fall in the center with progressively fewer observations distributed evenly on both sides of the average. When a graph is drawn to represent this data, it results in what is called a bell curve due to its bell-like shape. *See also* normal curve.

normative re-educative change
Inducing people to change through furnishing them with new ways to approach problems or address issues confronting them. *Compare with* coercive change, emulative change, indoctrination, interactional change, natural change, persuasive change, planned change, socialization change, and technocratic change.

norm of reciprocity
The mutual feeling that the provision of a benefit or service by one party in a relationship should be repaid in kind by the other party; tit for tat.

norm-referenced learning *basic term*
The traditional grading scheme. The principle of grading based on each learner's success compared to other learners. *See also* norm-referenced test. *Compare with* mastery learning.

norm-referenced test *essential 100 term*
A test that a measures a person's knowledge or skill relative to scores of other learners in the same group. Norm-referenced tests are useful for sorting people into groups. Grading "on a curve" involves norm-referenced measurement since an individual's grade depends on the position on the curve (performance of other students). Generally, norm-referenced tests are not appropriate in ISD and should not be used to evaluate either the learners or the instruction if there are explicitly stated objectives. *See also* standardized test. *Compare with* criterion-referenced test.

North American Simulation and Gaming Association (NASAGA)
Usually heard in its acronym form,

Continued on next page

normal curve *basic term*
A representation of the normal distribution. *Also called* bell (shaped) curve. *See also* normal distribution.

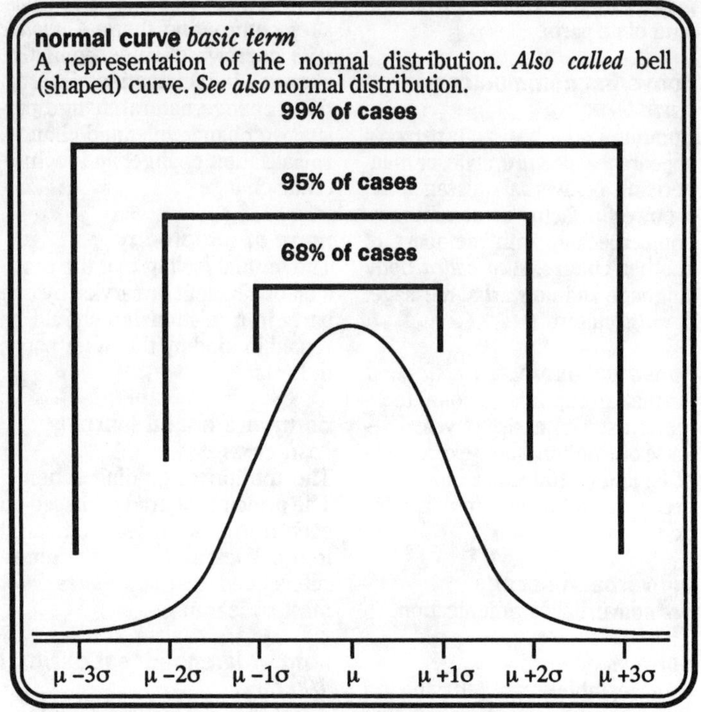

NASAGA is a professional society of interest to HRD professionals. with high interest in simulation and games.

Norwegian Society for Training and Development
A professional society for HRD practitioners in Norway

no skew
See normal distribution.

notebook computer
A small, portable computer. *Also called* a laptop computer.

notes, speaker's
Key words, points, or other material referred to by the speaker. Speaker's notes are often recorded on index cards. *Compare with* lecture notes.

notestorming
A structured brainstorming technique that uses written notes passed among silent participants. *See also* brainstorming.

note-taking
A method of recording the content of a meeting or learning activity. *See also* learning style.

novelty effect
In research, when the treatment, compared to the normal setting may effect the subject's behavior and confound the results of the experiment. *See also* Hawthorne effect.

NTSC 4.43 (video)
The video output of videotape or videodisc players used mainly in the Middle East.

NTSC video
The video standard used in the United States, Canada, and most other countries where 60 hz. power is used. NTSC video is 525 scan lines. NTSC represents the name of the body that set the standard, the National Television Standards Committee. *Compare with* PAL *and* SECAM.

Countries with NTSC video

Bermuda
Bolivia
Burma
Canada
Chile
Costa Rica
Cuba
Japan
Korea
Mexico
Montserrat
Panama
Peru
South Africa
St Christopher and Nevis
former USSR countries
USA

NTSC video
See Figure.

null hypothesis
In research, a statement that no differences exist between the groups studied. The experiment attempts to prove that the null hypothesis is false. Rejection of the null hypothesis is the desired outcome. This phrase is often confusing to new HRD practitioners.

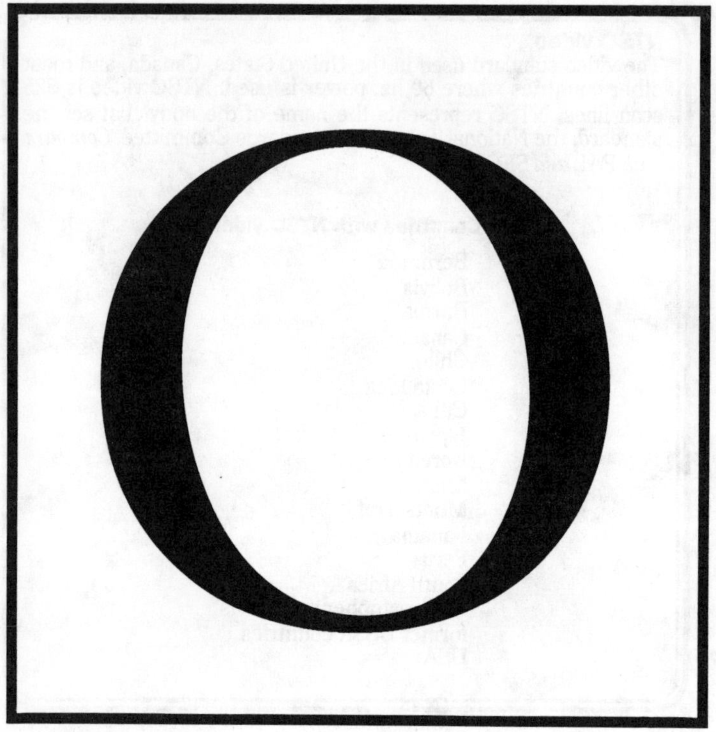

objective *basic term*
1. *See* learning objective.
2. Loosely, the desired outcome(s) of an exercise or activity, usually expressed in specific behavioral terms.

objectives-centered instruction *basic term*
A behaviorism-based theory of instruction that concentrates on observable and measurable outcomes.

objectives-preparation skill
The HRD competency of preparing clear statements which describe desired outputs. *See also* HRD Roles and Competencies Study.

observable behavior
Actions and performances that can be seen and measured. *See also* learning objective.

observation
1. One technique useful in assessment.
2. One technique useful in data collection for research.
3. *See* field trip.

observer-controller
An individual tasked to evaluate training and provide administrative control and constructive feedback to participants during a training exercise.

observing skill
The HRD competency of recognizing objectively what is happening in or across situations. *See also* HRD Roles and Competencies Study.

occupational analysis *basic term*
A detailed systematic listing of the tasks and performances of an occupation, and the general and technical knowledge needed to adequately perform the occupation.

occupational survey
A procedure used by the U.S. Air Force for the identification of the duties and tasks that comprise one or more shredouts, prefixes, specialties, career field ladders, or utilization fields and for the collection, collation, and analysis of information concerning such duties and tasks.

oculesics
Nonverbal communications involving the use of the eyes.

OD data gathering
The various techniques and methods used to gather information for organization development. OD data gathering differs from a needs analysis in that it often attempts to discover deeply suppressed feelings. Techniques used include do more/do less list, library, magic wand, organizational mapping, polling, and t-shirting. *See also* organization development (OD).

OD intervention
The usual name applied to an OD-based planned change effort. *See also* organization development (OD).

Odiorne, George
Best known as the father of MBO, Odiorne converted Peter Drucker's concept of management by objectives into a practical management tool. His books include *Management by Objectives*. *See also* Drucker, Peter; management by objectives; and organization development (OD).

OD Network
See Organization Development Network.

off-line
1. In technology-based learning, that learning that happens away from the learning station. *Compare with* on-line.
2. Loosely, not under the control of, or connected to, a computer.
3. Communication in an informal setting. Unofficial.

off-the-job training
Training that is conducted away from the participant's regular job site. The abbreviation OJT is *never* used for off-the-job training. *Compare with* on-the-job training (OJT).

off-the-shelf (instruction) (packages) (programs) (materials) *basic term*
Existing HRD learning activities for which little or no new design is required. Usually commercially supplied. Off-the-shelf activities usually are intended to meet an organization's general HRD programmatic needs, but may be available on a given topic. *Also called* canned instruction.

OK
In transactional analysis, one of the possible life positions. For example, I'm OK - You're Not OK. *See* transactional analysis (TA).

older worker
An arbitrary definition used to create a category of workers. Definitions may have legal implications—and differ. The Administration on Aging defines anyone who is at least 55 years of age as older. The Department of Labor defines anyone 45 or older as a mature worker. The Age Discrimination in Employment Act defines a mature worker as 40 or older.

old woman/young woman
One of the most common of all exercises used with groups, based on a drawing that can be interpreted two ways. Use of this exercise illustrates the impact of the participant's background or attitudes on their perception. *See also* connect the dots.

olfactory learning preference
An individual learning style based on preference for smell and taste. *See also* aural, haptic, interactive, kinesthetic, print, and visual learning styles.

one-on-one trial
Review of an evolving instructional package by an instructional developer, conducted with one member of the target population at a time. A one-on-one trial evaluates the then-current effectiveness of the under-development instructional product and provides for improvements, which are made before another such trial. The acquisition and analysis of data from selected members of the target population is used to identify and correct weaknesses. A formative evaluation step. *See also* formative evaluation *and* instructional systems development (ISD). *Compare with* pilot test *and* small group trial.

on-line
1. In technology-based learning, information currently available for direct access. Usually implies linkage to a computer. *Compare with* off-line.
2. Loosely, under the control of, or connected to, a computer.

on-line help system
A job aid built into the user's computer software. Provides just in time help. On-line help systems may be the most often used technological job aid.

Ontario Society for Training & Development (OSTD)
A professional society for HRD practitioners in the Province of Ontario. *See also* HR Canada.

on-the-job evaluation (OJE)
See on-the-job training (OJT).

on-the-job training (OJT)
essential 100 term
OJT has been called the most common training method. The worker-learner usually performs under the supervision of someone else already qualified to do the job. OJT provides observation with guided practice in a practical situation, while learners engage in productive work. Sometime the process is formally divided into OJT and OJE (evaluation) as two distinct phases. At its worst, OJT instills bad habits or attitudes in a new employee. OJT has been widely abused or given only lip service in organizations where it has loose structure. In order to differentiate the properly conducted OJT from the poorly done version, it is called formal OJT. *See also* apprenticeship training *and* job instruction training (JIT).

opaque projector *basic term*
Any device that projects an image from non-transparent originals, such as an open book. This useful technique has been seen less often in recent years because the opaque projector fell out of style: it was heavy equipment with a noisy fan and limited clarity. Recently a replacement item has emerged. The Video Visualizer achieves the same result by focusing a video camera on the opaque object and display through a video projection source. *See also* Video Visualizer.

open-book exam
1. A test in which the learner is permitted to use resources to answer questions. Many practitioners think open-book exams are of limited value when measuring learning.
2. A study technique providing the opportunity for the learner to find information in response to structured questions. Emphasis is on search skills more than on content.

open communication *basic term*
Sending and receiving of messages by individuals or groups with few constraints. Open communication is important in the instructional setting. *Compare with* closed communication.

open-ended key questions
Questions that cannot be answered either "yes" or "no." Open-ended key questions are used in planning instruction.

open-forum discussion *basic term*
A form of instruction, usually on an assigned topic, in which any member of the group may speak to any other member. Although open-forum discussions are facilitated, they are characterized by informality and high learner participation. *See also* organization development (OD). *Compare with* panel and symposium.

open question *basic term*
In oral questioning, a question that requires the respondent to compose an answer. Open questions expand communication based on the directing of the response. Open questions minimize defensiveness. *Compare with* direct question *and* clarifying question.

open response item
See open response question.

open response question
In written questioning, a question for which the respondent is asked to write out a short answer. *Also called* constructed response. *Compare with* closed response question.

open role playing
The role play situation in which all information is shared among all participants. No special instructions are given to any party. *Compare with* covert role playing.

open space technology *basic term*
An innovative approach, developed by Owen Harrison, to enhance individual and group performance in which up to 400 people self-organize and self-manage multi-day meetings and conferences around complex issues.

operant conditioning *basic term*
An approach to behavioral modification developed by B. F. Skinner.

Continued on next page

See also behaviorism; behavior modification; conditioned response; reinforcement; and Skinner, B. F.

operating objective
A formal statement detailing the measurable results planned to be achieved by the HRD department.

operational period
One of the phases of the life cycle model of cost-benefit analysis. *See also* life cycle model.

opportunity-centered instruction
A developmentalism-based theory of instruction that focuses on matching individual needs to appropriate instructional experiences. Opportunity-centered instruction is particularly useful for helping employees adapt to the changes that emanate from their life cycles.

opportunity training
Training conducted by section, squad, team, or crew-level leaders which is preselected, planned, and rehearsed, but not executed until unexpected training time becomes available. For example, when waiting for transportation, or completing scheduled training early, or when a break occurs in a training exercise.

optical character recognition (OCR)
The technology used in scanners.

optical disc
Any disc using optical storage technology. *See* compact disc read only memory (CD-ROM), optical storage, and videodisc.

optical media
Those media based on laser-read discs. Optical media does *not* refer to projection media with lenses such as a 35mm projector. *See* compact disc-interactive (CD-I), compact disc read only memory (CD-ROM), digital video interactive (DVI), optical storage, and videodisc.

optical spacing
A letter-spacing technique in which the space between individual letters is dictated by the unique shape of adjacent letters.

optical storage
The use of laser disc technology for the storage of data. *See* compact disc read only memory (CD-ROM) *and* videodisc.

oral questioning test
A measurement that offers an observation of employees' skills in working with others and in handling and solving typical job-related problems.

oral test
Any test in which the question and answer are spoken rather than given in writing.

ORBIT
A commercial information retrieval service that can be accessed by a computer over a telephone line. A large number of data bases may be searched. *See also* DIALOG *and* BRS.

organizational assessment
A process used by military senior leaders to analyze and correlate evaluations or various functional systems, such as training, logistics, personnel, and force integration, to determine an organization's capability to accomplish its wartime mission.

organizational audit
An intensive study of an organization to determine weaknesses and potential methods of improvement.

organizational career development
A planned effort to link the individual's career needs with the organization's workforce requirements. Organizational career development is a process for helping individuals plan their careers in concert with an organization's business requirements and strategic direction.

organizational climate *basic term*
Activities that establish acceptance among the learners for the learning activity. Climate setting is closely aligned with adult learning. The two components of climate are organizational climate and instructional climate. *See also* climate setting *and* instructional climate.

organizational climate survey
A method of gathering data for organization analysis and organization development. *See also* organization development (OD) *and* organizational climate.

organizational commitment
Strong involvement and support by the organization's management for an HRD program or activity.

organizational culture
The principles, ideas, and pronouncements that define an organization. Four levels of organizational culture are artifacts, perspectives, values, and assumptions. *See also* culture.

organizational curriculum *basic term*
The formal learning activities that are conducted, coordinated, or planned by the HRD department. The organizational curriculum includes all programs and is the long-term learning plan for the entire organization.

organizational curriculum objectives
Objectives directed at the development of the organization through the long-term development of individuals.

organizational design *basic term*
An organization's allocation of work duties and reporting relationships. Organizational design is a synonym for structure.

organizational development
See organization development (OD).

Organizational Dynamics
A periodical of interest to HRD practitioners involved in organization development. *Organizational Dynamics* is published by the American Management Association.

organizational environment *basic term*
That part of the broad external environment which influences the functioning of an organization directly. Any supplier, distributor, or stockholder is part of the organizational environment.

organizational goal
A general statement of an organization's desired end state or condition.

organizational mapping
In OD, a technique of data gathering. *See also* OD data gathering.

organizational mirroring
In organizational development, a technique used to show each element of the organization how it is viewed by the others.

organizational objective *basic term*
A general desired end state or condition, derived from an organizational goal, that can be measured.

organizational psychology
The study of the behavior of people working together.

organizational purpose
The reason that any organization exists. The mission of the organization.

organizational strategic planning
See strategic planning.

organizational structure intervention
In organizational development, an intervention focused on issues that confront the entire organization and its subunits.

organizational transformation
Insights into the human factors affecting the structure of the organization.

organization-behavior understanding
The HRD competency of seeing organizations as dynamic, political, economic, and social systems with multiple goals; using this larger perspective as a framework for understanding and influencing events and change. *See also* HRD Roles and Competencies Study.

organization-change agent
The HRD role of influencing and supporting changes in organization behavior. *See also* HRD Roles and Competencies Study.

organization chart
1. Any chart showing the organization's formal structure.
2. A project-related chart showing the organizational relationships for a specific project.

organization development (OD) *essential 100 term*
1. Within HRD, the field in which a long-term change effort is directed to an entire organization or some part of it, using techniques from the applied behavioral sciences.
2. A planned change effort, usually long-term, directed to an entire organization or some part of it, using techniques from the applied behavioral sciences. OD is generally aimed at increasing the organization's effectiveness and health through planned interventions that help groups initiate and manage change and integrate individual desires for growth and development with organizational goals. OD strategies for producing change are called interventions. For example, action research, action science, conflict resolution, process consultation, survey feedback, and teambuilding. *See also* action research, action science, change agent, consulting process, culture, data-based intervention, management by objectives, norm, sociotechnical systems, survey feedback, and teambuilding.

Organization Development Journal
A periodical of interest to HRD

practitioners involved in organization development. *Organization Development Journal* is published by the Organization Development Institute.

Organization Development Network
A professional society of interest to OD professionals. *Also called* (informally) the OD Network.

organization-development-theories-and-techniques understanding
The HRD competency of knowing the techniques and methods used in organization development and understanding their appropriate use. *See also* HRD Roles and Competencies Study.

organization expectancies
See organization development (OD).

organization specific
Related to a particular organization. *Compare with* specificity.

organization understanding
The HRD competency of knowing the strategy, structure, power networks, financial position, and systems of a specific organization. *See also* HRD Roles and Competencies Study.

organizer's guide, game
See game organizer's guide.

orientation *essential 100 term*
1. Any program conducted specifically for new employees of an organization. Orientations usually include the organization's history, benefits, and rules and expectations.
2. Any program conducted to help an employee move to a new position within an organization.
3. A process over time in which a new employee is integrated into the organization.

ornaments
Characters that are decorative elements rather than letters, which can be used alone or combined into borders or other patterns.

outcome
The expectation for results of a course or program. Outcomes may be stated in terms of organizational improvements as well as in terms of changes in the learners' performance. Learner-related changes are sometimes called educational outcome.

outcome imagery
Imagining the outcome of a task, either positive or negative. *Compare with* performance imagery.

outline
A planning tool that shows organization of a presentation and key points. *See also* lecture notes *and* notes, speaker's.

out of control
In quality measurement, a process is out of control if one or more points fall outside of the control limits, or if specific numbers of successive points fall on the same side of the center line. *See* control chart.

output
1. The tangible result of any process. *Compare with* input.
2. Any information presented on a computer display or in hardcopy. *Compare with* input.

oval diagram
A pictorial form of problem display. An oval diagram describes a problem as a set of complex rela-

Continued on next page

tionships among system variables and other variables in the system environment. *Contrast with* mind-map.

overhead projector *basic term*
A machine that projects an image from material on transparent sheets called transparencies. The transparencies can accommodate an extensive range of material, from artwork including color to simple handwritten material. Useful in general sessions as well as small groups. Generally, the room need not be darkened for acceptable visibility. The overhead projector is a versatile and useful device and is the most common instructional medium.

overhead question
Any question directed to the entire group, as opposed to one individual. Overhead questions seek volunteered answers. *Compare with* direct question.

overhead transparency
See transparency.

overlay *basic term*
1. Placing one transparency over another to increase the information conveyed by the projected image. The second and additional sheet(s) are flipped into position as the points they cover are presented. This technique is used to add complexity to an image once the viewer has seen the basic portion. Overlays are often in different color than the original. *Also called* revelation. *See also* overhead projector *and* transparency.
2. Additional pieces of information that are added to a display when the users press a key. Instead of showing all the information at one time, overlays reveal the information at the users' pace.

overlearning *basic term*
Encouraging learners to acquire more skills than needed to facilitate the retention and subsequent use of those skills.

overrating error
In research, when results are interpreted with a favorable bias.

overt
Unconcealed intentions.

overt response
An outwardly observable response of the learner. For example, a learner's oral, written, or manipulative act which is, or can be, recorded by an observer.

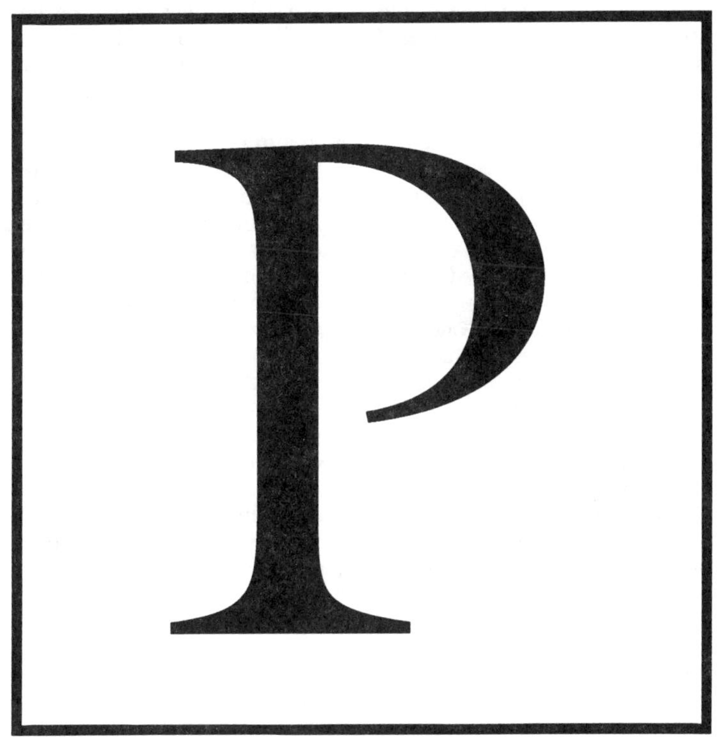

package
A full set of instructional courseware necessary to conduct an HRD activity. The term is not limited only to off-the-shelf materials. *See also* learning activity package.

packaged programs
See off-the-shelf instruction.

page proof
A copy of a document produced as a trial before the final press run.

paid study leave
See educational entitlement.

pairs
A group of two persons. *Compare with* dyad, triad, and quad.

PAL (video)
The world's most common video standard. PAL is used in most countries where 50 hz. power is used. Refers to phase alternate by line. *Compare with* NTSC video *and* SECAM.

palmtop computer
The preferred term to describe one of the smaller of today's microcomputers. *See* personal computer (PC).

pan
Video technique used to follow the movement of a subject through a scene or to achieve a panoramic effect. The camera is physically moved, usually in a horizontal way,

Continued on next page

from one side of a scene to the other. *Compare with* dolly *and* zoom.

panel
See panel discussion.

panel discussion *basic term*
A small group presentation based on purposeful discussion of an assigned topic and conducted in front of a larger group, or audience. Usually, a panel discussion is controlled by a moderator. There is little or no audience participation. *Compare with* lecture *and* panel-forum. *See also* colloquy, debate, forum, panel, speech, and symposium.

panel-forum
A panel immediately followed by audience participation. Compared with the low audience participation of a panel, a panel-forum has increased involvement. The forum involves free and open discussion by the panel members on questions submitted by the audience. *Compare with* panel. *See also* colloquy, debate, forum, panel, speech, and symposium.

paper-and-pencil test *basic term*
Any test based on the learner's written, rather than performance, input. Paper-and-pencil tests include standardized and instructor-made tests.

paper hanging
The practice of organizations to insert resumes of well-qualified outsiders (individuals who are not employees of the company) into proposals without stating the individual's status.

parabolic lens
A gridlike structure that focuses fluorescent light straight down. The parabolic lens reduces glare on video and computer displays without reducing the amount of light on work surfaces.

paradigm
A mental frame of reference that affects the way people think and behave. HRD professionals are frequently tasked with getting organizations to break old paradigms to learn new methods. This is called a paradigm shift.

paralanguage
The vocal tone or expression with which a message is communicated. *Also called* metalanguage.

parametric statistics
In research, used to compare groups where no assumptions have been made about the homogeneity of the groups. *Compare with* nonparametric statistics.

paraprofessional
1. An individual who assists professional personnel to carry out their responsibilites. *Also called* semiprofessional.
2. An occupation staffed by paraprofessionals. *Compare with* profession.

parent
In transactional analysis, one of the possible ego states. The three states are parent, child, and adult. The combinations of these states in human interactions is the basis of transactional analysis. *See* transactional analysis (TA).

parent company
Company with ownership and control of the investment.

Pareto chart
(Pronounced par-ay′-to. Rhymes with potato.)

A quality control chart that displays problems according to the magnitude of frequency of their effect, to identify the problem that causes the greatest effect. A Pareto chart is used to compare the relative importance of problems and draw attention to important aspects of a problem.

Pareto principle *basic term*
The 80/20 rule named for Vilfredo Pareto, an Italian economist. For example, 80 percent of the mistakes are made by 20 percent of the people. *See also* seven quality process tools.

participant
When learning is involved, the learner. *See also* learner.

participant aid
See learning aid.

participant evaluation
Evaluation of learning experiences by the participants.

participant program book
See program book.

participatory methods *basic term*
Those methods that are more learner- than instructor-centered. For example, a magic wand exercise is participatory, a lecture is not. *See also* experiential learning *and* facilitator.

part-task practice
An exercise, performed with or without a training device, that allows students to practice some portion of a task or set of tasks. *Compare with* whole-task practice.

part-task simulation
A technique for the use of computer-based learning in the simulation mode. A learning station may not be able to simulate an entire situation at once. By simulating only one of several parts, effective learning can take place. For example, simulation of a system on an aircraft, instead of the entire aircraft. *See also* simulation, simulator, and whole-task simulation.

part-task trainer
Systems used in military training that provide dynamic simulation of some subset of mission requirements. The subset may be defined in terms of crew positions and mission segments. A part-task trainer only includes those capabilities necessary for dynamic simulation of the tasks for which it is designed. Instrument flight simulators and aerial refueling part-task trainers both fit this definition.

passive participation
Instructional activities in which learners are only listening or observing. For example, a lecture or video. *Compare with* active participation.

patterns of organizational learning
Learning patterns that are based on tacit and explicit knowledge and their interaction. Ikujiro Nonaka identifies four patterns: (1) tacit to tacit, (2) explicit to explicit, (3) tacit to explicit, and (4) explicit to tacit. *See also* learning organization.

Pavlov, Ivan Petrovich
A Russian neurophysiologist who received a Nobel Prize in 1904. Pavlov is best known for his work in describing the classical conditioning of behavior in animals. *See also* behaviorism *and* Pavlovian conditioning.

Pavlovian conditioning
A basic pattern of how learning takes place, based on the work of the Russian psychologist Ivan Pavlov. For example, an event such as a bell sounding is repeatedly paired with a stimulus, such as food that always elicits a given response such as salivation. Continued pairings of the bell and food will eventually result in a "conditioned response"—the bell itself will elicit salivation. *Also called* classical conditioning. *See also* behavior modification, extinction, and reinforcement

payback period
A common method of evaluating a capital expenditure. A payback period is the multiple of income compared to the original investment. The period is usually in years.

payroll levy
See levy system.

PC resolution
See resolution.

pedagogical revision
Checking texts, video, lesson plans, course packages, and other materials to evaluate their instructional effectiveness.

pedagogy *essential 100 term*
1. An informal philosophy about teaching that can be traced to the instructional practice of medieval universities. Pedagogy is not a formal learning theory. It emphasizes what the instructor does rather than what participants learn. The word is derived from Greek *paid* (child) and *agogus* (leader). *See also* tabula rasa. *Compare with* andragogy.
2. Loosely, the art and science of teaching children.

peer coaching *basic term*
An activity of learners who agree to work together and coach each other in newly learned behaviors. *See also* transfer of training.

peer feedback *basic term*
Feedback from peers obtained by questionnaires or interviews on how participants have performed during or after an HRD program.

peer group *basic term*
Any group with similar age or background.

peer-mediated-learning
A small group session in which the leader is a member of the group.

peer session
Conference sessions providing participants the opportunity to discuss topics of interest to them in an informal atmosphere and without a designated leader or resource person. *Compare with* cracker barrel session.

peer teaching *basic term*
Instruction of a group by members of the group itself without regard to previous experience or standing. *Compare with* relay, sibling, and team teaching.

peer training
See peer tutoring.

peer tutoring
Instruction of a learner by another learner. For example, a learner who has completed instruction acts as an instructor to another learner in the skill or process to be learned. This procedure continues with each learner becoming an instructor for the next learner. *Also called*

peer training. *Compare with* peer teaching.

perceiving (P)
One of the 8 basic predispositions included in the Myers-Briggs typology. *See* Myers-Briggs Type Indicator (MBTI).

percentage compensation
A fee structure for a consultant's work, based on an agreed percentage of the growth in the client organization's sales or savings. *Compare with* performance-based compensation.

percentile (centile or percentile rank)
In statistics, points marking a distribution into 100 parts. The percentile is a score that shows approximately what percent of subjects scored below the given score. *Compare with* z-score *and* stanines.

perception
People's interpretation of what they sense. The process of information extraction. The process by which a learner receives or extracts information from the environment through experiences (sight, sound, feel, taste, or smell) and assimilates the data as facts.

perception principle
See gestalt perception principles.

performance *basic term*

1. One of the three required parts of a Magerian learning objective. What the learners must demonstrate to prove that they have grasped the task. These action words state the main intent of the objective. The performance should match the job task, describe the simplest and most direct behavior possible, and be stated clearly. Observable and measurable action words should be used, such as choose, describe, write, identify, or solve. To be useful, performance statements must tell plainly how the trainee's learning will be observed. Certain words should be avoided, such as to know or understand. Poor performance statements include "understand the Operator's Manual" and "know Ohm's Law." *Also called* behavior. *Compare with* condition *and* criterion.
2. The carrying out of an act to completion. Actual accomplishment of a task to some preset standard of completeness and accuracy.

performance aid
See job aid.

performance analysis
See needs analysis.

Performance & Instruction
A periodical of interest to HRD practitioners involved in systematic performance improvement strategies. *Performance & Instruction* is published by the National Society for Performance and Instruction.

performance-based compensation
A fee structure for a consultant's work, based the client organization's sales or savings increasing to an agreed-upon level. *Compare with* percentage compensation.

performance-based evaluation
Verification of the learner's acquisition of knowledge and skill by observing actual performance. *See also* evaluation, mastery learning, and performance-based instruction.

performance-based instruction *essential 100 term*
Learning activities designed to provide the specific on-the-job knowledge and skills required to perform the task to be learned. These are determined in a task analysis and expressed as learning objectives. Often includes performance-based evaluation. *Also called* criterion-referenced instruction (CRI). *See also* instructional systems development (ISD), learning objective, mastery learning, performance-based evaluation, and task analysis.

performance checklist *basic term*
The breakdown of a task into elements that must be correctly performed to determine whether each learner satisfactorily meets the performance standards described in the objective. The performance checklist is used to carry out a performance test.

performance criteria
See performance standard.

performance discrepancy *basic term*
The difference between desired and actual behavior for a specific situation. *See also* needs analysis.

performance imagery
Rehearsing the acts involved in performing a task. For example, imagining a performance and going through the steps in one's mind without imagining an outcome. *Compare with* outcome imagery.

performance improvement potential (PIP)
A concept developed by Thomas Gilbert to describe the possibility of making all employees into top performers. PIP refers to the gap between the top performer's performance and the others.

Performance Improvement Quarterly
A research journal of interest to HRD practitioners involved in systematic design and development of instruction. *Performance Improvement Quarterly* is published by the National Society for Performance and Instruction.

performance management
A managerial process linking strategic planning, performance standards, individual objectives, performance evaluation, training, and individual development.

performance measurement
The process of determining if the learner's performance on a given task reaches the standard for that specific task.

performance model
See performance-based instruction.

performance objective *essential 100 term*
The new capability the learner must demonstrate on the job. The instruction is intended to enable this performance. The learning objective can be satisfied in the classroom, but the performance objective must equal the task at the job site. *Compare with* learning objective.

performance-observation skill
The HRD competency of tracking and describing behaviors and their effects. *See also* HRD Roles and Competencies Study.

performance-oriented training
See performance-based instruction.

performance planning
Identification of a job's goals, priorities, and reward expectations. Usually accompanied by identification of training needs, performance activities, priorities, and explanations, as well as by financial compensation.

performance prompting
Guidance on what to do next provided by a performance support system. Performance prompting is usually provided automatically when the user makes an error.

performance standard
The quality of desired behavior for a specific task. Performance standard may be a level of accuracy. *Also called* performance criteria.

performance support system *essential 100 term*
An integrated computer program that provides any combination of expert system, hypertext, embedded animation, CAI, and hypermedia to an employee on demand. Performance support systems allow employees to perform with a minimum of support and intervention by others. Examples include help systems, electronic job aids, and expert advisors.

performance support tool
See performance support system.

performance technology
A set of methods and procedures, and a strategy for solving problems or realizing opportunities related to human performance. Performance technology is applicable to individuals, small groups, and large organizations. It is a combination of performance analysis, cause analysis, and intervention selection and design.

performance test *basic term*
Performance of a task under test conditions to determine the achievement of learning objectives by the learner. A performance test is usually evaluated on a go or no-go basis.

performance tryout
The opportunity to practice or demonstrate a newly learned skill or behavior as a feedback activity during the learning. The same conditions may be used as those in the performance test at the conclusion of the instruction. Performance tryout is one of the four steps of the job instruction training process. *See also* behavior modeling, job instruction training (JIT), on-the-job training (OJT), role play, and skill practice.

peripheral device
Any electronic or electromechanical devices that can be attached to a computer. For example, printers, graphics pad, and mouse.

peroratio
The conclusion of a speech. A summary whose purpose is to persuade listeners to take action. A rhetorical term. A key feature of a good speech.

personal computer (PC)
1. Any small computer.
2. Loosely, an MS/DOS computer.

personal development
The process of choosing educational and development activities for the furthering of one's own goals.

personality
Patterns or habits of behavior acquired during socialization.

personal philosophy
An individual's beliefs about a profession and the appropriate approaches and methods of practice.

personal selling
Direct face-to-face promotion of HRD offerings to potential users. *Compare with* public relations, sales promotions, and mass selling.

personnel/HR-field understanding
The HRD competency of understanding issues and practices in other HR areas (organization development, organization job design, human resource planning, selection and staffing, personnel research and information systems, compensation and benefits, employee assistance, union/labor relations). *See also* HRD Roles and Competencies Study.

Personnel Journal
A periodical of interest to HRD practitioners involved in personnel issues. *Personnel Journal* is published by ACC Communications.

Personnel Management
A periodical of general interest to HRD practitioners. *Personnel Management* is published monthly in the U.K. by the Institute of Personnel Management *See also* Institute of Personnel Management (IPM).

Personnel Management Plus
A periodical of interest to HRD practitioners involved in personnel issues. *Personnel Management Plus* is published by the International Personnel Publications (a U.K. publication).

Personnel Psychology
A periodical of interest to HRD practitioners interested in psychology. *Personnel Psychology* is published by Personnel Psychology.

perspective intervention
In organizational development, an intervention focused on a broader (historical) perspective to reorient present actions.

persuasive change
Inducing people to change through appeal to their self-interest. *Compare with* coercive change, emulative change, indoctrination, interactional change, natural change, normative-reeducative change, planned change, socialization change, and technocratic change.

PERT chart *basic term*
See Figure on next page.

Pfeiffer, J. William
Co-developer, with John Jones, of the *Handbook of Structured Experiences for Human Relations Training* and *The Annual Handbook for Group Facilitators* used for small-group theory and methods.

phase alternate by line
See PAL.

phenomenology
A philosophical movement based on the work of Edmund Husserl, with the view that individual, subjective perceptions of reality are more important than objective reality.

photographic symbol
A representation of reality that symbolizes a concept.

physiological needs *basic term*
One of the levels of needs in Maslow's hierarchy of needs. *See* Maslow's hierarchy.

PERT chart *basic term*
A method of planning and tracking project completion with attention to the critical path. The relationship for and between each significant step is displayed to develop an overall plan. The strength of PERT charts is display of the relationship and dependency of steps. *Compare with* Gantt chart.

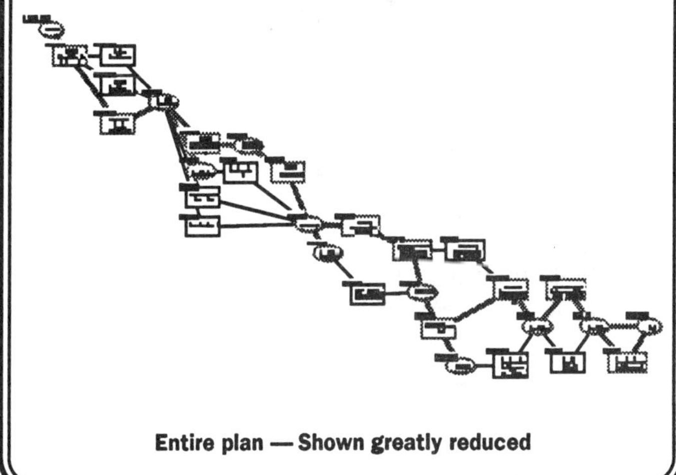

Entire plan — Shown greatly reduced

physiological variables
Differences in the physical and mental abilities of individuals.

Piaget, Jean
A Swiss developmental psychologist who spent many years evolving a theory describing the stages of thinking that children go through as they grow from early infancy to adulthood. *See also* cognitive development theory.

pie chart
A circular graph that shows relative size of categories of data. The area of the circle represents 100%. The circle is divided into sections that look like pieces of a pie. A pie chart is widely used because it is simple to interpret.

piggyback system
See embedded training.

pig in the python
See Figure on next page.

pilot program
See pilot test.

pilot test *essential 100 term*
1. The acquisition and analysis of data from outside the formal instructional environment to evaluate the instructional product in the operating environment. A formative evaluation step. In a pilot test, an instructional program is presented in final form to a portion of the target population. *Also called* field evaluation, field test, and field trial. *See also* formative evaluation *and* instruc-

Continued on next page

pig in the python
A graphic depicting the effect that results over time when two phenomena proceed in parallel, diverge away from each other, and resume their initial relationship. This is seen in HRD depicting the changes in use of a new technique that are not supported and abandoned. *See also* transfer of training.

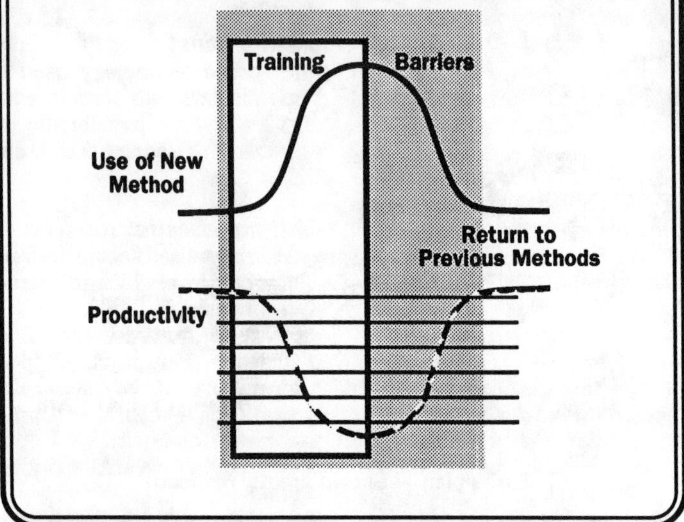

tional systems development (ISD). *Compare with* one-on-one trial *and* small group trial.
2. Loosely, the first trial of any instruction.

Pinto-Walker study
A study conducted by ASTD in 1978 to determine what members did in their professional work. The study produced 104 tasks, behaviors, knowledges, and abilities.

pitch
Slang expression for a presentation (especially sales). Also refers to vocal tone or scale.

pitch shift
Variation in the vocal pitch of a speaker. A desirable technique for a speaker.

pixel
One display picture element. The smallest unit of an electronic image. Pixel refers to the basic element of which displays are composed. Display resolution is directly related to the total number of pixels. *See also* resolution.

placard
A cardboard or posterboard visual aid normally used on a felt board or hook-and-loop board. *See also* felt board.

placebo effect *basic term*
Efficacy of a treatment having no authentic effect. Due to a subject's tendency to believe in the treatment's effectiveness because it is administered in an authentic setting.

place keeping
One feature of a technology-based instructional management system. The computer keeps track of what the users have completed. When users sign off, a place keeping system identifies the place to which they are returned when they sign on again.

plain vanilla instruction
See generic courseware.

plan, do, check, act (PDCA)
PDCA is called the Deming cycle. *See* Deming cycle.

planned change *essential 100 term*
In organizational development, a change process characterized by mutual goal-setting and equal power on both sides. *Compare with* emulative change, coercive change, indoctrination, interactional change, natural change, socialization change, and technocratic change.

planning
The fifth step in action research. Planning shifts the focus of attention from problem identification to solution identification. *See also* action research.

plan of instruction (POI) *basic term*
Often heard in abbreviation form P-O-I, the POI is used primarily for course planning, organization, and operation, and outlines a course broken down into lessons and modules. For every block of instruction within a course, it includes the lesson objective, learning objectives, duration of instruction, presentation plan, resources, and media support materials, and an indicator of how the student will be tested. The POI describes the instructional program in sufficient detail to enable a reader to grasp the requirements, strategy, activities, and outcomes of the instruction. Synonymous with program of instruction. *Also called* a syllabus.

plasma panel
The screen technology used in some displays that permits a flat display. Has a characteristic orange color. *Compare with* LCD *and* CRT.

platform *essential 100 term*
1. A slightly raised floor in the front of a room from which an instructor presents.
2. Reference to presenter-led instruction. For example, "platform instructor" or "on the platform." Sometimes called boards. *See also* standup trainer.
3. The instructor's area and function.
4. A reference to a particular computer setup. For example, a combination of hardware and software capable, or not, of supporting a particular instructional package.

platform presentation *basic term*
A formal lecture presentation style, as opposed to other methods.

platform skills
A synonym for presentation skills.

pleasant learning restimulation
An instructional technique based on recalling an early pleasant learning experience when the learner was eager to learn and classroom failure had not yet stymied learning. The learner is encouraged to return to that situation once again. Pleasant learning restimulation is

Continued on next page

useful in motivating some groups of learners.

plenary session *basic term*
A session involving all the participants in a meeting or conference.

plotter
An output device that draws with one or more pens, often on large size paper. Useful for graphics.

pocket job aid
A small or wallet-sized job aid. Pocket job aids are designed to be carried by an individual and accessible whenever needed. The Miranda card U.S. police officers use is a well-known example. An exception to the typical card size is the police officer's *Patrol Guide.* This is a small book always carried to provide needed help.

podium *basic term*
A specific place or raised platform for the speaker to stand. Often erroneously used to describe a lectern.

point
A key idea in a presentation. The point may be the main point or a subpoint.

point/counterpoint
See straw man.

pointer
Instrument used by presenter to direct audience attention to a specific part of a visual. May be a physical wand, flashlight-type instrument, or laser pointer.

policy
A broad description of preferred actions intended to ensure coordination within a department or between departments. A policy is activated through procedures.

policy deployment
A strategic management planning process to concentrate the organization's efforts into examining, managing, and improving the organization's key processes, and communicating this information throughout the organization. *See also* hoshin planning *and* strategic planning.

polling
1. A technique of OD data gathering. *See also* OD data gathering.
2. A methodology for research into opinions. Polling is sometimes used in needs analysis. *See also* Delphi technique *and* needs analysis.

population
1. In research, the universe of data under investigation from which a sample will be taken.
2. *See also* target population.

portrait
The orientation of a display. Portrait is vertical orientation, as this page. *Compare with* landscape.

position
The duties and tasks established as the work requirement for one individual. A position exists whether occupied or vacant.

positive benefit
In benefit computation, when a benefit produces a return greater than 1:1.

positive feedback *basic term*
A response to an act or event that serves to encourage repetition of the same type of action. Positive feedback is given when any sign of improvement occurs. *See also* negative feedback.

positive reinforcement *basic term*
Any favorable consequence or recognition directed at the learner. Positive reinforcement is provided upon the learner's demonstration of a desirable behavior. Learners are more likely to repeat activities for which they receive positive reinforcement. *Compare with* negative reinforcement.

positive skew
When scores are grouped near the low end of the scale. For example, if the value plotted was quality, it reflects a tendency for *all* units to have low quality.

positive transfer
In training transfer, when prior learning helps the learner acquire new knowledge or skills. Positive transfer is also known as proactive facilitation. *Compare with* negative transfer.

postcourse evaluation *basic term*
A survey conducted after the student has had time to use the skills learned in the classroom back on the job. *Also called* post evaluation or post training survey.

post-delivery (activities)
Any follow-up activities after a presentation.

poster
A cardboard or posterboard visual aid that rests on an easel or other mounting system.

post evaluation
See postcourse evaluation *and* post test.

postevaluation
See postcourse evaluation *and* post test.

post hoc fallacy
In research, when behavior is incorrectly associated with a cause for that behavior.

post-production
In video production, the stage after the original footage has been shot. Post-production includes editing, encoding, and computer program authoring.

post-secondary *basic term*
1. Any formal learning provided above the high school level.
2. Loosely, a synonym for vocational education.

post test *essential 100 term*
Any assessment of learners after they complete an exercise. Post tests are often used to measure the learner's mastery of the course objectives. The post test is sometimes compared to the pretest to determine learning gained. *See also* instructional systems development (ISD), learning objective, mastery learning, performance-based instruction, and mastery learning.

post training survey
See postcourse evaluation.

power pole
Metal columns used in a learning center to provide a ceiling-to-floor path for cables.

predictive validity *basic term*
The extent to which an instrument can predict future behaviors or results. Predictive validity can be calculated and expressed as a correlation coefficient relating the instrument in question to the measure of the predicted results or behavior.

pre-knowledge
The relevant knowledge that a par-

Continued on next page

ticipant should have before beginning an exercise. *See also* prerequisite.

pre-mastering
In videodisc production, when the master tape is checked and prepared for final transfer onto the master disc. All delivery discs will be pressed from the master disc.

pre-production
In video production, all design tasks that lead up to the actual shoot. For example, storyboarding and scriptwriting.

prerequisite *essential 100 term*
Any knowledge or skill that must be acquired by the learner before other new knowledge or skills can be learned. When these are taught in a specific course, that course may become the prerequisite.

prerequisite levels
Four Levels of Prerequisites are suggested by William Rothwell and Henry Sredl: Level 1—The minimum basis for selection into the organization or into a group; Level 2—The minimum basis for selection into a role or job class with specific entry requirements, such as an academic degree in a particular field, experience in an occupation, or skill/competence equivalent to a degree and experience; Level 3—The minimum basis for selection into a discrete learning experience; and Level 4—The minimum basis for selecting those who will progress from one unit or lesson to the next.

prerequisite session
Conference sessions that require a credential, prior knowledge, or prerequisite experiences. Prerequisite sessions are rarely seen in HRD.

prerequisite training
See prerequisite.

preretirement education *basic term*
Learning activities for persons facing retirement, designed to assist them in developing and implementing a personal plan for retirement.

prescription generation *basic term*
The process of matching a learner accurately with the instructional materials actually needed by that individual, based on the results of a test. One of the modes of CMI. The others are testing and record keeping.

prescriptive learning *basic term*
A learning design in which each learner is measured against a set group of skills and then assigned learning activities based on this measurement. *Compare with* performance-based instruction.

presentation *basic term*
Any communication delivered to an audience.

presentation dynamics
In a presentation, the eye contact, gestures, pacing, and voice variety.

presentation skill
The HRD competency of presenting information orally so that an intended purpose is achieved. *See also* HRD Roles and Competencies Study.

presentation system
In technology-based learning, the special software that enables the lessons to run on a particular computer without the presence of the authoring software. Some vendors

have a licensing fee for this software. *Also called* run-time system.

pre-service programs *basic term*
Pre-service programs include occupational education or job instruction developed or arranged by the organization for employees prior to beginning the job. Pre-service programs illustrate HRD activities for non-employees. *Compare with* in-service programs.

Prestel
A British videotex system. *See* videotex. *Compare with* Antiope *and* Telidon.

pretest *essential 100 term*
An assessment test given to participants before a learning activity to determine what level of knowledge, skill, or aptitude they bring to the instruction. Pretests are often used to generate an instructional prescription for needed learning. *Compare with* post test.

prevention
In quality, direction of analysis and action toward correcting a production process.

pride chart (pride document)
In executive development, an objectives document. Pride chart is derived from its content, which is a list of the 10 most important results to be achieved if the executive and staff are to be proud of themselves.

primary tension
The inhibitions of group members during the early period of group development. Primary tension is the group equivalent of stage fright. *See also* secondary tension.

principles approach
Facilitation of transfer to new contexts. The principles approach is based on presenting general principles and guidelines that have broad applicability.

print
The medium that involves words, pictures, or symbols on paper. *Compare with* audio.

print learning preference
An individual learning style based on preference for reading and writing. *See also* aural, haptic, interactive, kinesthetic, olfactory, and visual learning styles.

prioritization matrices
A quality process management and planning tool used to prioritize tasks, issues, or possible options based on known weighted criteria. Prioritization matrices are useful when narrowing options or ranking importance of similar items, or when resources are limited.

prior learning assessment (PLA)
The term PLA is related to accreditation of prior learning. Preferred in the U.S. *See also* accreditation of prior learning (APL) *and* recognition of prior learning (RPL).

prior-to-hire program
HRD activities provided by organizations to prospective employees. Prior-to-hire programs are usually free and without obligation to either party.

prisoner's dilemma
A popular case presented for group discussion to illustrate the trade-offs between cooperation and competition.

Private Industry Council (PIC)
Groups consisting of the local business community and labor, education, and economic development agencies. In cooperation with local government, PICs administer grants under the Job Training and Partnership Act to train unemployed workers with low incomes for new jobs.

proactive *basic term*
Taking action *before* events make it necessary. Proactive is the opposite of reactive or waiting to take action after an external requirement forces it. *Compare with* reactive.

probes
In interviewing, short comments or questions to stimulate the respondent. Used to guide the interview. *Compare with* closed response question.

problem-centered learning *basic term*
Use of actual organizational problems or situations as the focus for instruction.

problem solving *basic term*
1. Solving complex problems when there is no obvious, and possibly no single correct, answer. A problem-solving approach often requires the creative use of rules, procedures, techniques, and principles.
2. A group instruction method, based on discussion of a scenario. The small groups develop a set of proposals to solve the problem. In the large group, each proposal is critically discussed as it is presented. *Also called* scenario technique.

procedural analysis
Sequencing instruction based on the steps needed to perform an activity, task, or procedure.

procedural approach
Identification of the subordinate skills in a psychomotor goal. The procedural approach is used to expand the description of each component.

procedural intervention
In organizational development, an intervention based on evaluation of how OD steps may or may not help solve the problem at hand.

procedures *basic term*
Detailed guidance on how a task is to be done or how activities should be handled.

procedures trainer
A nondynamic system that allows procedural training to be accomplished. A procedures trainer may take the form of a mockup or a cockpit procedures trainer.

process *basic term*
1. The combination of people, machine and equipment, raw materials, methods, and environment that produces a given product or service.
2. A sequence of events or actions continuously changing over time. A process usually is a progression toward a goal.

process capability
The repeatability and consistency of a process. The statistically determined pattern or distribution can then be compared to specification limits to determine whether a process can meet established specifications.

process-centered game
A game in which the subject mat-

ter is far less important than the activities that the exercise involves.

process decision program chart
A quality process management and planning tool useful when faced with an unfamiliar problem or goal and a contingency plan is needed. The process decision program chart is useful when you need to identify likely things that can go wrong in a plan and to identify reasonable countermeasures.

process evaluation *basic term*
An evaluation that studies the interaction and dynamics of a group during an exercise rather than the achievement of learning objectives.

process mapping
A technique used to graphically depict processes across organizations for the purpose of analysis and improved management. Every step involved, no matter how small, is depicted.

Prodigy
A popular, commercial service that connects personal computers via modem and provides services such as electronic encyclopedia, news, weather, sports, and games. *See also* CompuServe.

producer
See executive producer *and* line producer.

product concentration marketing
A marketing method for HRD activities offerings. *Compare with* full coverage, market specialization, product specialization, and selective specialization marketing.

production
In video, the period when footage is actually shot. *See also* pre-production *and* post-production.

production assistant
In video production, an all-purpose assistant who replaces the production manager, assistant director, and associate producer.

production manager
In video production, the chief crewperson.

productivity
1. The sum of quality and quantity of work performed by a group.
2. The output of a group's task dimension.

productivity analysis
Comparison of the combination of effectiveness and efficiency of HRD programs. *See also* productivity model.

productivity mission
A formal statement of specific goals for different populations in terms of results, outputs, or resource inputs.

productivity model
In cost-benefit analysis, a model that measures both efficiency and effectiveness. In the productivity model, the results of matching specific learning variables resources with specific performance variables results in linked costs and outcomes. *Compare with* resource requirements, life cycle, and benefits models.

products
See package.

product specialization marketing
A marketing method for HRD activities offerings. *Compare with* full coverage, market specialization,

Continued on next page

product concentration, and selective specialization marketing.

profession *basic term*
1. Any field or discipline in which the central elements are distinct from other fields or disciplines. For example, HRD.
2. An occupation requiring licensure.

professional
1. Any person practicing in a profession.
2. Loosely, any person whose work is characterized by proficiency, timeliness, and integrity.
3. Anyone whose work requires lengthy formal educational preparation.

professional certification
A voluntary process by which a professional association or organization identifies individuals who are competent from those who are not. Professional certification does not exist in the HRD field. Credentialing of HRD practitioners has been studied by HRD-related organizations. In the U.S., the process resulted in the ASTD Model for Excellence study to determine professional HRD roles and competencies. *See also* certification. *Compare with* accreditation *and* licensure.

Professional Development Accreditation Program (PDAP)
OSTD's self-assessment process that accredits individuals in the field of Training Development. *See also* accreditation *and* Ontario Society for Training & Development. (OSTD)

Professional Organizational Development Network
A professional society of interest to some OD professionals.

professional practice area (PPA)
Organizational units of ASTD providing special interest affiliation for members.

professional services *basic term*
1. Consulting based on knowledge and skills of the consultant.
2. Professional staff time devoted to assisting an organization in conflict resolution, problem solving, needs analysis, or other activities aimed at developing the personnel in the organization.

proficiency
1. The degree to which a skill has been attained.
2. *See* criterion.

proficiency certification
Certification of the trainee-worker's proficiency for each task and objective. Proficiency certification is characteristic of on-the-job training and is often recorded on a task certification form.

profit center *basic term*
A form of financial arrangement for the HRD function. Under that system, the HRD unit is expected to sell its services, sometimes externally. There may also be the policy that if a component of the organization can obtain the same quality service from outside the company, it is free to do so. This encourages the profit center to compete with outside suppliers.

program *basic term*
Any learning activity with a definite beginning and ending. A program is composed of units and lessons. *Also called* course, seminar, or workshop.

program administrator
The HRD role of ensuring that the facilities, equipment, materials, participants, and other components of a learning event are present and that program logistics run smoothly. *See also* HRD Roles and Competencies Study.

program book
A conference guide for attendees. The program book includes the session's time, place, and description. It may also include information about the sponsoring organization, speaker information, and organization of the conference sessions into meaningful subdivisions called tracks. *Compare with* conference program book.

program design
See instructional systems development (ISD).

program designer
The HRD role of preparing objectives, defining content, and selecting and sequencing activities for a specific program. *See also* HRD Roles and Competencies Study.

program fees
Any fees for seminars, workshops, or HRD programs. Program fees may cover the costs for delivering an HRD program as well as factors for development and overhead.

programmed instruction *basic term*
A self-instructional method in which information is presented in precisely planned steps or increments, almost always in text form. The appropriate response immediately follows each step. Development of computers to perform the control and branching, as CAI, have led to the near disappearance of paper-based programmed instruction. *Compare with* CAI. *See also* behaviorism, operant conditioning, and participatory methods.

programmed learning
See programmed instruction.

programmer
1. The person who codes computer programs, including CBL and expert systems. *See* programming. *Compare with* author.
2. A device that controls sequencing of visuals and multiple equipment. A programmer is primarily used in multi-image presentations.

programmer ready materials (PRM) *basic term*
In technology-based learning, the output of the designer-developer during the development process. The programmer can completely program the instruction based solely on the content of the materials and without the need for further collaboration. Storyboards are the major component of PRM. *See also* storyboard.

programming
See programmer.

programming aid (utility) (system)
See authoring aid.

program objectives
The desired outcomes of a program.

program of instruction (POI)
A term favored in U.S. military instruction, synonymous with plan of instruction. *See* plan of instruction (POI).

Program on Noncollegiate Sponsored Instruction (PONSI)
Usually heard in acronym form, PONSI is a program sponsored by the American Council on Education in which companies invite college faculty to evaluate company courses to determine their equivalence to formal associate, baccalaureate, or graduate level courses. Higher education institutions may or may not accept the recommendation for transfer credit.

program package
See instructional materials package.

program plan
A description of what a program will cover.

program policy *basic term*
A description of purpose of the HRD department, major activities, services, responsibilities, and guidelines.

progress check
A question used to verify participant's progress and understanding. Sometimes called a double-check question.

progressive disclosure *basic term*
A technique often used with overhead transparencies to build complexity and add dramatic effect. Progressive disclosure involves showing only one part of a visual at a time and building up to the complete visual. The most common technique is to cover the points not yet discussed with a sheet of paper—preventing the audience from seeing them until wanted. The sheet of paper is then moved to reveal each point in turn. *Also called* revelation.

projected still video
The medium that involves projected still video images. For example, 35mm slides. *Compare with* print.

projection (voice)
The carrying power of a presenter's voice.

project management skill
The HRD competency of skill in planning, organizing, and monitoring work. *See also* HRD Roles and Competencies Study.

Project Opportunity
Programs for workers whose previous jobs have been eliminated.

projector
Machines that use light to put an image onto a screen. Projector types include 16mm motion picture, 35mm slide, overhead, opaque, and filmstrip.

project-related organization chart
See organization chart.

project structure
See matrix structure.

prompted systems
A synonym for menu-driven (systems). *See* menu-driven.

prompter operator
In video production, the person who operates a teleprompter, which allows the narrator to read long sections of dialogue without memorization.

propensity to transfer
A measure of learners' relative inclination to apply the knowledge and skills gained from training. Their propensity to transfer is an

assessment of commitment to change if the opportunity occurs.

proposmo
The conclusion or hypothesis of a speech. It can be tested intellectually. A rhetorical term. A key feature of a good speech.

protected profit center
A subsidized profit center. A protected profit center prices its products and services for essential programs below cost to ensure their availability to organizational units. The overall budget provides the necessary funds. *See also* profit center.

protégé
A person who is guided and supported by a mentor. *Compare with* mentor.

prototype *basic term*
A working model of any learning activity.

prototyping
Developing a limited working model of a system. The purpose of prototyping is to obtain user feedback about the system before committing resources to final system development.

proxemics
An area of nonverbal communications related to the use and structuring of physical space between people.

psychodrama
A therapeutic method using role playing, developed by Jacob Moreno, that encourages participants to confront their feelings by performing as actors and actresses in a planned drama. Psychodrama requires a well-qualified leader. *See also* role play.

psychological theory
In career planning, the theory that early childhood has a critical impact on an individual's subsequent career choices. Psychological theory claims that work is really a sublimation of infantile impulse, and that occupations can be described in terms of the needs they help satisfy.

psychological variable
Any difference between individuals that results from attitude, learning, perception, personality, and motivation.

psychometrics
The use of mathematical methods to measure and analyze socio-psychological data.

psychomotor *essential 100 term*
The area of learning associated with physical movement and skills. *Compare with* affective *and* cognitive.

psychomotor domain
See psychomotor.

psychomotor learning *basic term*
In Bloom's taxonomy, the demonstration of some physical skill or performance of some task—for example, repairing a diesel engine. *See also* Bloom's taxonomy and cognitive science. *Compare with* affective learning *and* cognitive learning.

psychomotor objective *basic term*
A learning objective that specifies muscular coordination and movement, manipulation of materials and objects, or an act which requires neuromuscular coordination. *See also* learning objective.

Continued on next page

Compare with affective *and* cognitive objectives.

psychomotor skill game
A game in which success depends mainly on the psychomotor skill of the player(s).

psychomotor skills
Coordinated mental and physical activities to accomplish a task.

public address system
Any equipment needed to amplify voice or other sounds to enable a large group to hear them. *Also called* sound system.

Public Personnel Management
A periodical of interest to HRD practitioners involved in personnel issues. *Public Personnel Management* is published by the International Personnel Management Association.

public relations
Any unreimbursed information about, or any promotion of, HRD offerings to potential users. An example is information about graduates in a company newsletter. *Compare with* sales promotions, personal selling, and mass selling.

punctuation
In a system, the process of organizing the sequence of acts or events in order to discover meaning and significance in the sequence.

punisher
Any consequence that tends to decrease the behavior it follows. For example, harsh words. *See also* behavior modification, cognitive learning, operant conditioning, and reinforcement. *Compare with* reinforcer.

purpose
The objective of a presentation.

Pygmalion effect *basic term*
The concept, confirmed by Albert Moll's research, that one's expectations about a future event can affect the likelihood of its occurrence. The Pygmalion effect is named after a figure in Greek mythology and a play by George Bernard Shaw that became the movie *My Fair Lady*. It is a positive example of the self-fulfilling prophecy. It means that the expectation by the person in charge that an individual will do well leads to the individual actually doing well. *See also* expectancy model, Hawthorne Effect, and self-fulfilling prophecy.

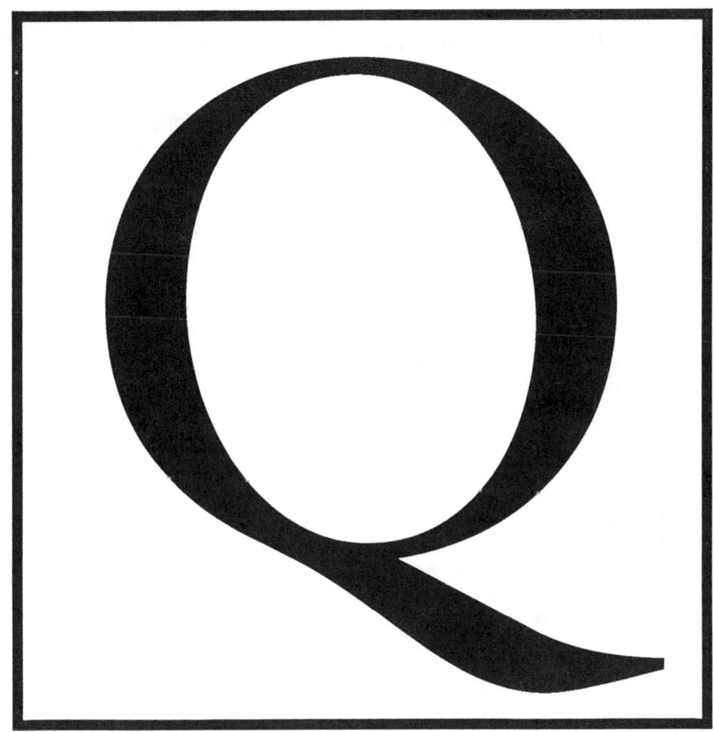

Q&A session
See question-and-answer session.

quad
A group of four persons.

quadrivium
The four subjects upon which an advanced education was based in medieval times. The quadrivium were arithmetic, astronomy, geometry, and music. *See also* trivium.

qualification training
"Hands-on" task performance instruction designed to qualify an incumbent in a specific duty position. Qualification training may be combined with on-the-job training to provide the performance skills required to do the job.

qualifying education
Any educational background that provides an individual with the necessary credentials for career advancement within the organization or outside.

qualifying training
Instruction designed to provide an individual with the basic knowledge, skills, and attitudes needed to satisfy job requirements. *See also* basic skills training. *Compare with* remedial training, retraining, and second-chance training.

quality
A measure of the extent to which an element in experience meets a need, solves a problem, or adds value for someone.

Quality and Productivity Management Association
A professional society of interest to some HRD professionals.

quality circles *basic term*
A technique for improving production quality based on the Japanese QC (quality control) circles methodology. One of several team-based techniques used in organizations' quality programs.

quality costs
A concept developed by Armand Feigenbaum that places costs in four categories: (1) prevention, (2) appraisal, (3) internal failure, and (4) external failure. *See also* hidden factory *and* total quality management (TQM).

quality of work life (QWL)
essential 100 term

1. Individual and collective perception on the part of employees that relates to their total experience as a member of the organization.
2. Programs in organizations focused on enhancing policies, procedures, and physical working conditions.

quality process tools
See seven quality process tools.

Quality Progress
A periodical of interest to HRD practitioners involved in the quality process. *Quality Progress* is published by the American Society for Quality Control.

quarterly training briefing (QTB)
A conference conducted by U.S. active component division commanders to approve the short-range plans of battalion commanders.

quarterly training guidance (QTG)
A U.S. active component training management document published at each level from battalion to division that addresses a three-month planning period. The QTG adjusts, as required, the training guidance contained in long-range plans, and further develops this guidance to include specific training objectives for each major training event.

quartet
A group of four persons.

quartile
In statistics, points marking a distribution into four parts. For example, the third quartile is located at the 75th percentile. *See also* percentile.

quasi-experimental design
In research, the collective term for designs similar to true experiments, except that assignment of subjects to groups is not random. *Compare with* experimental design.

question
See clarifying question, direct question, open question, or overhead question.

question-and-answer panels
basic term
An instructional technique based on a list of questions distributed before the Q&A session. At the session, the answers may be pro-

vided by a panel of the students or invited guests. *See also* question-and-answer session.

question-and-answer session *basic term*
At any meeting, the time set aside for audience questions. In formal presentations, question-and-answer sessions are typically scheduled at the end. Many presenters prefer to take questions whenever they occur to a learner. *See also* question-and-answer panels.

question-answer sessions
See question-and-answer session.

questioning skill *basic term*
The HRD competency of gathering information by stimulating insight in individuals and groups through interviews, questionnaires, and other probing methods. *See also* HRD Roles and Competencies Study.

questionnaire *basic term*
A list of questions used in gathering information on a specific subject. Questionnaires may be a formal part of a research project or an informal method of collecting HRD-related information.

Quick Start
A program based on grants to educational institutions to train employees for new business or industry.

quintile
In statistics, points marking a distribution into five parts. For example, the third quintile is located at the 60th percentile. *See also* percentile.

quiz mode
An instructional technique that provides learners with the correct response immediately after they have responded to a question.

qwerty keyboard
(Pronounced kwer′-tee.)
The qwerty keyboard is the usual keyboard arrangement found on standard typewriters in English-speaking countries. It is named by the keys in the upper row: the leftmost key is "q," the next is "w," and so on. In advertising, a qwerty keyboard is sometimes made to sound like a feature. The qwerty keyboard is (rarely) called the Scholes keyboard after its originator. An alternate keyboard format is Dvorak. *Compare with* Dvorak keyboard.

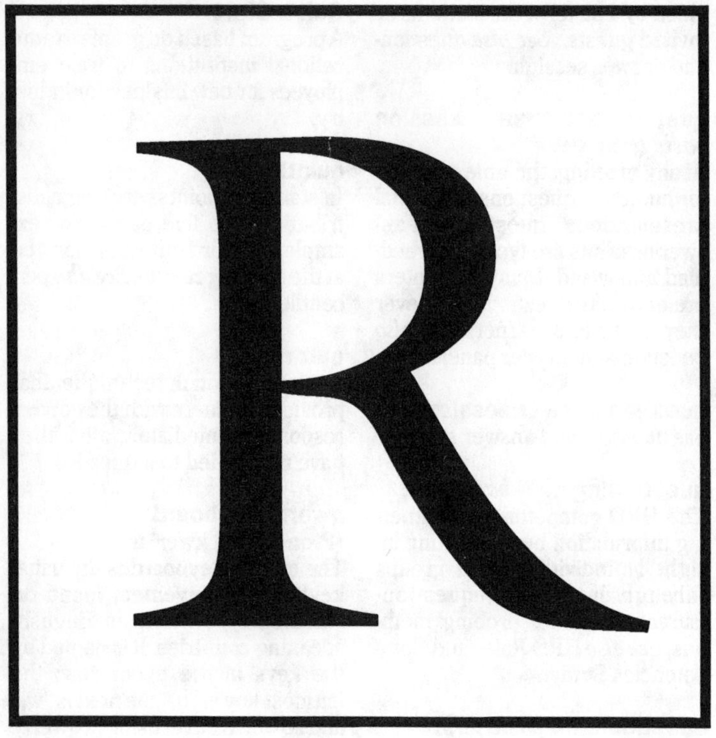

radial
Games in which several groups or individuals have different information that they feed into an information pool, based on which decisions can be made.

RADIOVISION
A radio broadcast coordinated with live instruction. RADIOVISION instruction is much like a slide-tape presentation presented by broadcast radio. Predistributed 35mm slides are advanced on a signal in the receiving classroom. RADIOVISION has been used in the U.K. and Francophone Africa.

ragged (justification)
Type with one or both margins uneven. *Compare with* centered *and* flush right or left justification.

raised floor
See access floor.

random access *basic term*
Refers to the ability to directly reach an information item without accessing other items. This capability is inherent in disc media. It is also a capability of a random access 35mm slide projector. Random access is usually associated with laserdisc technology.

random number
Numbers specifically generated to represent complete chance. Random numbers are used in research.

random number table
A computer-generated table of random numbers. *See also* random number.

random object play
A variation on random word play in which the attributes of an object are used as trigger words for generating original ideas. *Compare with* random word play.

random sample *basic term*
In research, a sample in which all members of the population had an equal chance to be selected. In HRD some practitioners use this term when they select a group without a planned obvious basis. Such selection is *arbitrary*, not random.

random selection
The process of choosing a random sample.

random test item
In computer-based testing, a test question drawn from a test bank for presentation to a learner. Structured, non-random methods of test item selection are also used.

random word play
A creative individual or group problem-solving technique, based on forced relations, developed by Edward de Bono. In random word play, a word is selected from the dictionary that has no logical connection to the problem. Then the word is played with to suggest new thoughts. The new thought may indicate a solution to the original problem. *See also* creativity training.

range
A measure of the variation in a set of data. It is calculated by subtracting the lowest value in the data set from the highest value in that same set.

rapid prototyping
In technology-based learning design, the early development of a small-scale prototype used to test key features of the design.

rating scale
An instrument that provides a scale of values that describe something or someone who is being evaluated.

rational emotive therapy (RET)
A methodology developed by A. Ellis based on the concept that people are unhappy because they "catastrophize" about what is merely annoying or inconvenient and respond to their exaggerated conception. *See also* stress management.

rational theory *basic term*
In career planning, a theory that assumes people consciously select their careers. Occupational choice depends equally on a sense of personal identity and information about labor market demand.

reach-testing
In group process, introducing a new idea from an anchored position of group agreement in the spiral model. Other members test that idea through discussion and may accept, extend, reject, or revise it.

reaction (evaluation) (measures) *essential 100 term*
1. The first level of Kirkpatrick's model of summative evaluation. Learners indicate opinions, attitudes, or feelings of satisfaction or dissatisfaction with the learning experience. Data are col-

Continued on next page

lected with reaction sheets. Reaction evaluation is used in a majority of HRD situations. *See also* Evaluation Model, Four Level; learning evaluation; behavior evaluation; and results evaluation.

2. A measure of how well the training environment has been managed.
3. Loosely, how well learners liked an instructional experience—a measure of customer satisfaction.

reaction sheets
A document used to collect reaction evaluation data. *See also* reaction.

reactor panel
At a conference, a predesignated group of people representing the audience. A reactor panel listens to the session and asks clarifying questions.

readability (level) *basic term*
A measure of the level at which a sample of text is written. Readability level specifies the education level required of the reader (learner). Readability level may be calculated to produce a Flesch Reading Ease Score (number represents a percentage of American adults who can read the material), Flesch-Kincaid index (Flesch score converted to a grade level), or Gunning-Fog index (also a grade level).

reading
An instructional method based on assignments to read particular written content.

real estate
In video, the space available on a videodisc or videotape.

realia
Real things. The media that involve real objects.

realism
Correspondence of a game to the situation being simulated.

reality check *basic term*
An instructional technique to remind trainees that it may not be easy to apply the new skills learned in the presence of difficulties and obstacles.

real time *basic term*
The actual time over which a learning activity operates as opposed to any simulated time scale built into its structure.

rear screen
A translucent panel used as a screen in rear screen projection *See* rear screen projection.

rear screen projection
See Figure on next page.

recall
See retention.

reciprocity
In most social systems, a typical norm that encourages members to respond to the behaviors of others with similar behaviors.

recognition of prior learning (RPL)
The term RPL is related to accreditation of prior learning. Preferred in Australia. *See also* accreditation of prior learning (PLA) *and* prior learning assessment (PLA).

record keeping
Computers can capture more data about a learner than can be reasonably used. Typically, the CMI system will record success on pre-

rear screen projection
Projection that comes from behind the screen, as contrasted with normal (from the front) projection. This method offers learners a view of the projected information unencumbered by the projection equipment. The image (reversed) is projected through a translucent panel to form a normal image to the viewers. The setup is sometimes made more complex by the use of mirrors to reduce the size of the rear projection area.

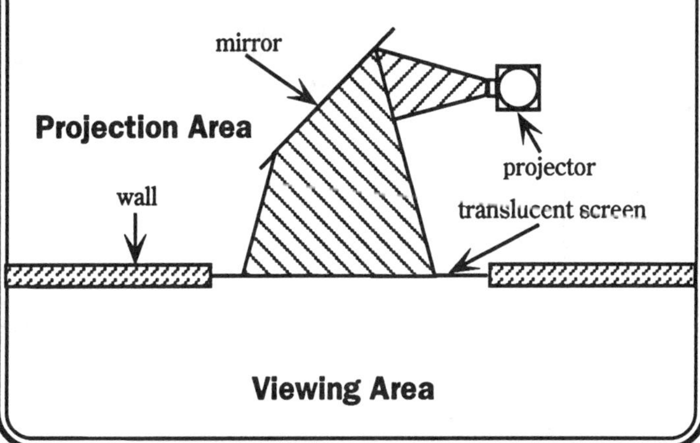

and post tests. One of the modes of CMI. The others are testing and prescription generation. *See also* grade book.

records-management skill
The HRD competency of storing data in easily retrievable form. *See also* HRD Roles and Competencies Study.

red, green, blue video
See RGB video.

redundancy
Repetition of information. Redundancy may be useful to improve reliability.

reel-to-reel
Audio- or videotape with physically separate lead and take-up reels.

reentry *basic term*
1. Return of an employee to the home country after completion of service in a foreign country.
2. Return of a learner to the work environment after instruction or a period of time away for any reason.

referent power
The power of charisma.

refreezing *basic term*
A phase in Kurt Lewin's Change Model. New skills must become habitual. New habits are best frozen through regular practice opportunities. Applicable to the transfer of training process. *Compare with* unfreezing. *See also* transfer of training.

refresher training *essential 100 term*
Training conducted to renew previously learned skills of people who have previously been proficient but require a reorientation to a task. Military refresher training includes a walkthrough and is conducted prior to sustainment training.

registrant
When learning is involved, the learner who has formally enrolled in the learning experience. *See also* learner.

registration
In technology-based learning, entering the necessary data about a learner into the system, so that a student will be recognized by the system at "sign-on." *See also* sign-on.

rehearsal
1. Physical rehearsal involves actually going through the steps of the planned performance.
2. Mental rehearsal consists of imaging the planned performance. *See also* imagery.

reinforcement *essential 100 term*
1. Actions designed to reward or encourage a desired behavior; a central tenet of the theory of operant conditioning. Reinforcement of the learner's correct performance should be rewarded in order to increase the likelihood of successful performance in the future. *See also* behaviorism *and* operant conditioning
2. Praise or encouragement of the learner's performance. Reinforcement will strengthen the learner's interest and motivation. *See also* positive feedback.
3. Provision of added learning tasks or data to aid the learner's comprehension and recall. *Also called* back-home or bridging tasks.
4. Loosely, strengthening skills or knowledge gained previously.

reinforcer
Any consequence that tends to encourage the reoccurrence of a behavior. For example, praise. *See also* behavior modification, cognitive learning, operant conditioning, and reinforcement. *Compare with* punisher.

relapse
The regression to a prior (less desirable) pattern of behavior despite previous training to perform differently. A relapse may allow a single slip to become the first step in a series of lapses.

relapse prevention
Specific activities undertaken to overcome a job environment that provides little or no support for newly acquired skills. *See also* transfer of training.

relationship-building skill
The HRD competency of adjusting behavior in order to establish relationships across a broad range of people and groups. *See also* HRD Roles and Competencies Study.

relationship intervention
In organizational development, an intervention focused on issues that arise when people work together.

relative benefit
In benefit computation, the comparison of the relative investment choices when two or more HRD options are available to address a performance problem.

relaxation training
Activities intended to help learners reduce elevations in such physiological indexes as heart rate, muscle tension, and blood pressure. Relaxation training focuses on reduction in external stimulation and focus on internal stimuli. *See also* stress reduction.

relay teaching *basic term*
An instructional delivery strategy to teach large numbers with a small cadre of ad hoc instructors. The cadre is taught, tested, and certified. In turn, each teaches 5 or 10 more who teach still others in a continuing succession. *Compare with* peer, sibling, and team teaching.

relevant practice
Practice of the substance of the learning objective. Relevant practice must be derived and provided for each objective. It includes any tools and equipment needed, as well as environmental requirements. Relevant practice also includes any other persons who may be required for practice to occur under realistic conditions.

reliability *essential 100 term*
The extent to which measurement results are free of unpredictable error. Tests that are reliable yield essentially the same results when readministered under different conditions. *See also* error and test-retest, alternate form, and split-half reliability. *Compare with* validity.

remedial education
See adult basic education.

remedial training
Instruction that provides job applicants or workers with the required entry-level knowledge, skills, and attitudes that they lack. *See also* basic skills training. *Compare with* retraining *and* second-chance training.

remote computer
A computer that is not at the learner's site. Typically, such a machine can be accessed through the telephone system and a computer terminal.

remote control
Control of audiovisual equipment from a distance.

remote production unit
In video production, a van that contains all of the video and audio equipment needed for production.

rental
A method of paying for temporary use of instructional materials. Rental of videotape and film based on a short period of use is common. *See also* leasing.

replacement planning
Planning that addresses who will fill projected vacancies. Replacement planning does not address how those individuals will be developed to become qualified to fill the vacancies.

repurposing
Modifying the content of an existing program to accomplish a task other than the one for which it was originally designed. Level One consumer videodiscs are often repurposed for Level Three use.

request for proposals (RFP) *basic term*
A request for proposals—RFP—invites bidders to submit proposals for a project and sets forth the particulars of the requesting organization's need. RFPs are is-

Continued on next page

sued by organizations that want a project done by an external individual or organization. The process begun with an RFP ends in a contract award. In some countries, the RFP is called a tender.

research *basic term*
Formal studies aimed at broadening the field of knowledge. Research may address issues regardless of the immediate applicability of findings. HRD practitioners are concerned with applied research. *See also* basic research *and* applied research.

research and development (R&D) *basic term*
1. Commonly referred to in its abbreviated form, R&D is any planned effort that does not support an immediate application, customer, or product. In its best use, R&D is focused on meeting the needs of customers with new or significantly improved products and services.
2. One of the phases of the life cycle model of cost-benefit analysis. *See also* life cycle model.

research cluster
The three roles of the HRD practitioner who is concerned with determining the need for formal, organized learning activities or the value of such activities in removing performance deficiencies. These roles are evaluator, needs analyst, and task analyst.

research design
The means by which evaluation is conducted.

researcher
The HRD role of identifying, developing, or testing new information (theory, research, concepts, technology, models, hardware, etc.) and translating the information into implications for improved individual or organizational performance. *See also* HRD Roles and Competencies Study.

research skill
The HRD competency of selecting, developing, and using methodologies, such as statistical and data collection techniques for a formal inquiry. *See also* HRD Roles and Competencies Study.

resistance to change *basic term*
Unwillingness to learn new skills; a learner phenomenon that works against HRD activities involving new procedures, roles, and traditions.

resolution *basic term*
The degree to which detail can be displayed. On a video monitor, resolution is measured in dots (pixel elements), vertically and horizontally. High resolution is necessary to display graphics. Low resolution is adequate for text. The best resolution of which an NTSC television screen is capable is low resolution. Overall size of the display does not alter the resolution. Resolutions are CGA (Color Graphics Adapter) 320 x 200 four color, 640 x 200 monochrome; EGA (Enhanced Graphics Adapter) 640 x 350 16 color; VGA (Video Graphics Adapter) 640 x 480 16 color. *See also* NTSC video.

resource allocation (cost allocation)
Considering costs as a resource for creating profit.

resource consultant
A professional who designs and implements HRD resource centers.

resource materials
The basic components of the package used in any exercise.

resource person
See consultant.

resource requirements matrix
A matrix of cells based on costs of personnel, equipment, facilities, and materials in association with analysis, design, development, implementation, and evaluation phases of ISD. A tool of the resource requirements model of cost-benefit analysis.

resource requirements model
In cost-benefit analysis, a model that identifies the relationships between costs and benefits. In this model, costs of personnel, equipment, facilities, and materials are associated with the five ISD phases: (1) analysis, (2) design, (3) development, (4) implementation, and (5) evaluation. *Compare with* benefits model, life cycle model, and productivity model.

resource-rich environment (rre) *basic term*
A display of resources that includes a variety of formats of instructional technology for enriching and enhancing traditional instruction. A resource-rich environment provides prerequisites before, and reinforcement after, classroom instruction.

response
Any activity induced by a stimulus. In instruction, *response* designates a wide variety of behaviors. For example, a response may involve a single word, selection among alternatives (multiple choice), solution of a complex system, or manipulation of keys. *See also* covert response *and* overt response.

response mode
The manner in which a learner responds. For example, writing a sentence, selecting an answer from a group of choices, or repairing a piece of equipment.

response time
The time between an entry on a computer terminal keyboard or screen and the resulting change of display. For example, the time it takes to have an answer judged by the computer system. Research shows that a response time of no more than .2 seconds is important.

restatement
One of the elements of a presentation's summary.

restraining forces
1. *See* barrier to transfer.
2. In organizational development, those forces that pull toward stability.

results *essential 100 term*
1. The fourth level of Kirkpatrick's summative evaluation model, focusing on measurable, tangible, positive changes in the organization due to training. For example, increased productivity. The results of instruction are compared to the purpose for which the instruction was originally planned. *Also called* impact. *See also* Evaluation Model, Four Level; learning; reaction; and results.
2. A bottom line measurement. Results measures include increased production, reduced scrap, or other benefit that was management's original goal for the training program. Ideally, a financial ROI calculation can be completed.

Resusci-Annie
A small simulator with a mannequin developed to enhance learning of cardiopulmonary resuscitation.

retention *basic term*
The degree to which newly acquired knowledge and skills are remembered by the learner after time has passed.

retention test
See criterion (referenced) test.

retirement planning
See preretirement education.

retraining *basic term*
1. Training employees to do two or more jobs as needed. *Also called* cross training.
2. Learning activities to provide additional employable skills, particularly to those who have lost their jobs or whose jobs are being phased out. *See also* upgrading training.

retreat *basic term*
A program conducted at a location that minimizes all outside communication in order to focus on a specific subject for a limited time.

return on investment (ROI) *essential 100 term*
In benefit computation, a ratio that expresses the relationship of the cost of performance value to the cost expended to achieve that value. *See also* cost-benefit analysis *and* evaluation.

revelation
See progressive disclosure.

reversal design
In research, when only one group is used and treatment is administered and then removed. Measurement is before, during, and after treatment.

reverse cycle training
Training which reverses the normal duty day so that training takes place during periods of reduced or limited visibility.

reverse engineering
A process of identifying steps and processes needed to produce a result by working backward from the result itself. The term is borrowed from the practice of preparing engineering drawings from an actual piece of equipment.

reverse image
A projected visual with content and background displayed opposite from standard projection, as in a photographic negative.

reverse role plays *basic term*
In role play, the situation in which participants switch roles at a critical moment in the role play. Reverse role plays are helpful for gaining understanding of another person's viewpoint or for seeing how oneself is perceived by others. *Also called* role reversal role play.

review *basic term*
1. A summary of information previously presented to a learner. It repeats key points, relates information to the whole, and helps learners to generalize to new situations.
2. Examining the presentation before it is actually given. A dry run.

RGB video
Universally called by its initials, the color video output of computers. RGB stands for red, green, blue.

rhetoric
The classical art of public speaking.

right brain
See whole brain learning.

right brain/left brain theory
See brain lateralization; creativity training.

right mode thinking processes
One of four whole brain learning descriptors. It includes cerebral and limbic right quadrants. Compare with left mode thinking processes. *See also* whole brain learning.

rightsizing
See downsizing.

RIO document
An objectives document used in executive development. The name is derived from its three parts: responsibilities, indicators, and objectives.

risky shift
The tendency of a group to make decisions involving greater risk. Risky shift decisions have a bigger payoff but a lower probability of attainment when compared with decisions made by individuals.

Rogers, Carl
The originator of client-centered therapy and encounter groups. Rogers had a significant impact on acceptance of the role of facilitator, as opposed to the role of teacher or instructor. *See also* facilitator *and* humanistic psychology.

role *basic term*
1. A set of behaviors expected of someone by virtue of job duties and status. A job title may match a role title, but a job often encompasses more than one role. *See also* HRD Roles and Competencies Study.
2. A position occupied by a group member in an interlocking network that includes all group members. Roles are defined in terms of the behaviors performed by the member.

role clusters
In the HRD Roles and Competencies Study, a group of related roles.

role modeling *basic term*
Providing a positive illustration of desirable behaviors for others to observe and imitate.

role play *essential 100 term*
1. An instructional technique based on learners assuming and acting out characters other than their own. Often the players are provided with scripts of background information on which to base their participation. Learners can examine previous behavior, try out new behaviors, or experiment with behaviors that might be potentially useful. Role play is often open-ended. Both players and the audience process the completed performance. Players self-critique the role play, with support from the facilitator, and may view a videotape of the role play. Role play is a descendent of psychodrama, a therapeutic technique developed by psychiatrist J. L. Moreno, in which patients act out their problems. *See also* multiple role play, reverse role play, and structured role play.
2. Practice of a newly learned or not yet mastered skill under observation. Learners are assigned their roles with specific instructions, sometimes includ-

Continued on next page

ing an ultimate course of action. The participant then practices the skill with other individuals to simulate the real-world setting to the greatest extent possible. *Also called* skill practice.
3. Loosely, an informal practice run of an on-the-job behavior.

role players
The key people potentially involved in bringing about successful transfer of training. Role players typically include the learner, learner's supervisor, instructor, higher management, peers, and subordinates.

role receivers
Role play participants who play a role.

role reversal role play
See reversal role play.

role rotation
A role play with only one play and role. The role is usually that of an individual who has a problem or is creating a problem. In role rotation, several learners attempt to use their skills to handle the situation. A number of persons rotate in the same role. Rotation can also be spontaneous.

role senders
Role play participants who deal with a person playing a role.

roman letter (type)
A category of letter style typified by thick and thin lines and the presence of serifs at the termination of strokes. *Compare with* italic.

ropes training
See adventure training.

Rosenthal effect
In research, the result of an experimenter unintentionally modifying the subject's behavior and confounding the results of the experiment.

rote learning *basic term*
Committing facts to memory without examination of purposes, logical relations, motivations, and consequences. *Compare with* meaningful learning.

rough
Preliminary material.

rough cut
In video production, a working copy of the final (edited master) tape.

router
In technology-based learning, a facility for directing the student from one place to another within the system. A router may present CAI automatically in a certain sequence, or it may route the learner through the CMI part of the system. *See also* computer managed instruction (CMI).

rule (of play)
The arbitrary constraints under which players of a game operate. Rules of play determine what players can and cannot do, who is winning, and when the game is over. Rules of play also provide a scoring system for the game.

Rul-Eg sequence
Rul-Eg is an abbreviation for from rule to example. An instructional approach to the teaching of concepts developed by M. David Merrill and colleagues. *Also called* expositive sequence.

Rummler, Geary
Well known for clear thinking in HRD, Rummler is the popularizer of the lean instruction concept. He

run chart
In quality control, a chart that plots data over a period of time to provide an indication of trends or patterns in a process. Run charts illustrate whether the average is shifting over time. Examples include equipment downtime or scrap produced per shift.

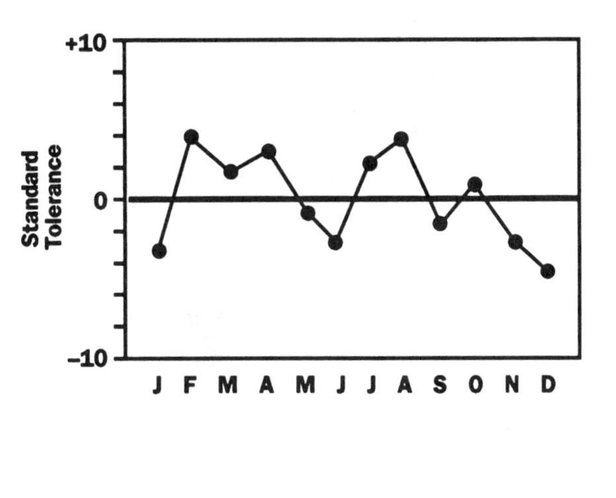

coauthored *Improving Performance* with Alan Brache. *See also* lean instruction.

run chart
See Figure.

runs
In quality control, the patterns in a run chart or control chart within which a number of points line up on only one side of the central line. Beyond a certain number of consecutive points (statistically based) the pattern becomes unnatural and suggests the need for attention.

run-time system
See presentation system.

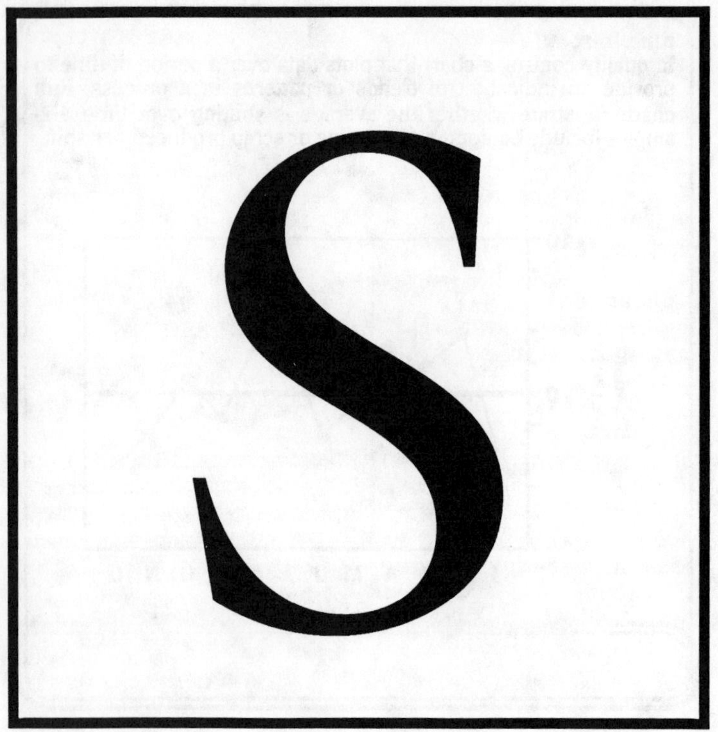

safe area
In video, the central area of a video frame that is certain to be displayed on any receiver or monitor. The outermost ten percent of the total picture is not reproduced in the same way on all displays.

safety needs *basic term*
One of the levels of needs in Maslow's hierarchy of needs. *See* Maslow's hierarchy.

sales promotions
Any non-personally communicated information or promotion regarding HRD offerings to potential users. An example is a catalog of offerings. *Compare with* public relations, personal selling, and mass selling.

sample *basic term*
1. In research, a subgroup of a population. *See also* random sample.
2. In quality process, one or more individual events or measurements selected from the output of a process. The sample is used to identify characteristics and performance of the whole.
3. A digital recording of an analog sound.

sand table
A type of terrain model similar to a sandbox. The sand table can be the source of a simple or elaborate approximation of terrain. A sand table can be easily reconfigured to represent a different location.

sans serif (type)
Type without serifs. *Compare with* serif.

Saskatchewan Training & Development Association (STDA)
A professional society for HRD practitioners in the Province of Saskatchewan. *See also* HR Canada.

satisfaction
Positive feelings about both outcomes and methods used to achieve them.

satisfiers
See motivation hygiene theory.

scaffolding
A cognitive apprenticeship technique. In scaffolding, the instructor performs parts of a task that the learner is not yet able to perform.

scaled format
A survey format. *See* Likert scale.

scatter diagram
See Figure.

scattergram
See scatter diagram.

scatterplot
See scatter diagram.

scenario
Background information regarding the setting of an exercise. The scenario may be brief or elaborate, with many charts and plentiful background and relevant data.

scatter diagram
A type of graphing technique that illustrates the relationships of one variable to another. Used to identify relationships and illustrate their strength. One type of quality control chart that shows the correlation between two variables. *Also called* scattergram and scatterplot. *See also* seven quality process tools.

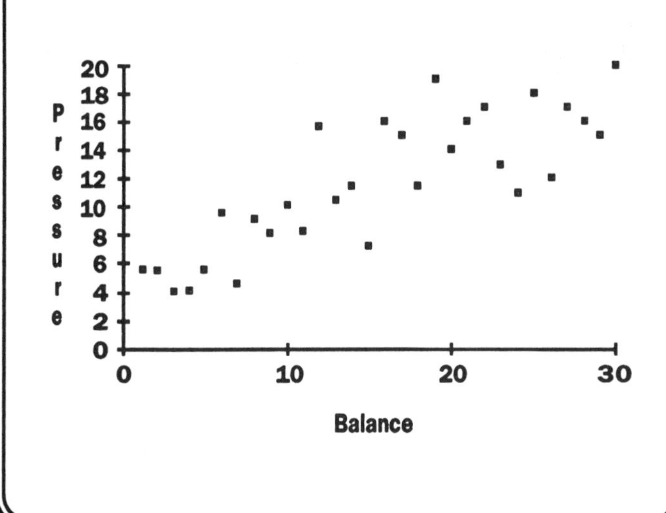

scenario technique
See problem solving.

scientific method *basic term*
A systematic process to investigate and draw conclusions about phenomena. The logic and procedures common to all the social sciences. The scientific method can be represented by the following steps.
1. Stating the problem
2. Forming a possible solution to the problem (hypothesis) based on a theory or rationale
3. Experimentation (gathering empirical data bearing on the hypothesis)
4. Interpretation of the data and drawing conclusions
5. Revising the theory or deriving further hypotheses for testing.

See also hypothesis.

scope *basic term*
The length or extent of coverage of a learning activity.

Scottish Vocational Education Council (SCOTVEC)
A system similar to the National Council for Vocational Qualifications operating in Scotland only. *See also* National Council for Vocational Qualifications (NCVQ) *and* national vocational qualifications (NVQ).

screen
1. A surface or special material onto which an image is projected.
2. The process of reviewing and making selections from among a greater amount of material.

script
1. In instructional delivery, a document based on a detailed outline that lists topics, subtopics, key points and the actual words that may be spoken by an instructor in delivering the instruction. A script is more specific than an instructor-independent outline. *Compare with* instructor-dependent outline *and* instructor-independent outline.
2. In video, the written directions for a program. The script includes dialog, camera directions, and setting.
3. In technology-based learning development, synonym for storyboard.
4. In transactional analysis, a lifelong plan for carrying out a particular game or series of games.

script person
In video production, the person who ensures that all of the script has been taped.

searcher
One of five career value structures identified by Edgar Schein. The others are technocrat, climber, builder, and stabilizer.

SECAM (video)
See Figure on next page.

secondary tension
Social discomfort typified by abrupt and abnormal departures from the routine functioning of a group. Secondary tension is induced by interpersonal conflict, environmental pressures, or feelings of frustration. *See also* primary tension.

second-chance training
Learning activities intended to remedy individual performance deficits. Second-chance training is focused on employees who have completed qualifying training but who do not yet meet the minimum job requirements. Second-chance training is a remedy when regular training fails. *Compare with* basic skills training, remedial training, and retraining.

SECAM (video)
The video output of videotape or disk players used mainly in France and some other countries where 50 hz. power is used. SECAM is an acronym for *sequential coúleur a memoire. Compare with* NTSC *and* PAL.

Countries with SECAM video

Afghanistan	Mali
Bulgaria	Mauritania
Cyprus	Mauritius
former Czechoslovakia	Monaco
Djibouti	Morocco
Egypt	Poland
France	Saudi Arabia
Greece	Surinam
Hong Kong	Togolese Republic
Iran	Uruguay
Libya	

second-person system
A virtual reality system based on a video camera input device. Users see images on a large video monitor or screen projection. *Compare with* total immersion system.

selected response question (item)
See closed response question.

selective specialization marketing
A marketing method for HRD activities offerings. *Compare with* full coverage, market specialization, product concentration, and product specialization marketing.

self-actualization *essential 100 term*
1. The fifth stage in Maslow's hierarchy. *See also* hierarchy of needs and humanistic psychology.
2. Loosely, the highest level of functioning of which an individual is capable.

self-actualization needs
One of the levels of needs in Maslow's hierarchy of needs. *See* Maslow's hierarchy.

self-analytic group
See sensitivity training.

self-awareness *basic term*
1. A developmental area addressed in organizational development. Self-awareness includes personal control or power needs, need to achieve, and need for affection. *Compare with* FIRO-B.

Continued on next page

2. Loosely, a deep knowledge of oneself and one's abilities.

self-contained electronic game
A game that makes use of an internal electronic data processing device.

self-development
The professional self-improvement efforts of an individual.

self-directed learning *essential 100 term*
An instructional design in which the learner takes the initiative to master predetermined material. Self-directed learning may be completed alone using self-instructional packages, or conducted with the help of others. Others may include instructors, tutors, mentors, resource people, and peers. *Also called* self-planned learning, self-education, self-instruction, self-study, or autonomous learning. *See also* andragogy, learner-centered instruction, learner-controlled instruction, and self-instruction. *Compare with* individualized learning, self-instruction, and self-paced instruction.

self-disclosure
Statements to others that reveal one's feelings, thoughts, beliefs, desires, or needs in the social situation.

self-fulfilling prophecy *basic term*
The principle that people tend to perform in accordance with what is expected of them. The self-fulfilling prophecy may originate from direct or indirect communication of a mental expectation regarding the probability of a future behavior, thus increasing its likelihood. The effects of the self-fulfilling prophecy can skew the results of program evaluation studies, most commonly in a positive direction. *Also called* the Pygmalion Effect. Self-fulfilling prophecy is not a synonym for Hawthorne effect. *See also* evaluation, expectancy model, Hawthorne effect, and Pygmalion effect.

self-instruction *basic term*
Any learning situation in which learners take responsibility for their own learning without relying on an instructor or other leaders of learning. *Compare with* individualized learning, self-directed learning, and self-paced instruction.

self-introduction
Introduction made to a group by each member, including their own name and other personal information.

self-knowledge
The HRD competency of knowing one's personal values, needs, interests, style, and competencies, and their effects on others. *See also* HRD Roles and Competencies Study.

self-managed work teams
An empowering method of task accomplishment in which the manager supplies the mission and the team takes on all managerial responsibility to complete it.

self-paced *basic term*
1. In individualized or self-directed learning, permitting learners to work at their own speed to complete the learning assignment.
2. In group instruction, operating at a speed set by learners as opposed to the instructor.

self-paced instruction *basic term*
Any method of instruction in which the learner determines the actual speed of progress within predefined limits. *Compare with* individualized learning, self-directed learning, and self-instruction.

self-reflective learning *basic term*
Personal learning directed at personal change. *Compare with* instrumental learning *and* didactic learning.

selling from the platform
A sales pitch by a presenter during a presentation. Selling from the platform is an objectionable behavior in a professional learning event.

semantic differential technique *basic term*
An evaluation technique involving the use of pairs of antonyms joined by a rating scale. The method is used to measure connotations of a given concept for an individual.

semantic (linguistic) memory
A form of long-term memory. Imaging can place episodes in our semantic memory. The image aids retrieval, and thus makes the episodes accessible. *See also* long-term memory.

seminar *essential 100 term*
An instructor-led learning activity. Often, the instructor is an expert or at least highly knowledgeable. Seminars are usually limited to a week or less and focus on a specific topic or problem. The seminar method is conceptually unsuited to introducing new material because each participant is expected to have something worthwhile to contribute to the session. Nevertheless, it is often used to present new material. *Compare with* workshop.

semiprofessional
See paraprofessional.

semiskilled workers
Those employees who require some special instruction. The instruction required is usually limited. For example, equipment operators.

senior
1. Those practitioners who have major career experience in any of the HRD roles and are acknowledged by their peers as people with expertise.
2. Any HRD practitioner who holds a responsible management position. The distinction is tied to the job rather than to the individual. For example, Director of HRD.

Also called senior trainer or senior HRD practitioner.

senior HRD practitioner
See senior.

senior trainer
See senior.

sensing (S)
In the Myers-Briggs typology, one of the eight basic predispositions included. *See* Myers-Briggs Type Indicator (MBTI).

sensitivity training *basic term*
Methods using intense interpersonal experiences to improve the individual's sensitivity to self and others. Sensitivity training should be conducted under the guidance of a trained person. *See also* encounter group, human relations training, L group, laboratory edu-

Continued on next page

cation, laboratory training, self-analytic group, and T-group.

sequence
In HRD, the order in which instructional components are delivered.

sequential learner
A person who learns by dealing with things and ideas one after an other or in order. *See also* learning style.

sequential learning *basic term*
An instructional technique that provides for increasingly difficult learning, based on previous knowledge and skills, and on planned desired outcomes.

serialist
A learning style describing people who follow a step-by-step learning procedure whereby they concentrate on one characteristic at a time to learn. *Compare with* holist.

serif (type)
Type with additional cross stroke at the end of the stroke, such as this type.

service
The work done by one person for the benefit of others.

service audit
A thorough assessment of the interaction between the organization and the customer at all known points of contact.

service leadership
Leadership with a focus on service. Service leadership includes attention to service to the customer, service to the organization, and service to the employees.

service management
A total organizational approach that makes the customer's perception of quality of service the driving force for operating the business.

service triangle
The three elements of service, identified by Karl Albrecht and Ron Zemke: strategy, people, and systems.

set
In video production, anywhere the shoot takes place.

seven quality process tools
A reference to the most commonly used tools in the quality process. The seven tools are (1) cause and effect diagram, (2) checklist, (3) control chart, (4) graphs (bar, line, and pie), (5) histogram, (6) Pareto diagram, and (7) scatter diagram.

shaping
A technique that reinforces successive approximations, starting with behavior that is already present. Gradually, more difficult material is presented and more sophisticated answers are required. For example, questions the student can answer already are followed by questions that the learner might infer.

sheer curtains
In learning centers, an open-weave drapery for windows to allow light without allowing clear vision outside.

sheer drapery
See sheer curtains.

Shewhart cycle
See Deming cycle.

short answer
A question format which requires the player to identify a person, place, or object in a few words or short statement.

short-range planning
The shortest of the planning processes used by organizations. Usually oriented to the following year. *Compare with* long- *and* mid-range planning.

short-term memory (STM)
basic term
Information of limited size (approximately seven information items) that is held in the brain for temporary use. In order to be remembered later it must be moved to long-term memory, encoded, and stored. Human beings use long-term and short-term memories unconsciously every day. *See also* information processing model. *Compare with* long-term memory.

showmanship
Any technique that an instructor can use to direct and hold attention during presentations.

sibling teaching
An instructional technique based on more experienced learners teaching newer ones. Both benefit and learn from this experience. *Compare with* peer, relay, and team teaching.

sigma
1. The Greek letter used to designate the estimated standard deviation.
2. A measure of quality. For example, six sigma represent high quality.

signal learning
That learning in which a conditioned stimulus signals an unconditioned stimulus.

sign-on (log-on)
1. The act of entering one's identity into the technology-based learning system to begin work or study.
2. The name one uses for recognition by a computer.

SIMNET
An acronym for Simulation Network, a U.S. Army project in which several military units and command and control functions are simulated so that the actions of any of the participants are reflected at the other simulation stations.

simple cluster sampling
In research, when a sample is selected from a fairly large population grouped into clusters. Simple cluster sampling can be useful anytime the population under consideration can be divided into a number of similar clusters. The ultimate savings is in preparation, cost, and administration of the sampling process.

simple random sampling
In research, when a sample is selected on a random basis. If a random sample is not used, the validity of the research can be questioned. The most common process for random selection from a relatively small population is through the use of random number tables. *See also* random number, random number tables, stratified random sampling, and systematic random sampling.

simplicity
The design principle that limits the number of visual components to those required for communication.

simulated case study
Any exercise which includes all the essential characteristics of simulations and case studies.

simulation *essential 100 term*
1. Any representation of an item of equipment, device, situation, system, or subsystem in realistic form. Simulation enables the learner to experience the operation of the target equipment without possibility of destruction of the equipment. The simulation may focus on a small subset of the features of the actual job-world situation.
2. Technology-based (usually part-task) simulation contrasts with the very costly, single-purpose special simulators typified by aircraft simulators. Each has a proper role. Simulation allows users to learn the operation of equipment without damaging it or harming themselves or others. Simulation is one of the modes of CAI. The others are drill and practice, instructional game, modeling, and tutorial. *See also* computer assisted instruction (CAI), Link trainer, part-task simulation, and simulator.
3. Any exercise that includes a simplified form of a real-life situation and games. Simulations usually have extensive designs with carefully determined decision points. Participants are given data about a number of conditions, situations, and critical decisions. The participants discuss the critical situations, make decisions, and get feedback about the consequences of those decisions. *See also* business game, game, in-basket exercises, case studies, and role plays.

Simulation Network (SIMNET)
See SIMNET.

simulator, full scale
A special, dedicated, single-purpose device with the sole purpose of simulating an entire object, device, equipment, or system. Full scale simulators are based on a combination of electronic and mechanical devices used in conjunction with computer programs. For example, a nuclear power plant control room simulator. *Also called* simulator training device. *See also* part-task simulation *and* part-task trainers.

simulator sickness
An unpleasant sensation common to users of virtual reality head-mounted displays. *See also* virtual reality.

simultaneous translation
Translation of a speaker's message into another language at the same time it is spoken. In HRD situations this requires special equipment and the listener to wear earphones. *Compare with* consecutive translation.

Singapore Training & Development Association
A professional society for HRD practitioners in Singapore

single loop learning *basic term*
Gaining information to stabilize and maintain the existing operational systems. Less complex and less valuable than the concept of double loop learning described by Chris Argyris. *Compare with* double loop learning.

site implementor
An individual at an instructional site who is responsible for the initiation and administration of in-

struct. Site implementors are often used in OJT.

sitting by Nellie
A euphemism for on-the-job training used in some English-speaking countries.

situational leadership
A model developed by Paul Hersey and Kenneth Blanchard in which the leader provides for the followers what they cannot provide for themselves. The leader identifies the development level of the followers and selects the style which best suits the situation. The followers contract with the leader for the style which best suits their perceived development needs.

situational performance analysis model
Any model focused on the particulars of a single event, problem, or situation.

situational technique
An evaluation technique involving participants in solving problems closely related to those under investigation.

situational training exercise
A limited, mission-related exercise designed to train through practice one collective task or a group of related tasks.

situation analysis
In presentations, a step in the predesign phase, assessing the effects of the setting and related events on the upcoming presentation.

situation simulation
Essentially, a CAI action maze. Learners choose from alternatives at decision points. After a decision, the learner is provided with the consequences of the decision, more information, and further choices. Often, a score is accumulated for comparison against a norm or self. *See also* computer assisted instruction (CAI), case study, and simulation. *Compare with* action maze.

6W
A projection rule based on the requirement of one foot of screen width for each 6 feet of viewing distance from the screen. The audience should be no further away than six times the width of the projected image.

skill *essential 100 term*
Any task-specific ability. A skill is a subset of a task. Skills involve physical or manipulative activities. They often require knowledges for their execution. All skills are actions having special requirements for speed, accuracy, or coordination. *Compare with* knowledges.

skilled craftspersons
Members of trades such as electricians, pipefitters, and carpenters. Skilled craftspersons require special training. *See also* craft training.

skilled trades
The crafts that include skilled craftspersons.

skill hierarchies *basic term*
Simple diagrams showing the dependency relationships between the skills taught in the course. Skill hierarchies are useful in determining which skills *must* be learned before others should be attempted. They are also useful in solving problems caused when the equipment available for student practice is limited.

skill perishability
The length of time it takes a skill to

decline below competency level after it has been initially learned.

skill practice *basic term*
In behavior modeling, the portion of the learning experience in which the learner can practice the skills previously demonstrated by the model. *See also* behavior modeling, performance tryout, and role play.

skills analysis
See also task analysis.

skills challenge
A learner friendly term for a practical test. A skills challenge usually comes at the end of a lesson or course.

SkillsLink
An on-line Information Service of training resources in Ontario, Canada. SkillsLink is sponsored by the Provincially funded Ontario Training Corporation. It lists organizations and individuals who offer services in the HRD field.

Skinner, B. F.
The main interpreter of behaviorism, Burrhus F. Skinner is particularly noted for the concept of operant conditioning. He has had a large effect on HRD activities. *See also* behaviorism, behavior modification, instructional objectives, operant conditioning, performance analysis, programmed instruction, and reinforcement.

Skinnerian
Related to the work and ideas of B. F. Skinner. *See also* operant conditioning *and* Skinner, B. F.

skit
An instructional technique based on a rehearsed drama presented by the learners. A skit usually has precise scripts provided for the learner-actors. Rehearsals are rare. Skits differ from role plays, in which a situation is provided but no lines are given. *Compare with* role play.

skunkworks
An informal system implemented to get things done, but not necessarily through approved, traditional channels.

sleep-assisted learning (SAI)
Those situations in which learning or enhancement of verbal material is attempted through its presentation to a sleeping person.

sleep learning
An instructional method based on presentation of audio material to a learner who is relaxed or asleep.

slide
1. A 35mm photographic image, mounted for projection. Can be synchronized with an audiotape recorder for an audiovisual presentation. *Compare with* transparency *and* lantern slide.
2. A lantern slide. *Compare with* transparency *and* lantern slide.
3. Loosely, a transparency. *Compare with* transparency *and* lantern slide.

Sloan Management Review
A periodical of interest to HRD practitioners involved in management. *Sloan Management Review* is published by the Massachusetts Institute of Technology.

slow-scan video
1. A device that transmits and/or receives still video pictures. Often used for distance learning.
2. A still frame video unit that accepts an image from a camera or other video source one line at a time.

small group discussion
See group discussion.

small group trial
Use of an instructional package by a limited number of members of the target population. A trial by a small group, usually under the supervision of an instructional developer, evaluates the effectiveness of the development instructional product to ensure market readiness. Weaknesses are corrected before release for use in the field. A formative evaluation step. *See also* formative evaluation *and* instructional systems development (ISD). *Compare with* one-on-one trial *and* pilot test.

smart room
A classroom that uses environmental sensing and controlling functions to automatically maintain the ideal learning environment by continuously monitoring and adjusting temperature, lighting, sound and other factors.

smile sheet
A derogatory synonym for reaction sheet. *See also* reaction sheet.

social architecture
The cultural, symbolic, relationship orientation of the organization. An open and positive social architecture enhances learning by encouraging teams, self-management, empowerment, and sharing. Social architecture is the opposite of a closed, rigid, bureaucratic architecture. *Compare with* knowledge architecture and technological architecture.

socialization *basic term*
The process of learning one's role in a setting such as work. Socialization consists of role anticipation, role development, and role stabilization. During the socialization process, individuals progressively internalize the values of their associates.

socialization change
In organizational development, a change process characterized by hierarchical control. *Compare with* coercive change, emulative change, indoctrination, interactional change, natural change, planned change, and technocratic change.

social learning *basic term*
The process by which trainees acquire skills through the vicarious process of observing others.

social learning theory *basic term*
A theory associated with Albert Bandura, based on the premise that people learn by observing and imitating the behavior of others. They remember what others did and also the outcomes of the observed behavior. Observation, imitation, and modeling are key ingredients in the process. *See also* behavior modeling.

social reinforcement
Any positive publicity, formal or informal, provided to trainees that supports their new behaviors.

social styles inventory
Any of several instruments used to identify the social style of the learner.

Society for Applied Learning Technology (SALT)
Usually called by its acronym, the Society for Applied Learning Technology is a professional organization comprised mainly of instructional systems practitioners.

Society for Human Resource Management (SHRM)
An international membership organization of interest to some HR professionals. Formerly called the American Society for Personnel Administration. *See also* Institute for International Human Resources (IIHR).

Society for Intercultural Education, Training and Research
See International Society for Intercultural Education, Training and Research.

Society of Insurance Trainers and Educators
A professional society of interest to HRD professionals who work in the insurance field.

sociodrama *basic term*
An expansion of role play, usually involving groups that have radically different values. Sociodrama often involves both learners and members of the population with which they will eventually work. *See also* role play.

sociological theory *basic term*
In career planning, a theory that family, religion, and school are crucially important in early career planning decisions. People learn from those with whom they come in contact.

sociotechnical systems
In organization development, an organization's total system of human activities along with the technical, physical, and financial resources and the processes for producing products and delivering services. *See also* organization development (OD).

Socratic dialogue (discussion)
basic term
1. An instructional method used by and named for Socrates. The instructor poses a question to the group, which jointly seeks a solution.
2. A technique in which learners are asked a question in relation to a specific topic. Based on the learners' response, more questions are asked that vary according to the response just given. The entire session follows this pattern.

Socratic instructional style
An instructional style based on intellectual exchanges between instructor and learner. *Compare with* balanced, facilitative, directive, and disseminational instructional styles. *See also* Socratic dialogue.

soft skill
A semi-derisive term to describe abilities not directed toward production of a tangible product. For example, interpersonal skills. This term is used primarily by non-HRD practitioners.

software
Programs that make computers work. Computer programs that deliver content are part of courseware, not software. *Compare with* hardware and courseware.

sole source
A situation where a consultant or vendor has been identified as the only resource available to provide a needed product or service. Used by organizations to bypass the bidding process when bidding is not appropriate.

solitaire game
An instructional game that is

played by an individual. Many computer games are solitaire games.

sound effects
Realistic sounds that can be added to audio or videotape.

sound person
In video production, the person responsible for recording the sound on a shoot. The sound person selects the microphones and makes certain that the sound is properly recorded on tape.

sound system
See public address system

space bubble
A concept developed by Edward Hall to describe a zone of personal space that surrounds each person. Intrusion into a person's space bubble will cause discomfort. The concept is useful because people from various cultures have space bubbles of differing sizes. *See also* cross-cultural instruction *and* proxemics.

spaghetti wiring
A jumble of cables that detracts from the visual continuity of the space.

span of control
The number and types of employees and jobs supervised by one person.

spatial learner
A person who learns by perceiving, understanding, and manipulating the relative positions of objects in space. *See also* learning style.

speaker's notes
Notes or a simple outline for a presentation, usually including only the major points. Often written on index cards, speaker's notes are used by a speaker to serve as a guide while speaking.

special cause
In quality processes, a source of variation that is intermittent, unpredictable, and unstable. Sometimes called an assignable cause. A special cause is signaled by a point beyond the control limits. The process should not be adjusted to deal with special causes.

special effects (generator)
In video production, a device to add various optical effects to video images.

specialty training standard
A U.S. Air Force publication that describes an Air Force specialty in general terms of the tasks and knowledge that an airman in that specialty may be expected to perform or to know on the job. It further serves as a contract between Air Training Command and the functional user, showing which of the overall training requirements for a specialization are taught in formal schools and in career development courses. *Compare with* course training standard.

specific-activity costs
In HRD budgeting, those cost items that include analysis, design, development, implementation, and evaluation.

specification
The engineering requirement for judging acceptability of a particular characteristic. A specification should not be confused with a control limit.

specificity
An attribute of instruction which is adapted to unique conditions found

Continued on next page

in only one organization, work group, job class, or position. Instruction with high specificity is said to be organization-specific.

speech
1. Oral communication.
2. An oral presentation, distinguished from a lecture by its informative or persuasive, rather than instructional, intent. A speech contrasts with an instructional presentation in which the purpose is learning. It is often characterized by formality and has little or no audience participation. *Compare with* lecture.

speech-forum
An oral presentation followed immediately by an open discussion. A speech-forum addresses the problem of limited audience participation usually associated with a lecture.

speech mannerisms
See mannerisms.

speed learning
See suggestopedia.

spider-web principle
A view of change. The spider-web principle is that a change in any one area is felt throughout other areas, as the vibrations on a strand of a spider web vibrates the entire web.

spiral curriculum
Continuous review and integration of previously covered subjects in further instruction. A term coined by David Ausabel.

spiral model
The process of decision making involving constant backtracking and reach-testing of ideas until the idea develops during group interaction to represent the consensus of the group members.

spiral principle
Early teaching of critical knowledge and skills followed by reinforcement in later lessons.

spirit duplicator
A reproduction machine based on an inexpensive process to duplicate typed images. No longer common in HRD.

split-half reliability
One method of determining the reliability of a test, based on treating and comparing two halves of the items as two administrations of the test. Split-half reliability requires that the selected items be as alike as possible. A reliable test will produce similar results from both halves. *Compare with* alternate form reliability *and* test-retest reliability.

spontaneous role playing
A role play used to help participants acquire insight into their own behavior and attitudes or the behavior and attitude of others. The instructor elicits some problem from the group and then directs an enactment of the problem.

spoon-feeding
Instruction that has been over-simplified and possibly delivered in a non-challenging learning environment.

springboard
A highly visible job within or outside an organization. A springboard job frequently leads to a higher level position in the same or a different organization.

SQ3R
A five step learning strategy. The

steps are (1) survey the materials, (2) develop questions, (3) read the material, (4) recall the information, and (5) review the material. *Compare with* MURDER.

stabilizer
One of five career value structures identified by Edgar Schein. The others are technocrat, climber, builder, and searcher.

stacks
General descriptive term for Hypermedia programs.

staff evaluation
An evaluation conducted by HRD staff members properly trained in observation techniques. The staff observes the learners and provides feedback on performance.

stage
See platform.

stage fright
The nervousness and tension that presenters feel just prior to beginning the presentation. *Also called* butterflies.

staging book
See conference program book.

stakeholder
Anyone with a vested interest in the outcome of an activity or project. Stakeholders may support or oppose a particular undertaking. For example, the union may be a stakeholder in a technology upgrade HRD program. *Compare with* client.

stand-alone delivery
Delivery separate from a large computer system or LAN. Achieved by, and synonymous with, personal computer delivery.

standard
1. A synonym for criterion. *See* criterion.
2. A short, concise statements of expected performance that serves as a gauge for measuring accomplishment. Standards are the subject of a number of U.S. federal agency studies and recommendations for setting industry and skill standards.

Standard Army Training System
Database software used by U.S. military forces that integrates the automation of unit METLs, the commander's assessment of proficiency, MTPs, and training management administration.

standard deviation *basic term*
A measure that tells how widely the majority of scores are scattered around the average score. A small standard deviation indicates that scores cluster around the mean, while a large one indicates that scores are widely dispersed about the mean. Standard deviation is represented by the Greek letter *sigma*. *See also* normal curve.

standardized test
A test that has been validated on large groups. The results of a local administration can then be compared to the level of success of the wider group. For example, a GED test. *See also* norm-referenced test.

Standards of Good Practice in Continuing Education
Self-appraisal guidelines established to assist HRD practitioners in conducting self-evaluations of their programs.

standup trainer *essential 100 term*
1. An HRD practitioner whose pri-

Continued on next page

mary responsibility is instructional delivery by presentation.
2. Loosely, an HRD practitioner whose primary reputation is as a skilled presenter.

stanines
In testing, a percentile-based score that shows approximately how many standard deviations above or below a mean a given score falls. *Compare with* z-score *and* percentile.

start up
One of the phases of the life cycle model of cost-benefit analysis. *See also* life cycle model.

start-up cost
Costs associated with one-time purchases, such as design work and equipment acquisition.

station
See development station, learning station, student station, and workstation.

statistical control
In quality processes, the situation in which all special causes have been removed from the process, evidenced on a control chart by the absence of points beyond the control limits and by the absence of non-random patterns or trends within the control limits. *See also* statistical process control (SPC).

statistical process control (SPC)
The use of statistical techniques, such as control charts, to analyze a process or its output. Statistical process control is the basis for appropriate actions to achieve and maintain a state of statistical control and to improve the capability of the process. *See also* statistical control.

status
A rank within a group ordered in a hierarchy from high to low. Status may be ascribed by some higher authority or achieved through behaviors recognized by other group members as beneficial to the group. *See also* leaderless group discussion.

steady state
The costs of an HRD system during the operational period. *See also* life cycle model *and* operational period.

step costs
Incremental increases in cost, based on a threshold. For example, one additional participant will not force rental of a larger classroom, but at a certain point additional participants will necessitate that expense.

stick figures
Simple drawings of figures (people) used in storyboarding and other planning processes.

still frame video
1. A video picture displayed in a single frame or one frame at a time. Still frame video is used in IVD.
2. A system of recording one frame of a video picture on a 2-inch (50-mm) magnetic disk. The still frame can be displayed on a video monitor, or a hard color picture can be printed. *See also* slow scan video.

stimulus
The event, situation, condition, signal, or cue to which a response must be made. *See also* association *and* operant conditioning.

stimulus-response (SR)
See operant conditioning.

stimulus-response method
basic term
In analysis, a method of gathering data based on listing the cue (stimulus) and action (response) critical to performing a task.

storyboard *basic term*
1. Documents used for film, video, and computer display planning. A series of sketches resembling a cartoon strip that help visualize the sequence of scenes or views to be presented. Plot, character, and action are all subjects of storyboarding.
2. Sketches of the visuals that are intended to support a presentation. The sketches are used to ensure that the message is supported by the visuals before the visual materials are actually made.

storyboarding
The process of producing storyboards. *See* storyboard.

strangers' group
A small group composed of participants from different organizations. Participants may or may not have dissimilar backgrounds and skills. Strangers' group is a term borrowed from OD. *Compare with* cousins' group *and* family group.

strategic HRD planning
essential 100 term
The process of developing a long-range plan for the HRD department. Strategic HRD planning takes into account present strengths and weaknesses and likely future opportunities and threats. Often defined as planning for the period 5-10 years in the future. *Also called* long-range HRD planning. *See also* strategic planning. *Compare with* short- *and* mid-range planning.

strategic plan
The result of the organizational strategic planning process. The strategic plan is usually a formal document.

strategic planning
A formal process by which an organization determines how it will achieve its purpose over the long term, given expected opportunities and problems presented by the external environment and the strengths and weaknesses of the organization itself. The result is a shared set of beliefs about the organization's future and goals that identifies the functions, priorities, and resources that are necessary to reach those goals. Special types of strategic planning include hoshin planning and policy deployment. *See also* hoshin planning *and* policy deployment.

strategic roles
The HRD role cluster including HRD manager, marketer, organization-change agent, and individual-career-development advisor. *See also* HRD Roles and Competencies Study.

strategist
The HRD role of developing long-range plans for training and development's structure, organization, direction, policies, programs, services, and practices, in order to accomplish the training and development mission. *See also* HRD Roles and Competencies Study.

stratification
In process control, a technique used to identify improvement opportunities. Stratification breaks down single element totals into component categories, classifications, or subgroups based on char-

Continued on next page

acteristics. Data may obscure patterns because several items are considered together.

stratified random sampling
basic term
In research, a sampling method to assure the desired sample makeup is representative of the true population. For example, the population can be stratified into the three groups, such as departments of different sizes. Then simple random sampling can be applied to each of the three groups. Other useful ways for the population to be stratified include age, sex, work location, output, sales volume, or geographic location. *See also* random number, random number tables, simple random sampling, and systematic random sampling.

stratified systems theory (SST)
A systematic theory of work in social organizations based on the work of Elliott Jaques.

straw man
1. A proposal presented to encourage discussion to reach a better outcome.
2. A technique used in presentations to establish an opposing position before presenting persuasive arguments against it. *Also called* point/counterpoint.

stress management
1. The techniques or structures designed for recognizing the signs of stress and for administering treatments in an organized context.
2. The handling of personal and organizational pressure, anxiety, and tension.

strokes
In transactional analysis, actions that satisfy people's need for recognition or attention. Strokes can be positive or negative. An exchange of strokes is a transaction.

structure
1. The characteristic of a group, organization, or system denoted by the hierarchical, physical, or spatial arrangement of the components at any given point in time.
2. The formal means of organization; the grouping of departments, divisions, work groups, jobs, and individuals.

Structure of the Intellect model
A three-dimensional representation of three intersecting categories, developed by J. Guilford. The model is based on the analysis of huge numbers of test-takers in operations, products, and content. Intersections of categories represented by a single letter result in combinations that define an area such as CMU—verbal comprehension.

structured brainstorming
A method in which every member of the group must contribute either in turn or pass until asked again in turn. *Compare with* unstructured brainstorming. *See also* brainstorming.

structured discussions
An instructional technique based on conversations between trainees, aimed at specific learning objectives. The learning objective is clearly announced in advance, or during the first moments of the discussion.

structured experience
A description for exercises coined by Pfeiffer and Jones. Structured

experiences exercises guide the participants in learning about human interaction. *See also* exercise.

structured HRD programs
Programs that are planned. *Also called* formal HRD programs. *Compare with* unstructured HRD programs.

structured interview
An interview based on specific questions in a prearranged order. *Compare with* unstructured interview.

structured job assignments
Assigned job tasks carried out in whole or part for HRD purposes.

structured on-the-job training
OJT with emphasis on structure and control. Use of the term results from poor reputation of loosely structured OJT programs. *Also called* supervised on-the-job training.

structured writing
See Information Mapping®.

student
See learner.

student accountability
Learners' acceptance of responsibility for their own classroom success.

student-centered learning
basic term
An instructional viewpoint. In student-centered learning, objectives are written from the learner's point of view and activities are developed to relate more to the learner than to the instructor. *See also* learner-centered instruction.

student disk
A diskette with technology-based lessons on it. The diskette may also require a presentation system. *See also* presentation system.

student/instructor ratio
essential 100 term
The actual or average number of students served by one instructor in an instructional program. Student instructor ratio is expressed as a ratio. For example, 20:1. A typical ratio is 30:1. The ratio in individualized instruction at any one point in time may be 75:1, although in other circumstances it may not differ greatly from traditional, depending on the subject.

student material
The courseware designed to aid students during a course of instruction and to act as a possible reference for them when they are back on the job. Student material can include manuals and learning-job aids.

student station
See learning station.

stylus
A pen-shaped instrument that is used for tactile interaction with a computer. For example, to enter text, draw images, or point to choices. *Compare with* mouse.

subject
In research, each individual that participates in an experiment.

subject-centered instruction
basic term
A pedagogy-based instructional approach. Subject-centered instruction focuses on what will be taught as opposed to learner-related characteristics. Subject-centered instruction focuses on learner acquisition of information.

subject matter expert (SME)
(Often heard pronounced by its initals—S-M-E—not as a single word, "smee.")
A person thoroughly knowledgeable of the content of instruction to be developed, who works with others on the design of instruction. The SME acts as advisor to the instructional designer. *Also called* subject matter specialist.

subject matter specialist
See subject matter expert (SME).

subject-matter understanding
The HRD competency of knowing the content of a given function or discipline being addressed. *See also* HRD Roles and Competencies Study.

substantive conflict
Intellectual clashes among members of a group on issues pertaining to the task.

substantive feedback
A form of feedback that provides the learner with meaningful information. Substantive feedback may vary in depth as determined appropriate. *Compare with* knowledge of results. *See also* feedback.

success factors
Those characteristics an individual must possess to advance within an organization.

succession planning *basic term*
Collective term for programs designed and conducted specifically to ensure that a qualified successor exists for every job in the management hierarchy. Includes HRD as well as non-HRD activities. Succession planning encompasses both replacement and development planning. *See also* executive development.

suggestive accelerative learning and teaching techniques (SALTT)
A group of techniques intended to substantially increase the speed of learning. *See also* suggestopedia.

suggestology
See suggestopedia.

suggestopedia
An instructional method, developed by Bulgarian Georgi Lozanov, to provide a short course in language training for adults leaving the country. Suggestopedia is primarily based on relaxation in a conducive learning environment. Suggestopedia features presentation of new material, review, and relaxation. This method is often cited as a basis for a wide range of accelerated teaching techniques, such as accelerated learning, suggestology, and superlearning. *See also* sleep learning.

summary
See conclusion.

summary question
In a presentation, a question used to bring closure. It recaps the applicable content for verification by the participant.

summative evaluation
essential 100 term
The evaluation of instruction conducted during and after delivery for the purpose of assessing the instructional environment, learning, on-the-job use, and return on investment. Summative evaluation is conducted during the evaluation phase of ISD. *See also* evaluation. *Compare with* summative evaluation.

sunk costs
See capital costs.

superego
A part of the personality described by Sigmund Freud. The superego is the voice for societal norms and values.

superlearning
See suggestopedia.

supervised on-the-job training
See structured on-the-job training.

supervisor development *essential 100 term*
Instructional programs designed to develop an organization's first line managers. Typical contents include communications, delegating, interpersonal relations, labor-management relations, leadership, project management, supervisory skills, and time management.

supervisor-trainer
A supervisor performing in the role of instructor.

supervisor training
See supervisor development.

supervisory development
See supervisor development.

Supervisory Management
A newsletter of interest to HRD practitioners involved in management. *Supervisory Management* is published by the American Management Association.

supplier
See vendor.

support
In a presentation, material such as statistics, examples, and testimony which backs up the main proposition.

support costs
In the HRD budget process, those items that include staff, materials, equipment, travel expenses, and consulting expenses.

support groups *basic term*
Collections of two or more people with similar needs who meet periodically to discuss current problems and ways to solve them.

support material, instructional *basic term*
Anything that the developer conceives, designs or fabricates to aid the student in the successful completion of the course objectives. Instructional support materials include written material, video, devices, and training aids.

supporting objectives
See enabling objectives.

surrogate travel
One multimedia application in which physical travel is precisely simulated using videodisc and computer. Surrogate travel allows the user to control the path taken through the virtual environment. For example, a tour of a nuclear power plant. Also known as vicarious travel. *See also* virtual reality.

survey feedback *basic term*
In organization development, a type of data-based intervention based on surveys of the members of a system. *See also* action research, data-based intervention, and organization development (OD).

survey test
A criterion-referenced test used before the development of an instructional system. A survey test is administered to a sample of prospective learners to determine what skills and knowledges should be included in the course of in-

Continued on next page

struction. *Also called* threshold knowledge test.

suspension bridge
In career development, a career ladder linking otherwise unrelated jobs. The suspension bridge is a reference to the education and experience needed to move between the jobs.

sustainment training
That instruction required to maintain the minimum acceptable level of proficiency or capability required to accomplish a training objective.

swap shop
See cracker barrel session.

Swedish Association for Human Resource Management
A professional society inclusive of HRD practitioners in Sweden.

syllabus
See plan of instruction (POI).

symbolic learner
A person who learns by perceiving objects, marks, and signs as representative of facts and ideas. *See also* learning style.

symbolic learning
An explanation for the enhancing effects of rehearsal on performance. Mental practice gives the performer an opportunity to rehearse the sequence of movements as symbolic components of the task. *See also* imagery.

symposium *basic term*
A series of related presentations, usually on different aspects of the same topic. Presenters make their own separate presentations to the audience and do not directly exchange ideas. It is characterized by formality and has little or no audience participation. *Compare with* panel.

symposium-forum
A moderator-directed session that consists of a symposium followed immediately by an audience-participation period of free and open discussion.

syndicates
Buzzgroups are called syndicates in many parts of the world. *See* buzzgroups.

synectics
A group problem-solving technique that stresses the use of analogy and metaphor, developed by William Gordon. *See also* creativity training.

synergogy
A model of education that combines pedagogical and andragogical methods developed by William Blake and Jane Mouton. *See also* andragogy, pedagogy, and synergy.

synergy *basic term*
The concept that the whole is greater than the sum of its parts, developed by Buckminster Fuller. Abraham Maslow applied the concept to his studies of self-actualizing people. *See also* gestalt *and* Maslow's hierarchy.

synthesis *basic term*
The fifth of six levels of learning described by Benjamin Bloom. *See* Bloom's taxonomy.

synthetic environment
See virtual world.

system *basic term*

1. An entity which behaves as a whole because of the interdependence of its component elements.
2. A method or procedure.
3. A network, as for communications.

systematic random sampling
In research, an appropriate method to select a sample from a large population. In systematic sampling, subjects are selected on some systematic basis, such as every tenth person. Systematic sampling is efficient and saves much time and effort. The sample is usually more representative of the population. As a result, the information per unit cost is greater. Systematic sampling is widely used when the population is large. *See also* random number, random number tables, simple random sampling, and stratified random sampling.

system measurements
Qualitative analyses of variables such as cost, productivity, and customer satisfaction.

systems approach *basic term*

1. The comprehensive and rigorous process of developing and conducting a project or activity to accomplish specific outcomes.
2. *See* instructional systems development (ISD).

systems approach to training (SAT)
A synonym for ISD used in the U.S. military. *See* instructional systems development (ISD).

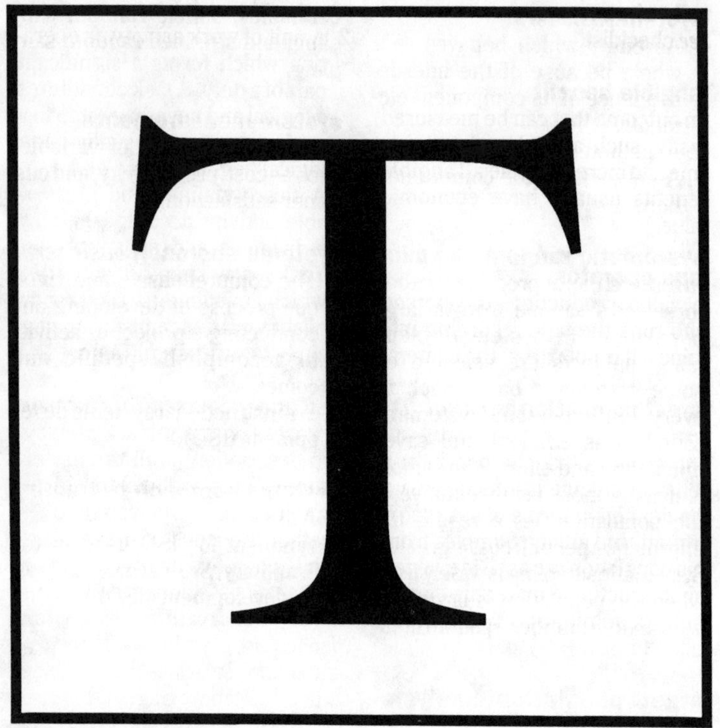

table game
A psychomotor skill game in which the playing area or surface is not big enough to accommodate the actual players.

tabula rasa
(Pronounced taa′-blah rah′-za.) A pedagogical theory of education in which the mind of the learner is perceived as a blank tablet upon which ideas are inscribed by a great teacher, lecturer, or professor. Based on the concept of tabula rasa (roughly Latin for blank slate) as expounded in the philosophy of John Locke (1632-1704), this theory still prevails in a great many universities.

tactics
Procedures employed in order to achieve a specific short-term objective (or set of objectives).

tactile input
Interaction with a technology-based program by use of touch, as compared with keyboard input. May be achieved by use of a light pen, mouse, digitizer, stylus, or touch panel screen. Experience shows that categories of users who never use a keyboard strongly prefer tactile input. The learner's status may also be involved. For example, doctors and pilots.

talent
In video production, a synonym for cast.

tally sheet
See checklist.

tangible benefit
An outcome that can be measured easily, such as reduced training time and increased sales. Tangible benefits usually have economic value.

tape operator
In video production, the person who runs the tape recording machine if it is not part of the camera.

target population *essential 100 term*
The group of people for whom a behavior change is intended, usually defined in terms of age, background, and ability. Samples from this population are used in evaluating instructional materials during their development. Sometimes called target audience.

target population analysis *basic term*
The process of assessing needs of a specific group of individuals. Target population analysis produces a description of the characteristics of that group. One of the parts of a needs assessment. Sometimes called audience analysis.

target population description
A concise description of the key characteristics of those who will be the recipients of an intervention. Based on the target population description, it is possible to select objectives, examples, terminology, and procedures that will better shape the instruction (or other intervention) for each individual.

task *basic term*
1. A set of skills performed to accomplish a specific objective. A subset of a job.
2. A unit of work activity or operation which forms a significant part of a duty. A task constitutes a logical and necessary step in a performance, and usually has a logical beginning and end.
3. A clearly defined and measurable activity accomplished by individuals and organizations. Tasks are specific activities which contribute to the accomplishment of encompassing missions or other requirements.

task analysis *essential 100 term*
A process of arriving at a step-by-step description of all the performance elements (tasks) that make up a job. Task analysis applies whether the steps of the task are mainly cognitive or psychomotor. Task analysis is done by questionnaires, observations of performance, and interviews with incumbents and supervisors. A term coined by Robert Gagne, it is also referred to as skills analysis. Task and skills analysis are subsets of the complete job. *Also called* skills analysis. *See also* DACUM, front-end analysis, needs analysis, and performance analysis.

task analyst
The HRD role of identifying activities, tasks, sub-tasks, human resource and support requirements necessary to accomplish specific results in a job or organization. *See also* HRD Roles and Competencies Study.

task certification form
A document to certify the trainee-worker's proficiency for each task. *See also* proficiency certification.

task force
See task-oriented group.

task lighting
The illumination located at and serving the immediate area of the learning station or workstation.

task-oriented group
Any group formed temporarily to complete a function. *Also called* ad hoc group and task force.

task simulation
See part-task simulation and whole-task simulation.

task simulator
See simulator.

task skills and behaviors
Those actions performed to move the team closer to the goal. Effective teamwork requires attention to both task and maintenance behaviors. *See also* maintenance skills and behaviors.

Tavistock Institute
An institution in England that produced early work in OD.

taxonomy *basic term*
A classification system. The best known HRD taxonomy is the *Taxonomy of Educational Objectives* prepared by Benjamin Bloom.

teachable moment *basic term*
An often unplanned, brief period in which learners are especially receptive to formal or informal training because they sense and accept their own learning needs.

teaching machine
A 1960s electro-mechanical device used to deliver programmed instruction. The teaching machine was replaced by CAI within a few years of its emergence.

teaching point
A particular element that is used by an instructor or medium to trigger understanding and convey knowledge or skill to the learners.

teaching style
See instructional style.

teambuilding *essential 100 term*
In organizational development, any of a variety of activities focused on improving work relationships or tasks. Teambuilding is especially used when a new group is formed. It is also common in management and supervisors instruction. *See also* organization development (OD).

team inventory
A technique using small groups (teams) in organizations to gather information. This method is particularly associated with job-related basic skills.

team learning
An instructional strategy in which the team takes the responsibility for, and facilitates, the learning of its individual members.

team presentation
See joint presentation.

team tasks
See buzzgroups.

team teaching *basic term*
Instruction delivered by two or more instructors working together.

Technical & Skills Training
A periodical of interest to HRD practitioners involved in technical and skills training. *Technical & Skills Training* is published by the American Society for Training and Development.

technical and skills training
essential 100 term
That area of HRD concerned with learning experiences related to equipment and processes. *Compare with* management development.

technical career ladder
A career ladder describing conditions where technical proficiency rather than management responsibility is linked to advancement. *Compare with* management career ladder.

technical career track
See technical career ladder.

technical competencies
Functional knowledge and skills identified in the HRD Roles and Competencies Study. The following competencies are included: adult-learning understanding, career-development-theories-and-techniques understanding, competency-identification skill, computer competence, electronic-systems skill, facilities skill, objectives-preparation skill, performance-observation skill, subject matter understanding, training-and-development-theories-and-techniques understanding, and research skill. *See also* HRD Roles and Competencies Study.

technical education
See technical and skills training.

technical proposal
A document prepared to respond to one requirement of an RFP that calls for a proposal to be submitted in two parts—technical and cost proposals. The technical proposal sets forth the details of each component proposed for the project. *Compare with* cost proposal.

Technical Trainer/Skills Trainer
A newsletter of interest to HRD practitioners involved in technical and skills training. *Technical Trainer/Skills Trainer* is published by the American Society for Training and Development.

technical training
See technical and skills training.

technocrat
One of five career value structures identified by Edgar Schein. The others are climber, builder, searcher, and stabilizer.

technocratic change
In organizational development, a change process characterized by goal-setting based on collecting and interpreting data and equal power on both sides. *Compare with* indoctrination, and coercive change, emulative change, interactional change, natural change, planned change, and socialization change.

technological architecture
basic term
The supporting, integrated set of technical processes, systems, and structure for collaboration, coaching, coordination, and other knowledge skills. Technological architecture may include such electronic tools and advanced methods for learning as computer conferencing, simulation software, and computer-supported collaboration, all of which work to create knowledge freeways. *Compare with* knowledge architecture and social architecture.

techno-structural intervention
See organization development (OD).

Techtrends
A periodical of interest to HRD practitioners involved in technology-based learning. *Techtrends* is published by the Association for Educational Communication & Technology.

telecine
See film chain.

telecommuting
Working at an alternate site instead of commuting in the traditional site. The alternate site may be the worker's home. Typically involving use of a computer for communication with the organization and transmission of work.

teleconference
basic term
1. Two-way electronic communication between two or more groups, or three or more individuals, in separate locations. Includes group communication via audio, audiographs, video, and computer systems. *See also* audio teleconferencing, audiographic teleconferencing, computer conferencing, and videoconferencing.
2. Loosely, a meeting where the participants are at separate locations. A telephone call with three parties would be a very simple teleconference. Some organizations have elaborate facilities for teleconferences. Teleconferencing offers an important alternative to the high cost of travel.
3. At a conference, a teleconference is useful for a general session when an important and significant resource person is invited but cannot be present physically. The resource person may speak to the large group through a telephone hook-up. The teleconference can arrange to provide two-way communication.

telelecture
Instruction delivered by telephone.

telephone conference bridge
A device designed to link three or more telephone channels for a teleconference. Usually refers to a bridge that provides only dial-up teleconferencing in which an operator calls each participant. *Compare with* meet-me bridge.

telephone survey
Any survey conducted over the telephone. Telephone surveys are usually based on a series of prepared branching questions.

telepresence
A computer-generated environment consisting of interactive simulations and computer graphics, in which a human being experiences being present in a remote location. *See also* vicarious travel *and* virtual reality.

teletext
A method of information dissemination with instructional potential. The user is able to select still frames of information. Videotex is distributed using otherwise unused portions of a broadcast video signal. Teletext is one-way and therefore not interactive. *See also* videotex.

Teletext
Formerly called Oracle. A system of information distribution via broadcast television, operated by the U.K. Independent Television Networks. *See also* CEEFAX *and* videotex.

television resolution
See National Television Standards Committee (NTSC) *and* video.

Telidon
A Canadian videotex system. *See* videotex. *Compare with* Prestel *and* Antiope.

temperament
See Myers-Briggs Type Indicator (MBTI).

templates
Instructional models that are frequently built into authoring systems. Templates offer increased productivity. For example, there may be a multiple-choice template. The author fills in the question, choices, answers, and feedbacks. The disadvantage is decreased flexibility.

tent cards
See name cards.

terminal
A peripheral device that enables a user to interact with a computer and use the power of that computer. Although a microcomputer may be used as a terminal, a terminal falls short of the definition of a computer. *Compare with* microcomputer.

terminal objective *essential 100 term*
The action, knowledge, or skills the learner is expected to have acquired at the end of instruction. *See also* course objective.

terminal performance objective
The final on-the-job results the student seeks to achieve from the learning process.

termination
In consulting, the end of the project. *Also called* closure *and* disengagement.

termination period
One of the phases of the life cycle model of cost-benefit analysis. *See also* life cycle model.

termination rule
A rule in a game that specifies how the game is concluded and how winners and losers are determined.

terrain model
An elaborate permanent training device. A terrain model is constructed to represent a specific area using whatever materials best represent reality at the selected scale. *See also* sand table.

test and evaluation
In a presentation, the final phase of preparation before actual delivery. Includes the dry run.

test anxiety *basic term*
The fact that some students do poorly on tests because of apprehension of the test itself.

testing *basic term*
1. One of the modes of CMI. In technology-based learning, testing is used to determine the gaps in a particular learner's knowledge. The information will be used to generate an appropriate instructional prescription. The others are prescription generation and record keeping.
2. A method of determining a learner's knowledge level in a given area. Testing may be used for a variety of purposes, including certification.

test-retest reliability
One method of determining the reliability of a test, based on readministration within a time period during which the skill, ability, or attitude of the learner is not expected to change. *Compare with*

Continued on next page

alternate form reliability *and* split-half reliability.

test validation
See validation.

text
1. Printed instructional media.
2. The computer's alphanumeric visual display. *Compare with* graphics.

text type
Type used in long passages for continuous reading. *Compare with* display type.

texture
Visualization of the sense of touch. The element of texture may be employed in much the same manner as the element of color.

T-group *basic term*
A group-based learning exercise to develop the individual's interpersonal skills by studying the effects of behavior and exploring alternative behaviors that might be more effective. T-groups (T for Training) use process observation, games, simulations, structured experiences, and other experiential methods. The T-group is rarely used today, except in a historical context. *Also called* encounter groups, confrontation groups, awareness groups, Synanon-type groups, discovery groups, sensory awareness groups, sensitivity training, and creativity workshops. *See also* laboratory training, human relations training, and sensitivity training.

theater style *basic term*
See Figure on next page.

T.H.E. Journal
A periodical of interest to HRD practitioners involved in technology-based learning. *T.H.E. Journal* is published by T.H.E. Journal.

theme, main
The single sentence which states the essence of the presentation.

theoretician
The HRD role of developing and testing theories of learning, training, and development. *See also* HRD Roles and Competencies Study.

theory *basic term*
Any plausible conceptual representation of a principle (or group of principles) used to predict and explain facts, observations, or events.

theory intervention
In organizational development, an intervention focused on differences between behavioral science assumptions and present behavior.

Theory X Theory Y *basic term*
A classic theory of management described by Douglas McGregor. Theory X is not "people oriented." It is based on the principle that people don't like to work. Theory Y is "people oriented." It is based on the principle that people can approach work positively.

thermal copier
Copier technology that uses heat to make the image. Used today only with thermal film to prepare transparencies.

thermal film
A special film for use with a thermal copier to prepare transparencies.

thinking (T)
In the Myers-Briggs typology, one

theater style *basic term*
A room arrangement with chairs only, set up in straight rows. *Compare with* classroom *and* conference styles.

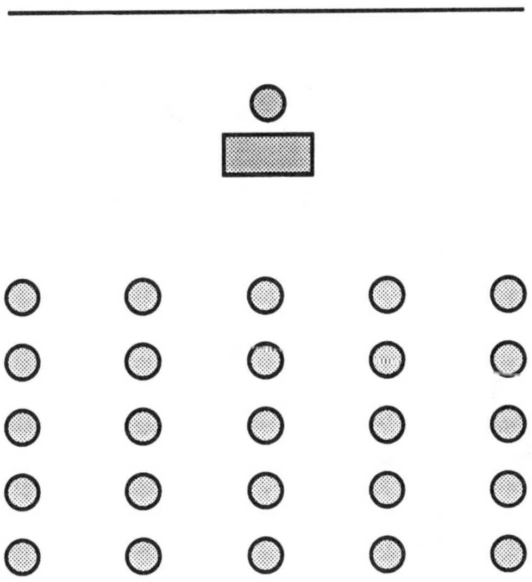

of the eight basic predispositions included. *See* Myers-Briggs Type Indicator (MBTI).

thinking styles *basic term*
The collective term for various styles that can be associated with the brain dominance profile. These include double dominant cerebral, cerebral right, double dominant right, limbic right, double dominant limbic, limbic left, double dominant left, cerebral left, and creative neutral. *See also* whole brain learning.

think tank
1. A synonym for brainstorming. *See* brainstorming.
2. Loosely, a formal or informal group organized for research and development.

third country national (TCN)
A person with citizenship in a country other than the host country or the country of origin of the organization involved. *See also* culture, native, and national.

third party facilitation
The intervention of a third person to help diagnose, interpret, and resolve problems between the first two parties.

35mm slide
See slide.

Thorndike, Edward
An educator who established some of the basic tenets of behavioral psychology. *See also* laws of learning.

Thorndike's seven laws of learning
See laws of learning.

threshold knowledge test (TKT)
See survey test.

thumbnail sketching
The practice of interpreting visual components as simple geometric shapes and experimenting with a variety of alternative shape relationships through a series of small sketches.

time and motion study
A job-engineering technique to determine the best way to do a job. The term often has a negative connotation to labor advocates.

time-compressed speech
See compressed speech.

time interval sampling
In research, observations may be spaced over specific time durations. The observer records the activity, behavior, or other data at the times specified on a checklist.

time utility
The timing of interventions or learning experiences.

tolerable cost
The total amount of money an organization can afford to spend on a training program.

tolerance threshold
The maximum degree of tension that will not prohibit a group from functioning normally. Social tension at a level above the threshold disrupts the ability of the group to function as a group.

topical discussion
A meeting on a general topic with minimal prescribed substructure. *Also called* general discussion.

top management commitment *essential 100 term*
The strategic support goal desired for HRD. Management commitment could be a pledge or promise of ongoing support from the top management group. To be effective, compelling actions must implement the commitment. For example, top management must always allot the resources needed for the training effort. *See also* managerial commitment *and* managerial support.

total immersion system
A virtual reality system based on wide-angle stereoscopic head-mounted display, simulated three-dimensional audio, and a remote hand-held or glove manipulator. *Compare with* second-person system.

total quality
See total quality management (TQM).

total quality management (TQM) basic term
A continuous improvement methodology for every process, supported by management to satisfy the customer. TQM includes every employee using tools, data, and teamwork. Armand Feigenbaum, the originator of the quality costs concept, is sometimes called the "Father of Total Quality Control" because of his assertion that every function in the organization is responsible for quality. *See also* Deming, W. Edwards; Juran, J. M.; quality costs; and seven quality process tools.

Total Quality Newsletter
A newsletter of interest to HRD

practitioners involved in the quality process. *Total Quality Newsletter* is published by Lakewood Publications.

total quality service (TQS)
A model developed by Karl Albrecht for enabling organizations to achieve competitive advantage by aligning their strategy, systems, and people around the needs of their customers.

touch panel
A special panel fitted in front of a display screen that permits the learner to indicate choices by touching a screen location directly, without use of a mouse or keyboard. The touch panel does not interfere with vision. *Also called* touch screen. *See* tactile input.

tour
See field trip.

trackball
In technology-based learning, fixed device including a ball moved by the user's fingers. As a result, the cursor moves in a like manner on the VDT. Pushing a button informs the computer system of the chosen location. *See also* tactile input. *Compare with* light pen, mouse, and touch panel.

track session
Conference sessions related to a particular topic. Track sessions offer the participant the possibility of customizing the conference experience in the topic of the track. Large conferences ordinarily have two or more tracks. *Compare with* breakout session, concurrent session, and general session.

trade
An occupation that usually requires a period of apprenticeship. *See also* apprenticeship.

Trade Adjustment and Assistance Program
U.S. legislation for a program limited to displaced workers.

trainee
See learner.

trainer *basic term*
1. An HRD practitioner.
2. One who helps individuals improve performance on their present jobs by providing organized learning experiences. *See also* facilitator, human resource development (HRD), and training.
3. Loosely, the person in charge of a class or anyone responsible for providing the instructional process. A generic term used to describe a range of instructional personnel in business, industry, and government.
4. A job-performance-oriented device designed to simulate conditions inherent in the equipment that it represents.

trainer of trainers
A person who conducts train the trainer sessions.

Trainer's Workshop
A periodical of interest to HRD practitioners involved in supervisory and management instruction. *Trainer's Workshop* is published by the American Management Association.

Training
A periodical of general interest to HRD practitioners. *Training* is published by Lakewood Publications.

training *basic term*
1. In HRD, instructional experiences provided primarily by employers for employees, de-

Continued on next page

signed to develop new skills, knowledge, and attitudes that are expected to be applied immediately upon (or within a short time after) arrival on or return to the job. One of the HRD activity areas.
2. Instruction which emphasizes job-specific, near-transfer learning objectives; traditionally skills-based instruction, as opposed to education.
3. Loosely, any learning that is focused on the present job of the learner.

training aid
Any item that is developed or procured primarily to assist in instruction and the process of learning.

Training and Development
A periodical covering a broad range of articles of interest to HRD practitioners. Formerly called *Training and Development Journal. Training and Development* is published by the American Society for Training and Development.

Training & Development
The professional periodical published monthly by the Institute of Training & Development,. *Training & Development* serves as the national forum for HRD in the U.K. *See also* Institute of Training & Development (ITD).

training and development
See human resource development (HRD).

Training & Development Alert
A periodical of general interest to HRD practitioners. *Training & Development Alert* is published by Advanced Personnel Systems.

training-and-development-field understanding
The HRD competency of knowing the technological, social, economic, professional, and regulatory issues in the field; understanding the role training and development plays in helping individuals learn for current and future jobs. *See also* HRD Roles and Competencies Study.

Training & Development in Australia
A periodical of general interest to HRD practitioners. *Training & Development in Australia* is published by the Australian Institute of Training and Development.

Training & Development Society for British Columbia (TDBC)
A professional society for HRD practitioners in the Province of British Columbia. *See also* HR Canada.

training-and-development-theories-and-techniques understanding
The HRD competency of knowing the theories and methods used in training and development; understanding their appropriate use. *See also* HRD Roles and Competencies Study.

Training & Enterprise Councils (TEC)
Independent companies, set up in 1990, and numbering 82 in England and Wales. TECs are directed by business leaders and include local authority, trade union, and Employment Service representation. They link public and private resources in developing enterprise and training services to meet local needs. *See also* Local Enterprise Council (LEC).

training and evaluation outline (T&EO)
A summary document prepared for each training activity that provides information on collective training objectives, related individual training objectives, resource requirements, and applicable evaluation procedures.

training assessment
An analytical process used to determine an organization's current levels of training proficiency on mission essential tasks.

Training Cost Model
A cost-benefit model specifically for HRD, developed by Glenn Head.

training department
See HRD department.

Training Directors' Forum Newsletter
A newsletter of interest to HRD practitioners who are Managers of HRD. *Training Directors' Forum Newsletter* is published by Lakewood Publications.

training evaluation
The process used to measure the demonstrated ability of individuals and units to accomplish specified training objectives.

training game
See instructional game.

Training Guarantee Act
An Australian act of parliament that requires employers to spend a minimum percentage of total payroll on eligible training as defined by the legislation. If expenditure on training does not meet the required level (currently 1.5% of payroll) the shortfall must be paid to the Australian Taxation Office.

training management
The process used to identify training requirements and subsequently plan, resource, implement, and evaluate training.

training manual *essential 100 term*
A document designed for student use during a course and often afterward on the job. A training manual may include preprinted lecture notes, lab/job/worksheets, appropriate drawings and other graphics, and self-check tests.

training materials
See instructional materials.

training meeting
1. A periodic meeting conducted by platoon, company, and battalion key leaders to review past training, to plan and prepare future training, and to exchange timely training information between participants.
2. Any HRD-related meeting.

training needs *basic term*
Needs linked specifically to job or role requirements. *See* instructional need.

training objective
See learning objective.

training plan
A document that includes program information and data concerning the system or equipment program, event, or situation that originated the training requirement, and that describes the training required and the training program(s) needed to satisfy the requirement. Training plans are designed to provide for planning and implementation of training and to ensure that all resources and supporting actions

Continued on next page

required for establishment and support are considered.

training quality audit *basic term*
Audits of instruction, directed to learners and graduates. Tools include checklists for assessing tests for validity, the curriculum for job-relevance, and administration for timely and effective support. Written and performance tests measure learning. Surveys reveal the effect of training on the targeted jobs.

training quality tracking
A method to ensure that corrections and improvements are actually carried out. The tools are implementing documents (these vary with the organization). TQT tracking charts compare items identified, corrected, and verified.

training records
The documents that provide historical information about the organization's instructional activities. Today, training records are required to support the employer's conduct of legally mandated instruction. Employers also maintain records to defend liability by evidence that an employee was instructed on various working conditions and hazards.

training requirements (TRs) *basic term*
1. The difference between demonstrated and desired levels of proficiency for tasks.
2. In military training, the difference between demonstrated and desired levels of proficiency for mission essential or battle tasks. TRs are those skills and knowledges that are required for satisfying the job performance requirements, and that are not already in the students' incoming repertoire.

training resources *basic term*
1. Those human, physical, financial, and time resources used to support instruction.
2. In military training, they may be internally controlled by an organization or externally controlled by a headquarters that allocates their use to units as required.

training schedule
A document that specifies the "who, what, when, and where" of training to be conducted.

training standard
See course training standard *and* specialty training standard.

training strategy
1. The method(s) used to help learners attain desired levels of proficiency.
2. In military training, the method(s) used to help attain desired levels of training proficiency on mission essential tasks.

training vendor
See vendor.

train the trainer (session) *basic term*
Sessions intended to prepare instructors.

transaction
In transactional analysis, an exchange of strokes. *See also* strokes *and* transactional analysis.

transactional analysis (TA) *essential 100 term*
A concept developed by Eric Berne. Considered effective at the applied level, it is also comprehensive at the theoretical level. It is based on the combinations of the

three ego states; parent, child, and adult. The combinations of these states in human interactions is the basis of transactional analysis. The combinations, such as parent-child result in positions such as I'm OK—You're Not OK.

transactionally-focused evaluation
Evaluation based on *how* planned learning experiences are carried out.

transactional perspective
An acknowledgement of the two-way nature of social influence.

transactional theory
See transactional analysis.

transfer agent
The HRD role of helping individuals apply learning after the learning experience. *See also* HRD Roles and Competencies Study.

transfer audit
An activity designed to determine the strengths and weaknesses of an organization's transfer management system. *See also* transfer of training.

transfer climate
The distinguishing attributes of an organization's (or unit's) support for transfer of training by its employees. The transfer climate projects varying degrees of an organizational encouragement conducive to the application of new knowledge and skills.

transfer curve
See Figure.

transfer curve
A plot of the relationship between the extent of training transferred to the job and the time elapsed after training. These are usually plotted on the vertical and horizontal axis respectively. Preferred patterns are upward-sloping and begin immediately following training.

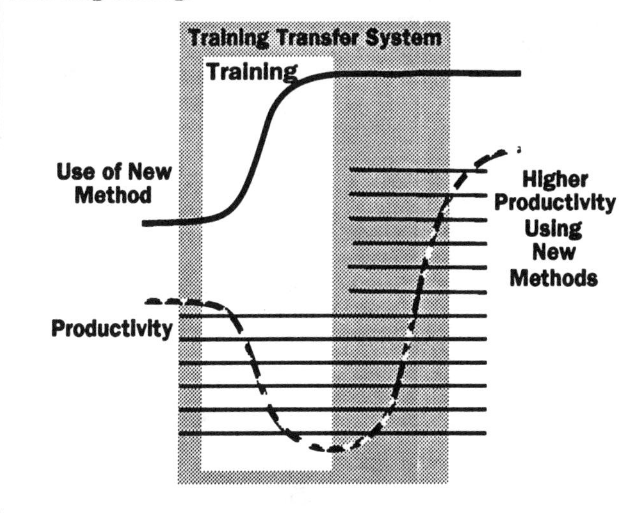

transfer management system
An organization's program to ensure that the knowledge and skills employees gain in HRD activities are applied to their job. A system of preplanned activities to ensure the effective and continuing job application of the knowledge and skills learners gain in instruction *See also* transfer of training.

transfer matrix
A 3 x 3 (nine-ceil) combination of two dimensions (time and role) useful for classifying both barriers to transfer and transfer-aiding strategies.

transfer of learning *basic term*
The term for the transfer of training process preferred by HRD professionals with a learner-centered orientation. *See also* transfer of training.

transfer of training *essential 100 term*
The extent to which trainees effectively and continuously apply the knowledge and skills gained in instruction (both on and off the job) to their jobs. Transfer may encompass both maintenance of behavior and its generalization to new applications.

transfer partnership
A concept developed by Mary Broad and John Newstrom to formalize the cooperation of three key groups—managers, trainers, and trainees— who have a strong interest in a particular training program and have agreed to work together to support the full application of the training to the job.

transfer test
See criterion (referenced) test (CRT).

transfer ultimate value
In HRD, the highest level of evaluation, focusing on the full impact of a change effort.

transition
Any statement or visual that bridges sections.

translation
See consecutive translation and simultaneous translation.

transnational
An organization with origins in one country that conducts or plans to conduct activities in several other countries, integrating focus on realities, and adapting to conditions to the exclusion of only the original country.

transnational structures
An organization or entity that is above or beyond any nation or border. Many global corporations and public international organizations such as the United Nations would be considered transnational structures.

transparency
A specially prepared transparent original containing an image. Used with an overhead projector. Light from the projector passes through the transparency to form an image on a screen. *Also called* acetate, foil, and viewgraph. Acetate refers to the plastic sheet used for overhead projection. At one time the transparency sheet was made from acetate. *See also* overhead projector.

transparent
A goal state for the user's lack of perception of a technology-based system. Machines that are simple, non-intimidating, and inviting to

use make technology transparent. This allows the user to concentrate on the substance of the instruction supported by the technology.

transportable

1. Extent to which courseware can be transferred from one computer to another without a person having to rewrite the program. Lessons developed with most authoring systems are not transportable.
2. A computer that is portable. The term suggests that it is at the heavier end of the weight range.

tree diagram

A quality process management and planning tool used to break down tasks or projects into details and/or paths. The tree diagram is useful when planning projects, to ensure that everything will get done.

trends

In quality, the patterns in a run chart or control chart that feature the continued rise or fall of a series of points. As with runs, attention should be paid to such patterns when they exceed a statistically based predetermined number.

triad *basic term*

A group of three people. *See also* triplet. *Compare with* dyad *and* quad.

triplet

A group of three persons. *See also* triad. *Compare with* dyad *and* quad.

trivium

The three subjects upon which a medieval education was based. The trivium were Latin grammar, logic, and rhetoric. *See also* quadrivium.

tryout

See pilot test.

T-scaled score

See stanines.

t-shirting

A technique of OD data gathering in which participants design t-shirts that express their feelings. *See also* OD data gathering.

T-test

An inferential statistical procedure used to compare groups based on their mean scores. Limited to comparison of two groups. *Compare with* analysis of variance.

tuition reimbursement

See employee educational assistance.

tuning

Fine adjustment of an activity's or program's structure and rules so as to ensure optimum effectiveness.

Turing test

A test of artificial intelligence named after the famous British mathematician Alan Turing.

turnkey *basic term*

An off-the-shelf product or system that is ready to run as and when delivered—simply turn the key.

tutorial *basic term*

The most typical form of CAI. The program and the learner interact one-on-one. Ideally, the process advances just as the best tutor might personally conduct the process. One of the modes of CAI. The others are drill and practice, instructional game, modeling, and simulation.

12W
A formula to test visuals that will be projected. For example, if the original artwork or graphic display measures 12 inches wide (including the necessary margins), the evaluator will view the materials from 12 feet.

2 x 2 grid (2 x 4 grid)
1. A suspended or dropped ceiling that uses a 2-foot by 2-foot grid. Panels that are 2-foot by 4-foot panels are also common.
2. Any of a variety of graphic models portraying two related variables or factors, with horizontal and vertical axes forming a 2 x 2 window or grid representing four possible combinations of the two variables. *See also* Johari window.

two-step procurement
A contracting procedure in which the technical proposal is prepared as step one and the cost proposal as step two. *See also* cost proposal *and* technical proposal.

two-way interactive television
A communication system that links remote sites with one another, allowing a simultaneous exchange of voice, video, and data transmission. The students and instructors see each other in real time over the system.

typeface
A complete set of letters and other characters of a given type design.

type 1 HRD department
A characterization to describe an HRD department that has few, if any, independent transactions outside the organization.

type 2 HRD department
A characterization to describe an HRD department that has some independent transactions outside the organization.

type 3 HRD department
A characterization to describe an HRD department that has substantial dealings outside the organization.

type 4 HRD department
A characterization to describe an HRD department that is autonomous. A type 4 HRD department transacts business more with those outside the organization than within.

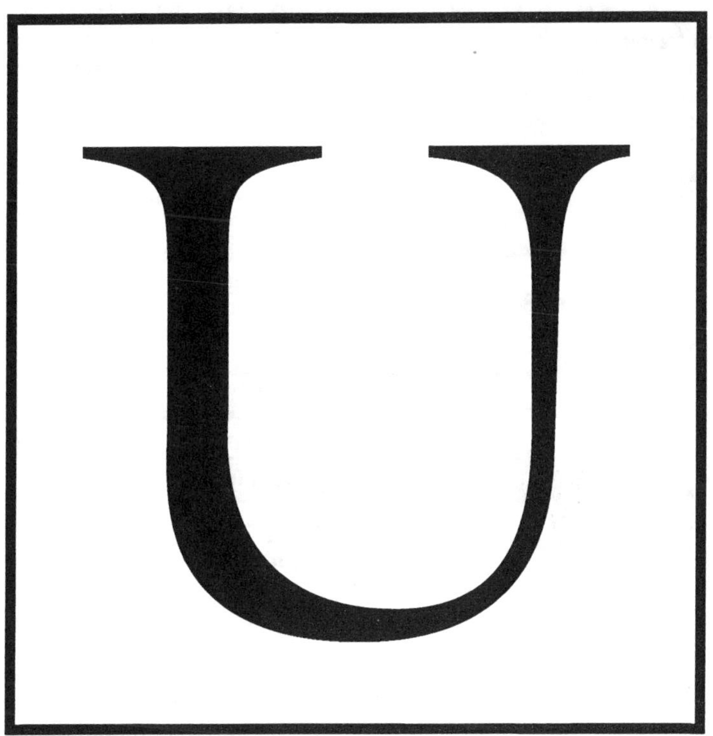

unapplied billing entry
Overhead and time spent on things not associated with a project. Time for which a client cannot be billed. *Also called* non-billable time.

underground employee self-development
A variety of self-help activities undertaken by an individual without the support of the organization. The risk is that the organization can, at any time, abort the individual's efforts.

underrating error
In research, when results are underassessed.

unfreezing *basic term*
A phase in Kurt Lewin's Change Model in which learners are encouraged let go of old habits and practices. Habits interfere with the acquisition of new learning. Old habits are best unfrozen through conscious intention and recognition of rewards for doing so. Applicable to the transfer of training process. *Compare with* refreezing. *See also* transfer of training.

unit
See Figure on next page.

unit objective
The learning objective associated with a particular unit of instruction.

unit
1. In technology-based learning, the smallest instructional component. A unit covers one learning objective.
2. A part of an instructional program.

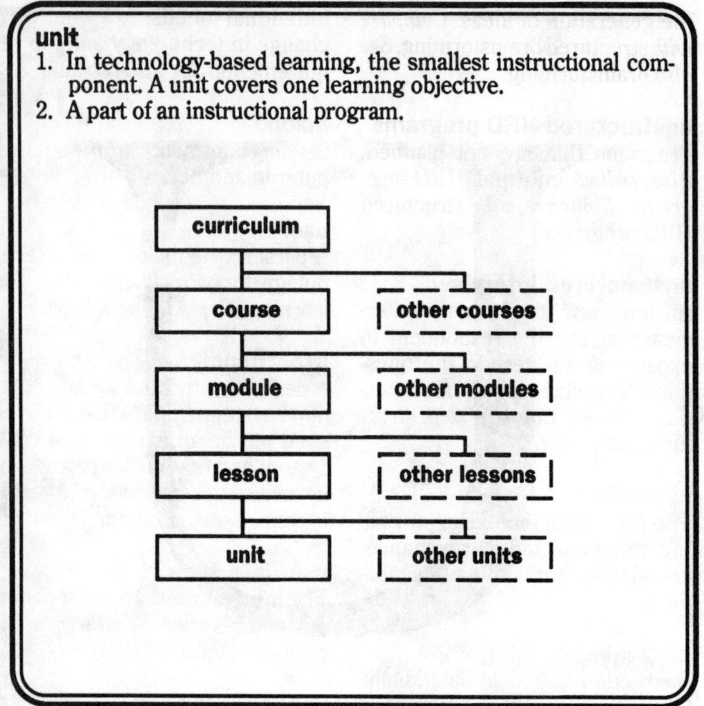

unit of instruction
See unit.

unit plan
A description of what a unit should cover.

unlearning *basic term*
Removal of old habits that interfere with the acquisition of new learning. Applicable to the transfer of training process. *Also called* extinguishing or diminishing. *Compare with* refreezing. *See also* unfreezing *and* transfer of training.

unskilled
A category of occupations usually involving routine and primarily physical tasks that do not require specialized training.

unskilled labor
Workers in jobs that do not require formal skills, training, or education. For example, housekeeping services for females, military conscription for males, and street vending for both sexes.

unskilled personal service
See unskilled labor.

unskilled worker
A person without specialized occupational competencies.

unsolicited proposal
A proposal submitted when there is no RFP. If accepted, leads to a sole-source procurement.

unstructured brainstorming
A method in which any member of a group can contribute freely to

the generation of ideas. *Compare with* structured brainstorming. *See also* brainstorming.

unstructured HRD programs
Programs that are not planned. *Also called* informal HRD programs. *Compare with* structured HRD programs.

unstructured interview
An interview in which the interviewer(s) ask the respondent to expand on answers to the questions. No specific sequence of questions is used. *Compare with* structured interview.

upgrading
The process of increasing or raising the expected performance, knowledge, and skills of occupations.

upgrading training
Instruction to update individuals. Upgrading training focuses on the knowledge, skills, and attitudes an individual needs to cope with change in technology and job requirements. *See also* retraining.

upload
Sending information from one computer to another.

user
A person who makes use of technology for work rather than for learning. *Compare with* learner.

user-friendly
A desirable attribute for any computer system. Implies that the user need not be an expert to use the system and that mistakes are easily overcome or avoided by the system. *See also* human factors.

user interface
The integration between technology and it's user. *See also* graphical user interface (GUI).

user-oriented
See user-friendly.

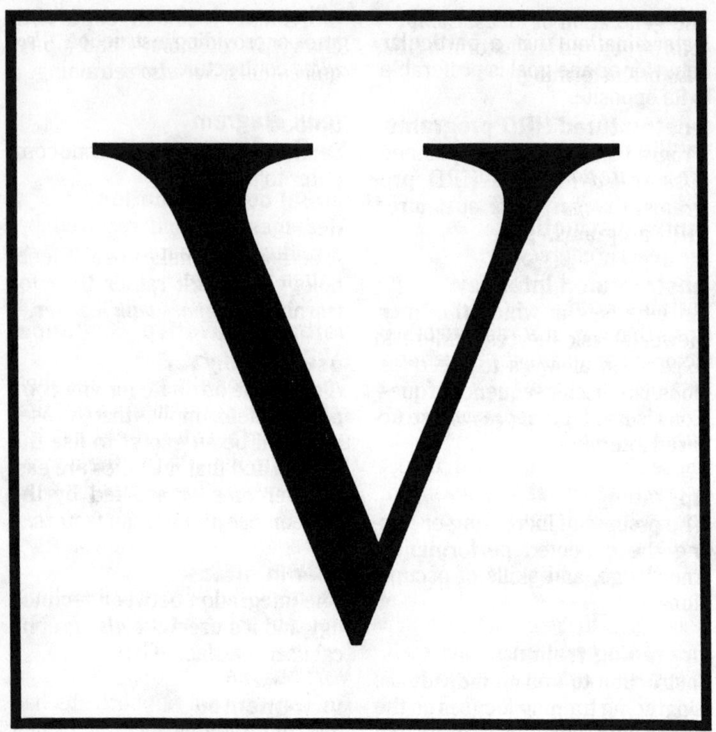

validation *basic term*
Ensuring that a learning activity, instructional product, measurement instrument, or system is capable of achieving its intended aims and functions. For example, validation of instruction includes developmental testing, field testing, and revision of instruction to ensure that the instructional intent is achieved. Validation allows instructional designers to guarantee specified results.

validity *essential 100 term*
The extent to which a test is a worthwhile measure for its intended purpose. Tests that are valid yield essentially true results. The degree to which a test performs this function satisfactorily is usually called the relative validity. Actions taken to make the test instrument valid are called *defending* the validity of the instrument. *Compare with* reliability. *See also* construct validity, content validity, concurrent validity, and predictive validity.

value-added benefit
Any additional benefit to be derived from a system.

value clarification
Helping individuals identify their individual values and how these values may influence their behavior. Value clarification is important in developing self-directed individuals.

values
Determination that a particular behavior or one goal is preferable to its opposite.

vanilla courseware
See generic courseware.

vanilla instruction
See generic courseware.

variable cost
Costs that vary according to other factors. For example, travel and lodging.

variables
Those characteristics of an object or process that can be measured. For example, length. *See also* attributes.

variance
A statistical measure of how much a set of scores differs within itself, as opposed to central tendency.

variation
In quality processes, the inevitable difference among individual outputs of a process. The sources of variation can be grouped as common causes or special causes.

variety
See voice variety.

Velcro board
See hook-and-loop.

Velcro software
See clip media.

vendor *basic term*
Any organization or individual that sells an HRD product or service to a customer organization. Vendors are always external to (i.e., not part of) the customer organization. Some vendors call themselves "consultants" even though they are selling a product or learning program, or providing instruction. *Also called* contractor.

Venn diagram
See Figure on next page.

verbal communication
Messages sent and received by individuals or groups using oral or written language.

verbal innovative deviance (VID)
The behavior of a group member reflecting agreement with the group goal but disagreement with the group majority on the appropriate means for achieving that goal.

vertical audience
Learners who will participate in a program in the future.

vertical file
An instructional support mechanism based on a collection of file folders containing various supporting materials on alphabetically arranged topics. Learners have free access to the vertical file. For example, short articles or brochures.

vertical job loading
See job enrichment.

vertical sensing
In organizational development, a small group diagnostic technique involving interviews of a vertical slice of the organization.

vertical thinking *basic term*
A concept developed by Edward de Bono to describe a thinking method controlled by a preexisting pattern or idea. Vertical thinking displays characteristics associated with left brain hemispheric functions. Vertical thinking con-

Continued on next page

Venn diagram
A graphical problem-solving device with two or more intersecting circles. The diagram can be used in both problem identification and problem analysis.

Electricity
Electric
Clocks
Clocks

trasts with creative lateral thinking—a process of looking at a problem from multiple perspectives. *See also* brain lateralization, creativity training, and lateral thinking.

vestibule training *essential 100 term*
Instruction for new employees before they start regular work. Vestibule training is conducted off the factory floor or work site, using duplicate equipment and recreating or modeling the work environment, or some aspect of it. The term is rarely used today, although the method is widely used. Simulation is sometimes used to refer to vestibule training. *See also* on-the-job training (OJT), orientation, and simulation. *Compare with* OJT.

veterans panels
An instructional technique based on a group composed of people who have already experienced the situation about which the students are currently studying. In a panel format, veteran panelists discuss the experiences they have encountered in that particular situation.

VHS
The most common 1/2-inch video tape format. The advent of VHS video equipment made economical video production possible for smaller organizations.

vicarious learning *basic term*
1. Using observation of others to acquire new skills.
2. Unconscious patterning of behavior after that of coworkers.

vicarious reinforcement *basic term*
Encouragement of retention and use of a new behavior based on the learners' interaction with others who are applying the learning. Vicarious reinforcement methods include observation, discussion, or reading descriptions.

vicarious travel
See surrogate travel.

video
An instructional medium. Video can be accessed from tape, disc, or semiconductor memory. In some cases, video is meant to include audio and other signals that are part of a complete video signal. *Compare with* text, audiotape, and CAI.

video-based instruction
Any learning activity conducted through the use of video in any form. *Compare with* CAI *and* instructor-led instruction.

video compression
Any technique used to reduce the bandwidth required for the transmission of the video signal.

videoconferencing
See video teleconferencing.

videodisc *basic term*
A medium based on video accessed from a laser disc. Videodisc is the principal form of video combined with CAI to constitute interactive video. The spelling with a "c" is preferred by video and HRD professionals over the spelling with a "k" (videodisk), which is also seen. *Compare with* CD-ROM *and* optical storage.

videodisc player
A video playback device that retrieves information from a prerecorded videodisc. Full-motion video segments or still frames can be retrieved in random order. A videodisc player is often coupled with a computer for interactive instruction. *Compare with* video player.

videodisk
Alternative spelling of videodisc. Not used by player or disc manufacturers, HRD professionals, or video production professionals.

video display terminal (VDT) *basic term*
The preferred term for computer display, commonly referred to in its abbreviated form, VDT. VDT is preferred, since it accurately describes a monitor using any display technology such as CRT, LCD, or plasma panel. *See also* cathode ray tube (CRT), LCD, or plasma panel.

video graphics array (VGA)
A very high resolution signal used in personal computers. VGA graphics are adequate for technology-based learning. *Compare with* color graphics adapter (CGA) *and* enhanced graphics adapter (EGA)

video monitor
1. Any screen used for displaying video pictures.
2. A screen used in computer terminals in which the display is based on video technology. A video monitor is not a TV set. *See also* display.

video player (videotape player)
Any equipment that plays recorded videotapes.

video recorder (videotape recorder)
Any equipment that records video

Continued on next page

images from a wired or transmitted signal. A video recorder may also be a video player.

videotape *essential 100 term*
1. Any video system using cassette or reel-to-reel tape. Currently popular playback systems include 3/4-inch U-matic and 1/2-inch VHS.
2. A medium using a videotape capable of recording a session and then playing it back. Videotape can also be used in conjunction with cable TV or CCTV.

videotape playback-critique
An instructional technique based on videotape playback and critique of the recorded performance. Videotape playback-critique is often used for learning specific motor and interpersonal skills. For example, sales training.

video teleconference *basic term*
A distance learning method using audio and television images between two or more locations. Video teleconferencing is best for *classroom groups* located distantly from the instructor. For example, National Technical University courses. NTU transmits by satellite. *Compare with* audio teleconferencing, audiographic teleconferencing, and computer conferencing.

videoteleconference
See video teleconference.

videotex
An interactive method of information dissemination with instructional potential. The user is able to select still frames of information. Videotex is distributed from a data base created for that purpose by either telephone lines or cable TV. *See also* teletext.

Video Visualizer
A device that projects an image from non-transparent originals, such as an open book, by focusing a video camera on the opaque object and displaying it through a video projection source. It achieves the same result as an older device called an opaque projector. *See also* opaque projector.

viewdata
See videotex.

viewgraph
See transparency.

viewing angle
The horizontal and vertical angles formed by the learner and the screen. Curved screens usually have smaller viewing angles than flat screens.

virtual reality (VR)
An experience in a computer-generated simulated environment. Virtual reality is particularly used to simulate conditions that do not actually exist, but may also be used to simulate actual potential conditions. Immersive virtual reality uses special peripherals, particularly data gloves and special, close to the user's eyes, computer graphic displays called head-mounted displays (HMD). Immersive VR gives the user the feeling of being present in a scene and able to move around in it. Desktop virtual reality is based on standard desktop computers. *Also called* artificial reality. *See also* surrogate travel *and* virtual world.

virtual world
Any environment modeled in a virtual reality system. The virtual world may represent "real" locations and objects or those created for the virtual reality system, including imaginary and yet to be built worlds. *Also called* synthetic environment. *See also* virtual reality (VR).

vision (visioning)
See visualizing the future.

visioning skill
Projecting trends and visualizing possible and probable futures and their implications. *See also* HRD Roles and Competencies Study.

vision statement
An overall statement of the goal of an organization, usually found at the beginning of that organization's business plan. For example, to become the best HRD department in the hospitality industry.

visualization
Creating dominant mental images of desired future states and envisioning the satisfactions and rewards that would accrue as a result of attaining those states. *Compare with* imagery.

visualizing the future
The collective process of identifying the desired future state of the organization. Visualizing the future is an important preliminary step in strategic planning.

visual learning preference
An individual learning style based on preference for observation. *See also* aural, haptic, interactive, kinesthetic, olfactory, and print learning styles.

Vocational Education Journal
A periodical of interest to HRD practitioners involved in vocational issues. *Vocational Education Journal* is published by the American Vocational Association.

voice bits
Short recordings of human voices spliced together to create a fast paced audio or videotape.

voice variety
The technique of varying inflection, intensity, pitch, and volume in a presentation.

Vroom, Victor H.
Originator of the Expectancy Model. *See* Expectancy Model.

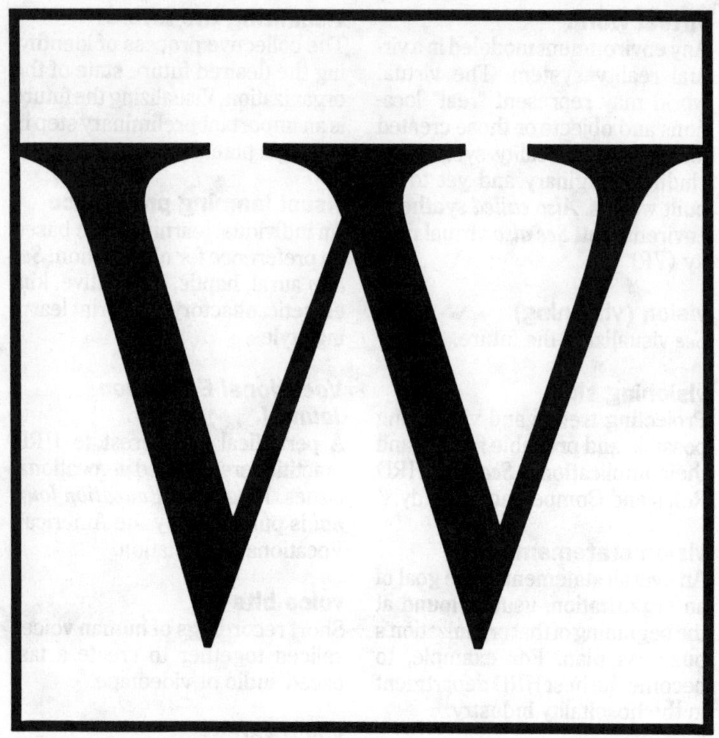

waiting-list control group
A design to control for Hawthorne-type effects, subjects are told that they will be in the experiment but actually receive no treatment. *See also* Hawthorne effect.

want
1. A desire usually encountered while attempting to determine a need. Needs analysis must distinguish between wants and needs. *Compare with* need.
2. A motivation to learn.

war game *basic term*
A competitive exercise based on a simulated battle.

warm up
An activity designed specifically to facilitate people getting to know each other. *Also called* an ice-breaker or mixer.

weights of attributes
See attribute weights.

wellness program *basic term*
Activities with the goal of improving a person's physical and psychological health. For example, fitness, nutrition, and weight control.

whiteboard
A surface that can be written on with a special, colorful, dry erase marker. Since airborne chalk is

harmful to computer drives, technology-based classrooms use whiteboards. *Compare with* chalkboard.

white space
The amount of blank space between and around areas of print in a printed document.

whole brain learning *basic term*
Implementation of brain lateralization and brain dominance technology in the classroom.

whole brain teaching
Synonymous with whole brain learning. *See* whole brain learning.

whole brain technology
A wide array of concepts, models, tools, and techniques developed by Ned Herrmann and others. *See also* whole brain learning.

wholeness
A principle inherent in a group which stipulates that every person in a group affects and is affected by every other member and that a change in any one person inherently effects change in all others.

whole-part-whole learning
An instructional technique based on parts of the instructional matter. Whole-part-whole learning starts with the big picture, proceeds to the component parts, and builds up to end with the total picture.

whole-task practice
An exercise, performed with or without a training device, that allows students to practice an entire task at one time. *Compare with* part-task practice.

whole-task simulation
The most difficult simulation technique to achieve. Whole-task simulation requires provision of all of the relevant elements of a work environment. For example, a simulator for a particular aircraft. *See also* part-task simulation, simulation, and simulator.

wide area network (WAN)
A network composed of local area networks (LANs). *Compare with* LAN.

word chart
Any visual consisting only of words. Word charts do not contain drawings or pictures.

workbook
An instructional document. Learners are expected to progress through the workbook in the specified fashion. Workbooks can be used for individual activities or in general and small group sessions.

work breakdown structure (WBS)
A systematic technique for analyzing large, complex projects. A WBS diagram is prepared to portray the project graphically into a series of subprojects. The subprojects are further refined into elements each of which is a manageable task.

Workforce 2000
An influential study by William Johnson and Arnold Packer. It projects U.S. worker demographics, skill levels, and trends that will obtain at the end of the century with implications.

work group *basic term*
A small group of organizationally-associated individuals, usually fewer than fifteen. Work groups include everyone who works in the same location and reports to the same supervisor.

working memory
See short-term memory.

workout
A problem-solving meeting. Workouts include 40 to 100 members of an organizational unit are often held in a retreat setting. The meeting begins by a presentation of the problem by top management. The group uses brainstorming and other techniques to derive recommendations which are presented to top management at the end of the workout. Workouts are often directed at improving the quality and productivity of the organization.

work rule
Defined conduct or behavior that applies in the workplace.

worksheet *basic term*
One form of job aid. Worksheets, like cookbooks, are best for sequential tasks. They differ in that they collect written responses from the user. The responses may be from calculations, to summarize data, or to gather information for further use. Worksheets come in three types: information collection, matrix, and computation. For example, when following a procedure that includes a calculation, the user records the results before proceeding to the next step. Familiar examples of this type of activity are IRS income tax worksheets.

workshop *essential 100 term*
1. A limited length learning activity led by an instructor. Workshops focus on improving proficiency in a specific subject. In comparison with a seminar, a workshop is practical and learners expect to have new skills at completion. *Compare with* seminar.
2. A practical session designed to illustrate the mechanics of an exercise without necessarily playing it all the way through.
3. A group of professional or vocational persons with a common interest or problem who meet together for an extended period of time. These workshops use study, group exercises, research, and discussion techniques.

work standard
The production of an individual or group that will be considered minimally acceptable.

workstation *basic term*
A work location, sometimes confused with learning station. A workstation may feature a computer and any associated input or output devices, based on the particular job need. *Compare with* authoring station *and* learning station.

World Federation of Personnel Management Associations (WFPMA)
An international HR body formed in 1976 as an umbrella institution linking national human resource organizations. *See also* International Federation of Training and Development Organizations (IFTDO).

write once, read many (WORM)
A compact disc format, known best by its acronym WORM. *See also* compact disc read only memory (CD-ROM).

writing skill
The HRD competency of preparing written material which follows generally accepted rules of style and form, is appropriate for the

audience, is creative, and accomplishes its intended purposes. *See also* HRD Roles and Competencies Study.

WYSIWYG
(Pronounced wiz′zy-wig′.) Abbreviation for "What you see is what you get." A computer display that shows the exact appearance of the final printed page. WYSIWYG is important in all applications that are delivered in another media.

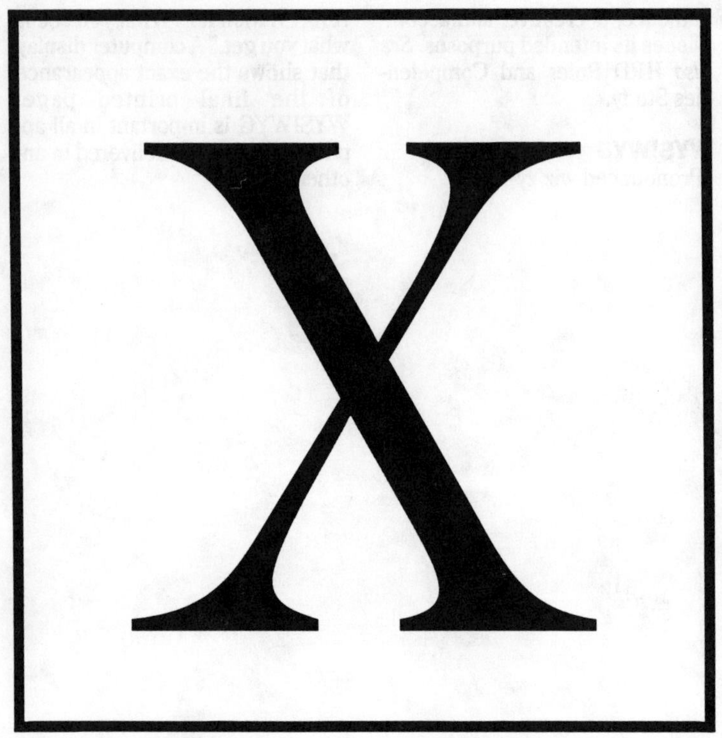

xerographic process
See electrostatic copier.

xerox
Improper synonym, used by some HRD practitoners, for a copy made using the electrostatic process. Xerox® is a trademark of the Xerox corporation and should not be used as a verb. *See also* electrostatic copier.

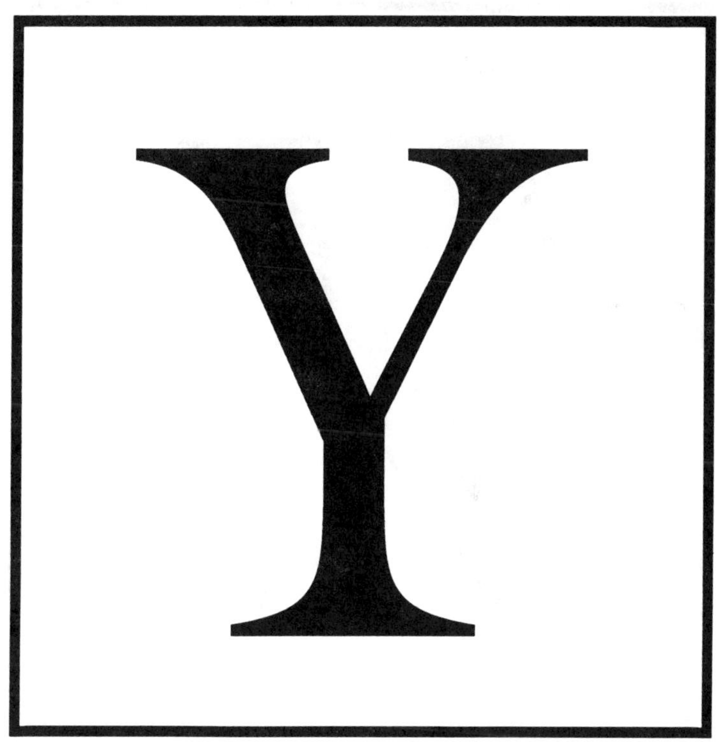

yearly training briefing (YTB)
A conference conducted by U.S. reserve component division commanders to approve the short-range plans of battalion commanders.

yearly training guidance (YTG)
A U.S. reserve component training management document published at each level from battalion to division that addresses a one-year planning period. The YTG adjusts, as required, and further develops the training guidance contained in long-range plans, to include specific training objectives for each major training event.

Youth Apprenticeship
U.S. programs to equip non-college-bound students with the required skills for and exposure to the world of work. Youth Apprenticeship programs include a four-year curriculum that combines academic, technical, and occupational education for students who have completed the 10th grade. Participants are paid wages and complete the program with a high school diploma. *Compare with* apprenticeship .

Youth Training Scheme (YTS)
An apprenticeship system used in the U.K. to combat low education participation rates. YTS offers basic workplace training combined with off-the-job training for students who have finished their compulsory education.

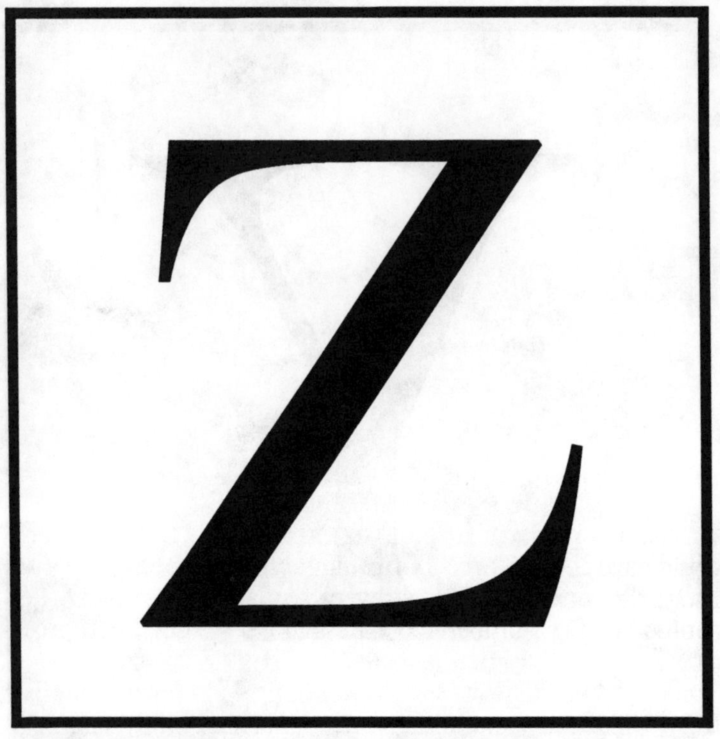

zero-sum game
A game in which winning is at the expense of losers. In general, zero sum activities are avoided in HRD. *See also* instructional game.

zoom
1. In video, apparent movement closer to, or farther away from, the subject. *Compare with* dolly and pan.
2. To scale a display so that it is reduced or magnified.

zoom principle
An instructional technique based on providing the learner with a broad picture to establish a cognitive framework in memory before getting to details.

z-score (T-score)
In testing, a score that shows how many standard deviations above or below a mean a given score falls. *Compare with* percentile *and* stanines.

Essential HRD Vocabulary

The terms selected for the essential HRD vocabulary were limited to a practical and convenient number. That number could have been 250 or 500. The bigger the number, the more useful the vocabulary. But, an overabundance of terms can be confusing. The number 100 seems to offer a good compromise.

It was difficult to select only 100 terms to form a "jump start" vocabulary for someone unacquainted with the HRD field. The panel of experts selected the terms they felt belong in this group. All expressed difficulty in identifying such a small number of terms. Agreement was wide, but not complete. Those printed here were determined by "averaging" their selections to arrive at a final list.

Some terms may seem obviously essential but are not on the list. For example "learning" was originally selected, but it is located in a series of learning-related words near "learner," which is on the list. Also, some terms suggest others that will be found in their *See also, See,* or *Compare with* entries. Such terms were removed from the final list to permit addition of a totally different term to create a richer vocabulary.

The resulting list includes terms from a wide array of HRD areas. They may not include the term used most in your organization, and all terms listed here may not be used regularly where you work, but they serve as a reasonable starting point for the field in general. These terms should be helpful in coming up to speed in most organizations.

The Trainer's Dictionary

A
affective
andragogy
apprenticeship

B
behavior modification
behaviorism
Bloom's taxonomy
brainstorming

C
career development
case (study) method
change agent
client
cognitive
competency
consultant
continuing education
courseware
critical incident
curriculum

D
demonstration
discovery learning
distance learning

E
evaluation
executive development
experiential learning

F
facilitator
feedback
force field analysis
formative evaluation

G

H
handout
heterogeneous
human resource development (HRD)

I
in-basket exercise
individualized instruction
instructional game
instructional systems development (ISD)
instrument
intervention

J
job aid

K

L
learner
learning objective
lesson plan
Likert scale

M
management development
Maslow's hierarchy
mastery learning
mean
mentoring
mnemonic
motivation
motivation-hygiene theory
multimedia
Myers-Briggs Type Indicator (MBTI)

N
needs analysis
nominal group technique
norm-referenced test

O
on-the job training (OJT)
organization development (OD)
orientation

P
pedagogy
performance-based instruction
performance objective
performance support system
pilot test
platform
planned change
post test
prerequisite
pretest
psychomotor

Q
quality of work life (QWL)

R
reaction
refresher training
reinforcement
reliability
results
return on investment (ROI)
role play

S
self-actualization
self-directed learning
seminar
simulation
skill
standup trainer
strategic HRD planning
student/instructor ratio
summative evaluation
supervisor development

T
target population
task analysis
teambuilding
technical and skills training
terminal objective
top management commitment
training manual
transactional analysis (TA)
transfer of training

U

V

validity
vestibule training
videotape

W
workshop

X

Y

Z

Acronyms and Abbreviations

Introduction

This section provides an added way to use the dictionary. After trial use, it has been reworked to help you find needed terms.

The Acronyms and Abbreviation section has four features:

1. It provides the spelled-out forms of all the terms in the dictionary that possess acronyms or abbreviations, but that are entered into the dictionary under their spelled-out forms (according to the general format of the dictionary). This method of listing serves two functions:

   - It is a quick reference for a reader who only wants to know the spelled-out form of an acronym or abbreviation.
   - It guides a reader who is unfamiliar with the spelled-out form of an acronym or abbreviation to the location of the term in the dictionary.

2. It provides a cross-reference of those few terms that are *not* entered into the dictionary under their spelled-out forms. These terms are exceptions to the basic format of this dictionary because they lack a specific and easily spelled-out form and, consequently, are known almost exclusively by their shortened forms (their abbrevia-

tions are more like technical shorthand for complex meanings).

An example of such a term is "6W." It is included in this section although it does not have an easily corresponding spelled-out form. Its listing in this section helps prevent confusion over where it can be found in the dictionary, thus acting as a "safety net" for readers who, searching here first for a term whose spelled-out form they do not know (and whose spelled-out form was untenable as a dictionary entry), might conclude that the term has been omitted from the dictionary if it were omitted here.

In short, listing terms of this type here alerts a reader to the term's status as an exception to the dictionary's general format. These exceptions are marked *See under* [term as entered in dictionary].

3. It provides a cross-reference of those terms whose spelled-out forms are entered into the dictionary, but whose *definitions* are entered under their acronym forms. These are terms that are virtually *always* used and seen in acronym form.

   An example is the term "DACUM." Its spelled-out form ("developing a curriculum") is provided here and is entered into the dictionary, but because the acronym is used almost exclusively and in a variety of ways (e.g., as an adjective), the definition for this term appears in the dictionary under its acronym form.

   These very few exceptions are also marked *See under* [term as entered and defined in dictionary].

4. It provides the spelled-out forms of terms whose definitions are self-evident and do not warrant entry in the dictionary. These terms, listed *only* in this section, are marked with an asterisk (*).

For some readers, this acronym and abbreviation section will function as the threshold into the dictionary proper. I hope that all readers will profit from its use.

Acronyms and Abbreviations

A

AAR	after action review
AAT	automated apprenticeship training
ACA*	American Creativity Association
ADA	Americans with Disabilities Act
AHRI	Australian Human Resource Institute
AID	Agency for International Development
AIM	Australian Institute of Management
AITD	Australian Institute of Training & Development
AMA	American Management Association
ANOVA	analysis of variance
AOR	areas of responsibility
APA	accreditation of prior achievement
APA	American Psychological Society
APE	accreditation of prior experience
APEL	assessment of prior experiential learning
APL	accreditation of prior learning
AR-PRINT	Army Program for Individual Training
ARTDO	Asian Region Training and Development Organization.
ARTEP	Army Training and Evaluation Program
ASHROD	Alberta Society of Human Resource & Organization Development
ASTD	American Society for Training and Development
ASTS	Army School of Training Support
AV (A/V)	audiovisual

B

BESEP	Basic Skills Enhancement Program
BIM	British Institute of Management
BPS	British Psychological Association
BRS	*See under* BRS.
BS 5750	*See under* BS 5750.
BSO	behavioral skills output

C

CAI	computer assisted instruction

CAL	computer assisted learning
CAT	computer assisted training
CBD	*Commerce Business Daily*
CBE	computer-based education
CBI	computer-based instruction
CBL	computer-based learning
CBR	computer-based reference
CBT	computer-based training
CCEU	Council on the Continuing Education Unit
CCTV	closed-circuit TV
CD	compact disc
CD-I	compact disc-interactive
CD-ROM	compact disc read only memory
CD-ROM XA	*See under* CD-ROM XA.
CDTS	computer directed training system
CEEFAX	*See under* CEEFAX.
CEM	Critical Events Model
CER	conditioned emotional response
CEU	continuing education unit
CGA	color graphics adaptor
CJS	Canadian Jobs Strategy
CMI	computer managed instruction
CMT	computer managed training
CO*	contracting officer
COB*	close of business
cognet	cognitive network. *See under* cognitive network.
COR*	contracting officer's representative
COTR*	contracting officer's technical representative
CPAF*	cost plus award fee
CPFF*	cost plus fixed fee
CRI	criterion-referenced instruction
CRT	cathode ray tube
CRT	criterion-referenced test
CSLR	computer supported learning resources
CT	criterion test
CTG	command training guidance
CYCLOPS	*See under* CYCLOPS.

D

DACA*	days after contract award
DACUM	developing a curriculum. *See under* DACUM.
DIALOG	*See under* DIALOG.
dpi	dots per inch
DVI	digital video interactive

E

E	extraversion
EAP	employee assistance program
EDTP	Employee Development and Training Program
EGA	enhanced graphics adapter
E-group	experimental group
Eg-Rul	from example to rule. *See under* Eg-Rul sequence.
EIDS	Electronic Information Delivery System
E-Mail	electronic mail
EOC	Equal Opportunities Commission
ESL	English as a second language
ETDO	European Training & Development Organization
ETSA	Education and Training Support Agency
EWS	experienced worker standard

F

F	feeling
fax	facsimile
FIRO-B	*See under* FIRO-B.
FTA	fault tree

G

GED	general educational development
GUI	graphical user interface

H

HBR	*Harvard Business Review*
HDTV	high-definition television
HR*	human resources
HMD*	head-mounted display
HRD	human resource development
HRE	human resource environment
HRIS	human resource information system
HRM	human resource management
HRP	human resource planning
HRU	human resource utilization
HVAC*	heating, ventilating, and cooling
Hz.	Hertz

I

I	introversion
ICP	individual career plan
IDP	individual development plan
IFB	information for bid and award
IFTDO	International Federation of Training and Development Organizations
IIHR	Institute for International Human Resources
ILO	International Labor Organization
IM	interactive multimedia
IPA	Interaction Process Analysis
IPD*	Institute of Professional Development
IPM	Institute of Personnel Management
IPMNZ	Institute of Personnel Management New Zealand
IPS	inches per second
IQC*	indefinite quantity contract
ISD	instructional systems development
ISDN	integrated service-digital network
ISO 9000	*See under* ISO 9000.
ITD	Institute of Training & Development
ITV	instructional television
IVD	interactive videodisc
IVI	interactive video instruction

J

J	judging
JCA	job competency assessment
JIT	job instruction training
JPM	job performance measure
JPR	job performance requirements
JQS	job qualification standard
JTA	job task analysis
JTPA	Job Training and Partnership Act

K

K*	thousand
K&S*	knowledge and skills
KASH*	knowledge, attitudes, skills, and habits
kilo	thousand. *See under* kilo.
KOR	knowledge of results
KRA	key results area

L

LAN	local area network
LAP	learning activity package
LCD	liquid crystal diode. *See under* LCD.
LCI	learner-centered instruction
LDS	lesson design system
LEC	Local Enterprise Council
LGD	leaderless group discussion
L group	*See under* L group or sensitivity training.
LTM	long-term memory

M

M	mean
M*	million
MAIT	Maintenance Assistance and Instruction Team
MAPEX	map exercise
MATES	mobilization and training equipment site
MBO	management by objectives

MBOR	management by objectives and results
MBTI	Myers-Briggs Type Indicator
MBWA	management by walking around
M.C.*	master of ceremonies
MDTA	Manpower Development and Training Act
METL	mission essential task list
mic	microphone
MIDI	musical instrument digital interface
mike	microphone
MILES	multiple integrated laser engagement system
MPOI	master program of instruction
MSTD	Manitoba Society for Training & Development
MTA	major training area
MTP	mission training plan
MTT	mobile training team
MURDER	*See under* MURDER.

N

N	intuiting
nAch	need for achievement
NASAGA	North American Simulation and Gaming Association
NCVER	National Centre for Vocational Education Research
NCVQ	National Council for Vocational Qualifications
NLP	neurolinguistic programming
NLQ	near letter quality
NOOSR	National Office of Overseas Skills Recognition
NSPI	National Society for Performance and Instruction
NSSTE	National Society of Sales Training Executives
NTB	National Training Board
NTL	National Training Laboratories
NTSC	National Television Standards Committee. *See under* NTSC video.

NTSC 4.43	*See under* NTSC 4.43 (video).
NTU	National Technological University
NVQ	national vocational qualifications
NZATD	New Zealand Association Training & Development
NZIM	New Zealand Institute of Management
NZQA	New Zealand Qualifications Authority

O

OCR	optical character recognition
OD	organization development
OEFD	*Organisation Europeene pour la Formation et le Developpement. See under* European Training & Development Organization (ETDO).
OJE	on-the-job evaluation
OJT	on-the-job training
ORBIT	*See under* ORBIT.
OSTD	Ontario Society for Training & Development

P

P	perceiving
PAL	phase alternate by line. *See under* PAL.
PBT*	performance-based training
PC	personal computer
PDAP	Professional Development Accreditation Program
PDCA	plan, do, check, act
PERT chart	*See under* PERT chart.
PIC	Private Industry Council
PIP	performance improvement potential
PLA	prior learning assessment
PO*	purchase order
POI	plan of instruction
POI	program of instruction
PONSI	Program on Noncollegiate Sponsored Instruction
PPA	professional practice area
PRM	programmer ready materials

Q

Q&A*	question-and-answer
QTB	quarterly training briefing
QTG	quarterly training guidance
QWL	quality of work life

R

R&D	research and development
R&E*	research and experimentation
RDTE*	research, development, test, and evaluation
RET	rational emotive therapy
RFP	request for proposals
RFQ*	request for quotations
RGB	red, green, blue
RIO	responsibilities, indicators, and objectives. *See under* RIO document.
ROI	return on investment
RPL	recognition of prior learning
rre	resource-rich environment
Rul-Eg	from rule to example. *See under* Rul-Eg sequence.

S

S	sensing
SAL	sleep-assisted learning
SALT	Society for Applied Learning Technology
SALTT	suggestive accelerative learning and teaching techniques
SAT	systems approach to training
SCOTVEC	Scottish Vocational Education Council
SECAM	*sequential coúleur a memoire. See under* SECAM.
SHRM	Society for Human Resource Management
SIETAR	International Society for Intercultural Education, Training and Research
SIMNET	Simulation Network. *See under* SIMNET.
6W	*See under* 6W.

SME	subject matter expert
SOW*	statement of work
SPC	statistical process control
SQ3R	*See under* SQ3R.
SR	stimulus-response
SST	stratified systems theory
STDA	Saskatchewan Training & Development Association
STM	short-term memory

T

T	thinking
TA	transactional analysis
T&D	training and development
T&EO	training and evaluation outline
T&M*	time and materials
TASA*	task and skill analysis
TCN	third country national
TDBC	Training & Development Society for British Columbia
TEC	Training & Enterprise Councils
Tele-con	teleconference
TKT	threshold knowledge test
TOW*	training objective worksheet
TQM	total quality management
TQS	total quality service
TQT*	total quality training
TR	training requirements
12W	*See under* 12W.
2 x 2 grid	*See under* 2 x 2 grid (2 x 4 grid).

U

V

VDT	video display terminal
VGA	video graphics array
VHS	*See under* VHS.
VID	verbal innovative deviance
VR	virtual reality

W

WAN	wide area network
WBS	work breakdown structure
WFPMA	World Federation of Personnel Management Associations
WORM	write once, read many
WYSIWYG	What you see is what you get. *See under* WYSIWYG.

X

Y

YTB	yearly training briefing
YTC*	yearly training calendar
YTG	yearly training guidance
YTS	Youth Training Scheme

Z

About the Author

Dr. Angus Reynolds is Instructional Technologist for EG&G Energy Measurements. His work centers on the development of advanced technology-based learning systems. Previously, he was Professor of Instructional Technology at the New York Institute of Technology. As Associate Dean, he built the Institute's HRD-related graduate programs to serve the needs of students employed in various capacities by the major organizations in the greater metropolitan New York area. For a decade he was Control Data Corporation's senior corporate HRD consultant. As Chief Consultant for CDC's Instructional Technology Consulting Center, his major work centered around high-level technology transfer consulting assistance to client organizations worldwide. A long-time consultant, he has identified and implemented solutions to problems in major multinational organizations in the aluminum, automotive, chemical, computer, food, hospitality, law enforcement, market research, nuclear, petroleum, power, steel, and telecommunication industries, as well as for the United Nations. He edited *Technology Transfer: A Project Guide for International HRD* and coauthored *Selecting and Developing Media for Instruction, Third Edition; The Global HRD Consultant's and Practitioner's Handbook;* and *The Global Learning Organization: Creating Competitive Advantage Through Continuous Learning.* He has contributed to a number of important works, including *Handbook of Human Resource Development, Instructional Technology Guidebook,* the *AMA Handbook of Human Resource Management and Development*, and the *ASTD Handbook of Instructional Technology.*

An Invitation

Authors and Publishers

Permission is granted to authors who wish to include not more than 25 terms from this dictionary in the glossary or elsewhere in their publication, provided that the following notice is printed:

> "Definition of terms reprinted with permission from *The Trainer's Dictionary* by Angus Reynolds, published by HRD Press, 1993. All rights reserved."

Authors who wish to include more than 25 terms must contact HRD Press.

Dictionary Users

You can join me and the HRD expert panelists in preparing the next edition of this dictionary. You are invited to become a contributor. I welcome any suggestion for improving the usefulness and practicality of the dictionary.

Also, please share the identity of any HRD term that may be heard or read by a new HRD practitioner during the first 90 days on the job or by any HRD practitioner joining a new organization.

Send your suggestions or new term and definition to me at the address below. If your idea or term is adopted for the next edition of this dictionary, your name will be included as a contributor.

Send defined terms to:

Angus Reynolds
EG&G Energy Measurements, Inc.
Box 4339, Station A
Albuquerque, NM 87196
USA